THE ARMCHAIR TRAVELLER SERIES

JOURNEY TO A WAR
W.H. Auden & Christopher Isherwood

LETTERS FROM ICELAND
W.H. Auden & Louis MacNeice

THE DONKEY INSIDE
Ludwig Bemelmans

RIDE ON THE WIND
Sir Francis Chichester

THE LONELY SEA AND THE SKY
Sir Francis Chichester

BRAZIL ON THE MOVE
John Dos Passos

JESTING PILATE: An Intellectual Holiday
Aldous Huxley

THE BLACK HEART: A Voyage Into Central Africa
Paul Hyland

DON FERNANDO
W. Somerset Maugham

ON A CHINESE SCREEN
W. Somerset Maugham

THE GENTLEMAN IN THE PARLOUR: A Record of a Journey
from Rangoon to Haiphong
W. Somerset Maugham

ADVENTURES IN ARABIA: Among the Bedouins, Druses,
Whirling Dervishes, & Yezidee Devil Worshipers
William Buehler Seabrook

THE MAGIC ISLAND
William Buehler Seabrook

HUNTERS OF THE GREAT NORTH
Vilhjalmur Stefansson

A RUSSIAN JOURNAL
John Steinbeck

HOT COUNTRIES
Alec Waugh

LOVE AND THE CARIBBEAN: Tales, Characters and
Scenes of the West Indies
Alec Waugh

ADVENTURES IN ARABIA

THE MOUNTED CAMEL MASTER OF THE BENI SAKHR WITH A
PURE-BRED WHITE RACER NUZZLING HIS CHEEK

Adventures in Arabia

Among the Bedouins, Druses, Whirling Dervishes, & Yezidee Devil Worshipers

By W. B. SEABROOK

Illustrated with many
photographs and pen drawings
by Miss A. G. Peck

PARAGON HOUSE
New York

First Paperback edition, 1991

Published in the United States by

Paragon House
90 Fifth Avenue
New York, NY 10011

Library of Congress Cataloging-in-Publication Data

Seabrook, William, B. 1887.
    Adventures in Arabia : among the bedouins, Druses, whirling
  dervishes & Yezidee devil worshipers / by W.B. Seabrook.
        p.   cm.—(The Armchair traveller series)
    Reprint. Originally published: New York : Harcourt, Brace, 1927.
    Includes index.
    1. Middle East—Description and travel.   2. Seabrook, William, B.
  1887—Journeys—Middle East.   I. Title.   II. Series.
  DS49.S43   1991
  915.604'3—dc20   90-7276
                                                                   CIP

Manufactured in the United States of America

The paper used in this publication meets the minimum requirements of
American National Standard for Information Sciences—Permanence of Paper
for Printed Library Materials, ANSI Z39.48-1984.

TO

AMIR AMIN ARSLAN
ARAB OF THE ARABS

Acknowledgment

For hospitality, friendship, and protection, I wish to thank:

Mitkhal Pasha el Fayiz, hereditary sheik of sheiks and overlord of the allied Beni Sakhr Bedouin tribes; and Mansour, the slave.

The Amir Abdullah, ruler of Transjordania.

Sultan Pasha Atrash, war chief of the Druses.

Hussein Pasha Atrash, lord of Anz.

Ali be Obeyid, civil judge of Souieda, in the Mountain of the Druses.

Sitt Nazira el Jumblatt, the "Veiled Lady of Mukhtara."

Suleiman bey Izzedin, the Druse historian, and Daoud Izzedin, his son.

The Most Reverend and Holy Sheik Shefieh el Melewi, governor-general of the Whirling Dervishes in Syrian Tripoli.

Howeja Mechmed Hamdi of Baghdad; Dr. and Sitt Mirza Yacoub of Baghdad; and Prince Suleiman Pashati of Baghdad.

The Mir Said Beg, ruler of the Yezidees; and Nadir-Lugh, high priest in the temple of Satan at Sheik-Adi.

The late Dr. Arthur Dray of Brumana.

I wish to thank *Asia* for permission to publish in altered form certain chapters of this book.

W. B. S.

Contents

AMONG THE BEDOUINS

PAGE

I. "IN THE FACE OF ALLAH"   21
II. BLACK TENTS AND WHITE CAMELS   43
III. A VAMPIRE OF THE DESERT   66
IV. MANSOUR, THE SLAVE   88
V. THE ROBBER-SAINT   106
VI. WE RIDE IN GHRAZZU   127
VII. "FOR THE EYES OF GUTNE"   143

AMONG THE DRUSES

VIII. AT THE CASTLE OF SULTAN PASHA ATRASH   169
IX. THE GOLDEN CALF   192
X. THE VEILED LADY OF MUKHTARA   218

AMONG THE DERVISHES

XI. IN THE PALACE OF THE MELEWI   235
XII. DAIDAN HELMY'S LEAP (AN INTERLUDE)   255
XIII. IN THE RUFAI HALL OF TORTURE   270

AMONG THE YEZIDEES

XIV. THE MOUNTAIN OF THE DEVIL-WORSHIPERS   289
XV. IN THE COURTYARD OF THE SERPENT   314
INDEX   335

Author's Preface

WHEN a man goes wandering into outlandish places, he usually has a reason. At any rate, reasonable people feel that he should have one. Therefore, it seems necessary and proper, in this preface, to explain why I went to Arabia.

Actually, I have never understood the *why* of anything —my own obscure but insistent motivations least of all.

One of my first memories is a picture-book my grandmother gave me in early nursery days. Its frontispiece showed three majestic figures from another world, cloaked mysteriously, riding upon the backs of strange, towering beasts, following a star.

That picture filled my childish mind with indescribable excitement. A second picture showed a baby, with people kneeling. It failed to interest me. My grandmother explained that this was a particular sort of baby—but I was stubborn. I kept turning back to the three men on camels.

Some years later, when I was nine or ten, we moved from Maryland out to Kansas, and were living in Abilene, a prairie town. The prairie was flat in all directions to the skyline. The nearest town, an adjacent county seat, was called Enterprise. The town itself was hidden by the curve of the globe, but on very clear days the tops of a small church steeple and a stand-pipe could be vaguely seen. To the boys of Abilene, Enterprise spelled mystery. It was before the day of automobiles. To walk there, across the prairie, was a long-discussed adventure. We had a Daisy air rifle and an old bowie knife, and persuaded ourselves that we might encounter Indians. Six of us planned to start, unknown to our parents, at dawn on a certain morning. But the night before, back of my father's barn where we gathered for conference, dissension broke out. Enterprise, the gang agreed, should be "the World's Fair at Chicago." But I obstinately insisted that Enterprise should be Samarkand.

I had read the *Arabian Nights* and Marco Polo. I tried to tell them what we would find at Samarkand— temples and palaces, golden domes, black giants with curved swords, and beautiful Circassian slaves chained to marble columns—but they derided me, voted to leave me behind, and marched off the next morning to "the World's Fair at Chicago," singing "Ta-ra-ra-ra boom-de-ay."

Ten years passed, and after college, when my beard had begun to stiffen, I made a second effort to take the road for Samarkand—which was to me a symbol rather than a place—and suffered a second disappointment. I had crossed on a cattle boat to Cherbourg, with the idea of tramping round the world. I had been begging, stealing, occasionally working my way through France, down the valley of the Rhone, and came at last to Marseilles. On that amazing waterfront, the Quai de la Joliette, I saw, for the first time in flesh and blood, hawk-nosed Arab merchants in striped robes who had come with dates from the coast of the Red Sea; turbaned Nubians and red-

fezzed Turks; once a tall-hatted Dervish from Baghdad.
I scraped acquaintance with a youth of my own age who
wore a bright red tarboosh and greasy overalls. He was
a Moslem from Smyrna, a wiper and assistant to the lamp-
trimmer on a Messageries Maritimes boat that made all
Near-Eastern ports.   Next trip, it would touch at his
home city, on the Turkish coast.   I had about 200 francs
(the equivalent then of $40), sewn in a little leather sack
hung round my neck, saved for emergency.   I believed
that if I got to Smyrna, I could tramp my way across
Turkey as I had done through France. My young friend
saw a way to help me and gain a little profit for himself.
A small bribe, shared between him and the lamp-trimmer,
got me aboard as their "helper."   They assured me I
would pass unnoticed by the officers.   But at Naples I
was caught and kicked ashore.   I fell ill in Naples, and
the adventure ignominiously ended.   I had to cable for
help and return to America—but vowing that some day
I would "do it," and not as a vagabond either.

Normal events intervened.   I was married in Atlanta,
gassed a little at Verdun, and came to write in New York,
while my dreams slept.

The writing was not astonishingly successful, and
Katie, my wife, opened a sort of coffee house at 156
Waverly Place, in Greenwich Village, where queer and
sometimes famous people occasionally dropped in from
all corners of the world.

One night there came a young Oriental with sad black
eyes and exquisite manners—Daoud Izzedin by name.
He was from Arabia, a Druse, a gentle member of that
strange, fierce race of painted warriors who were then as

legendary in America as the hosts of Gog and Magog, but who have since become more definitely known because of the wild revolt they led last year against the French in Syria.

I listened fascinated while Daoud talked, of his cousins who lived in feudal castles built of lava rock, among the mountains on the edge of the great Arabian desert; of slaves with jeweled scimitars; falcons, hounds; white-veiled *hareem* beauties; horsemen with long, braided hair and flashing spears.

My sleeping dreams surged—this time irresistible. Money stood in the way, and also the current belief that Christians who ventured among those legendary mountains did not always come back alive.

But when Daoud, after other evenings, realized how much I was in earnest, he said:

"You will find my father easily in Beirut. He is the Druse historian, Suleiman bey Izzedin. You have but to get off the boat at Beirut and ask of the first native Arab you see, '*Wein beit Izzedin?*' [Where is the house of Izzedin?] and they will take you to him. When my father learns that you are my friend, he will give you letters and camels. And with these, you will go to the sheiks of the mountain. Once in the mountain, you will require no money, and you will be *dakhile* [sacred as a guest], in my father's face and in the face of Allah."

It was not, however, toward the Druses alone that Arabia drew me. I had read Doughty's immortal book, and I wanted, above all else, to go among the Bedouins, the true desert tribes who dwell in the black tents. In that part of the adventure, Daoud declared, neither he nor his father could help me—but there was a certain great man his father knew, the Amir Amin Arslan, an Arab of the Arabs whose forebears had been governors and princes since the eleventh century—I might read about the family if I cared to, in the *Encyclopædia Britannica*—and who himself had been a governor of the desert people under the Ottoman empire.

Amir Amin Arslan, he said, was now a city dweller, living in the old Arslan palace at Beirut—but he had dealt honorably with the great tribal sheiks in the old days of the Sultanate, and was reputed now, throughout Arabia, to be the one city Arab whom the desert people loved and trusted.

He, more surely and safely than any other man or group of men, could send me to the furthermost black tents, if he would. And Daoud would write his father about the matter at once.

So Katie and I began to plan and get ready. For she was going too. (As a matter of fact, she shared many—though not all—of the hazards and experiences which followed.) Meanwhile, there were many things to learn. I did not go to books. I went to people. I sought out Arab cooks and amiable sons of Sinbad in the Washington Street slums, and Arab scholars on Columbia Heights. On the whole, I learned more from the former; I spent hours—whole evenings—with them, frequently over an *arak* bottle, learning, parrot-like, colloquial phrases in modern, current Arabic, and gradually whole sentences.

They frequently asked why and for what purpose I was going to Arabia. And now I have been trying once more to answer that natural question. I am afraid it has become only too apparent that I went for no useful, moral, scholarly, political, humanitarian, or reasonable purpose whatsoever. I went for the joy of it, and because I believed I should love it.

Now that the *why* is disposed of, it may be well to explain also, briefly, *how* we got there. The answer is "roundabout," like a couple of lunatics.

When we started by yellow taxi across Manhattan Bridge to a long wharf lost on the Brooklyn waterfront, beside which lay the little S.S. *Asia* of the Fabre Line, we had every intention of landing sensibly at Beirut.

But the S.S. *Asia* had, and still has, a gorgeous habit of starting for one port, or set of ports, and missing them temporarily by a thousand miles or so, to arrive at wholly unexpected places where the passengers never dreamed of going. This is due to aberrations neither of the captain nor of the compass, but to freight-office radio messages concerning figs, dates, ivory, apes, and what-not. The passengers are usually delighted, and lose nothing by it, in the end.

So it occurred, while coasting along Crete, that our boat turned her nose unexpectedly northward, and one evening at flaming sunset we dropped anchor in the Bosphorus. As we stood on deck watching the domes and minarets of old Stamboul turn purple in the twilight, we must have gone a little crazy, for we decided to disembark there if we had to swim.

It was more easily arranged than that. The Fabre Line people were helpful. We landed and saw Constantinople, and later went wandering down to Arabia, by wagon and train through Anatolia, across the Taurus Mountains—and eventually came to the house of Izzedin in Beirut, where a lucky surprise awaited us, for Daoud himself had meanwhile tired of New York and returned to the parental roof-tree, and we were taken to the family bosom.

Before the week ended we all went to dinner, one evening, at the palace of Amir Amin Arslan, and sat up until midnight discussing whether they should send Katie and me first to the Mountain of the Druses, or give her time to become "acclimated," while they sent me alone to the Bedouins.

Ten days later I was in the desert.

W. B. S.

New York
November, 1926

Among the Bedouins

Chapter I

"IN THE FACE OF ALLAH"

FOUAD TAIMANI, my guide, was plainly nervous. Indeed, the landscape was not calculated to inspire confidence. We had ridden for days through flat desolation, down from the Hauran toward the ancient wilderness of Moab, and were now approaching a range of ugly, barren hills.

The English that Fouad had learned in mission school was quaint but not courageous:

"Alas, my sir, the grain is few. The Beduw are enhungered. I fear that they may fall upon us and spoil us."

As we entered the hills, he continued:

"I pray you, sir, let us go swiftly, for this spot is evil. It was here but yesterday, hard by, as we were warned in Ramtah, that the Beduw fell upon a man and despoiled him of his camel, and when he cried out and ran after them, they deprived him also of his life."

I was not particularly afraid of being deprived of my life, for while the Bedouins are professional robbers, they seldom kill *farengi* as close as we were to the French and British posts. A mere robbery—even though accompanied by occasional native bloodshed—entails little consequence for the marauders; but the murder of a European is habitually followed by airplanes and hangings. If they can't catch the guilty ones, they hang a few of their cousins or fellow tribesmen.

As a matter of fact, we passed through these hills un-molested, without seeing a living soul.

On the following day, however, among the rock gorges less than six hours' ride from Amman, Fouad, who was some paces ahead of me in the narrow defile, turned a sharp angle, and exclaimed with bitter finality:

"*Ya wail immi!* [Alas, what grief for my mother!]"

In the instant before my mare's head also came around the angle, I failed to understand the significance of his mournful ejaculation. I couldn't imagine what we had come upon in this lonely spot that might cause grief to an old woman back in the hills of the Lebanon. I in-vented a long-lost second son, lying dead or wounded in our path.

I was totally surprised when confronted instead by six dirty and evil-looking men on horseback, with rifles across their saddle pommels.

Even then, I was not sure they meant to rob us, for not a weapon was leveled, and no rifle or pistol was raised at any moment during the queer little drama that ensued. It turned out afterward that we had been "covered" by two of their companions who were dis-mounted and hidden among those rocks.

After his first cry of pain, Fouad behaved splendidly. He had exchanged some words, which I could not follow, with the Bedouin who seemed to be in command, and now said to me:

"Our lives shall be spared, but we must be deprived of all our goods. And they mean also to deprive us of our horses. Yet the garments upon our backs may re-main to us, and our water bag, that we may proceed by foot to Amman."

This program, which Fouad was ready to accept with Oriental fatalism, seemed highly distasteful to me. Amir Amin Arslan had discussed such emergencies at great length, back in his palace at Beirut, and had drilled me thoroughly in what he advised as the best way to meet them.

I held up my right hand, palm forward, and said, partly in bad Arabic, and partly in English which Fouad had to translate:

"*Ana bwajh el Beduw* [I am in the face of all Bedouins] and bear upon my body the proof. I come unarmed, and not under the protection of the *farengi* flying machines, but under that of your own desert laws. I am already *dhaif* [a guest protected by the sanctuary laws] in the black tents, for I go to my brother, Mitkhal Pasha, sheik of sheiks. I am *dackhile* [inviolate] to you and to all Bedouins, so that if you take aught from me, shame will be upon you and upon your tribe. If you are in great want, I will give you freely all that I possess, even my horses, and my water bag, and the little gold you know to be in my purse, even the clothing from my back. But I must offer them as gifts, and you must accept them as gifts; for if you take by force one nail from my horse's shoe, your faces will be blackened and the shame will be upon your tribe."

My little oration was met with scowls and mutterings.

"They say," Fouad explained, "that these are strange words from a *farengi*—and that the desert laws are only for the people of the desert—also that you are without doubt a liar—but they are puzzled that you should offer all that you have as gifts."

"Are there those among you who can read Arabic?" I

asked. Fortunately for us, two of them could. I produced my precious letters, signed by Amir Amin Arslan, the first a general letter of safe conduct in the desert, which read:

"In the name of Allah, the Merciful, the Compassionate. This man is in my face, and in the face of Mitkhal Pasha el Fayiz, sheik of sheiks of the Beni Sakhr, with whom, if he is touched, will be blood feud."

THE TOMB OF FATIMA

The Resting-place of the Daughter of Mohamet in the Damascus Oasis Gardens

They peered at it together, mumbling the words, and then read it aloud to their surly companions. They passed it about from hand to hand, and all had a look at it.

It would make a charming dénouement to say that they became immediately friendly, embraced us as brothers, and took us to their tents as honored guests—but human nature is not like that, except in fiction. They were angry and disappointed. Luckily for us, they were straggling members of a tribe that couldn't risk trouble with the powerful Beni Sakhr, and after a few words of muttered apology, they reined their horses aside, and motioned us to pass on.

"Would it not be better," I whispered to Fouad, "to offer them a couple of pounds in friendship?"

"No," he said; "if they had dared to take anything, they would have taken all."

The city of Amman, which we reached that afternoon —ancient Philadelphia to the archeologists who take keen interest in its Greco-Roman ruins, and famed in still earlier Bible history as capital of the Ammonite kingdom whose people David conquered and tortured with "saws and harrows of iron"—was like a little paradise with its green trees and streams and fountains, after our hard, hot journey.

Old Jeremiah's prophecy that the Lord would "roar from on high" and make Amman "a desolate heap, no more remembered," had—fortunately for my convenience —been unfulfilled. Amman today is the busy capital of Transjordania, ruled over by the Amir Abdullah, under British supervision. The handsome modern Oriental palace they have built for him braves Jehovah's wrath and floats the green flag of Islam from Amman's highest hill.

More to my immediate purpose was the native hotel, where I had a noble bath, in a stone outhouse, off the cat-infested back yard, deluged to my heart's content by gallons of water that poured down from a huge zinc tank suspended by chains from the ceiling. A fat, motherly old woman, no whit embarrassed by my nakedness, stood in the doorway with towels and a three-legged stool and my clothes. I guessed her to be Christian, and so she was —a native of Beit-Lachem [Bethlehem].

And from her, later in the evening, we had the last Christian meal I was destined to taste for many weeks— a meal that I looked back on longingly when in the desert. It consisted of four quarts of beer, fresh butter, bread in the loaf, and an enormous platter of fried eggs.

We slept like logs, atop the counterpane of the bed, with our own blankets as covering—a simple trick that frequently discourages the "biter of strangers." A bright light kept burning in the room offers an additional protection.

The next morning, while I lay lazily abed, sore from three days in the saddle, Fouad went scouting for news in the cafés and market.

We knew that Mitkhal Pasha would probably be encamped somewhere in the edge of the desert out from Amman. His principal village, Um-el-Akmid, lay only one long day's journey eastward in a little oasis on the old caravan route to Baghdad, and it was in this neighborhood that his allied tribes, more than fifteen thousand strong, with their thirty thousand head of camels, sheep, and goats, assembled in the autumn for their great winter *rahla* south in search of pastures.

But he might be anywhere within a circle of three hundred miles or more. He might be off to the eastward on one of his occasional *ghrazzwat* [raids] or visiting the sheik of some friendly tribe.

Amir Abdullah, the native ruler, would probably know exactly where Mitkhal could be found, for he and the powerful sheik called each other "cousin" and had been intimate friends and cronies for years. I had planned to pay my respects to the Amir, and counted on obtaining from him not only directions, but a guide and escort.

Of course, there was the British military headquarters, but I had learned already that the man who wishes to hold the confidence and friendship of the Arab will do well to steer clear of all "foreign entanglements" and trust himself entirely to native protection and hospitality. Not only did this policy open doors for me that no European "official" traveler had ever entered, but I think that on one or two occasions it saved my life.

Fouad returned to the hotel about eleven o'clock saying that Amir Abdullah was in Jerusalem and would not return for three days, but that Rakaby Pasha, his prime minister, would receive me at two o'clock.

A dilapidated Ford driven by a fourteen-year-old boy —the best vehicle our hotel garage could supply—transported us to the palace, and a native guard in khaki showed us into the prime minister's reception hall—a high-ceilinged, square, plastered room, with a mélange of European and Oriental furniture, horsehair sofas and chairs of the ugliest Victorian period, rugs, low divan couches, and taborets.

After keeping us waiting for a quarter of an hour, Rakaby Pasha entered. He was a man past sixty, with an aggressive and disagreeable personality. He was florid, white-haired, inclined to unhealthy stoutness. Except for his red fez, he was dressed in conventional European clothes, frock coat, a heavy gold watch chain across his paunch. He was a Syrian Moslem, a Damascene; but from his appearance one might have guessed him to be a Greek banker.

We spoke in French. He asked me with cold politeness what I "required." Cold politeness from an Oriental under such circumstances was equivalent to deliberate discourtesy.

I regretted that I had come to him, but told him simply who I was and what I wanted—an American friend of Amir Amin Arslan, with letters to Mitkhal Pasha, whom I hoped to visit. He asked my business or profession, and I told him that in America I lived by writing.

"I have heard," said he, "of writers who enter our country pretending friendship and literary interest, but who really have some secret secondary motive, and who always end by making trouble—"

Without reflecting on the consequences, I lost my temper and replied:

"I have heard also of native prime ministers in Syria who were suspicious because they themselves were notoriously dishonorable and corrupt, and who frequently sold their own people traitorously to the French and English for personal gain. I shall ask you to try to believe that I am not the type of writer you have so courteously described—and assure you of my conviction that you are not the kind of prime minister I just mentioned. I shall also bid you good day."

Fouad had turned white as a sheet, and so far forgot himself as to precede me out of the door—but when we reached the ramshackle flivver in the courtyard below and were once outside the palace gate, he heaved a deep sigh, and said: "Ah, sir, how greatly do I admire at your indiscretion!"

I think he meant it as a compliment, but I have never been quite sure.

"What'll we do now?" I asked him. I didn't want to waste three days which might easily stretch into a week waiting for the return of Amir Abdullah, and I didn't want to apply to British headquarters.

Fouad had an excellent idea. "Let us go into the market place and the cafés," he suggested, "and search diligently for men of the Beni Sakhr. If haply we find one, he will give us tidings of Sheik Mitkhal."

In less than an hour we had "haply" found four, including one who had come in to sell a colt, and who knew Amir Amin Arslan. When the facts were explained, we became more important to that Bedouin than his colt, or any of his own private affairs. His one duty in life was to serve Mitkhal, he said, and since I came as Mitkhal's friend and guest, it was now to serve me. He wasn't sure where Mitkhal was, but he took my letter, tied it in the folds of his *kafieh*, left his colt unsold in the hands of a friend, refused my gold, and was gone at a gallop.

I learned afterward that he rode all that night, picking up a second horse and the proper direction from a group of tribesmen he encountered on the trail, and arrived at Mitkhal's tent next day.

Two mornings later I was awakened by a clattering of hoofs, loud shouting outside my window, and then a pounding on my door. I hurried out in my pajamas. Praise be to Allah! Twelve mounted Bedouins with braided hair and bronzed faces, their flowing *abbas* of camel's hair dyed black or brown, with rifles slung on straps across their shoulders, and breasts gleaming with cartridges, lifted their hands and touched fingers to forehead in friendly salute.

With them was a coal-black negro, armed and dressed as the rest, except that the shoulders of his *abba* were heavily embroidered with gold braid, and at his waist hung a huge scimitar with glittering jeweled handle and curved silver scabbard—the symbol of his office as chief body servant and favorite slave to the sheik of sheiks.

There was no slave-like humility about him, however. He was grinning, confident, and proud as a peacock, for he was not merely a slave and major-domo, but a warrior among the warriors, and one of the most influential members of Mitkhal's household—also, as I learned later, one of the most popular. We were destined to become fast friends.

He led a beautiful little blooded white Arab mare, which he explained was "*atieh men ami* [a gift from his 'Uncle'—a euphemism meaning master]," for me.

The town Arab who was proprietor of the hotel came running out, in shirt-sleeves and suspenders, bowing and spreading his hands. The true desert tribesman is the real aristocrat of Arabia, and be he wealthy sheik or simple warrior, he is so regarded by the native townspeople when he comes in from the black tents. They may not always love him. They may curse him behind his back for a bandit and brother of wolves. But he commands their respect and fear.

The proprietor shouted to his servants and to passing street urchins to come tend the horses as the Bedouins dismounted, and he eagerly helped unsling their rifles. They entered the best parlor of the hotel gravely, ignored its chairs, and squatted on the floor rugs in a circle. Though friendly, they were reserved and silent—all save the black, whose name turned out to be Mansour. He bustled about, hobnobbing and chattering with the hotel man.

Presently servants entered with tall glasses of pink,

sweetened water and boxes of cigarettes. When coffee came later, Mansour himself served it.

They wanted to make an early start. I was taking little luggage, and it was already packed in my saddle bag. They refused food, saying they had eaten on the road. When the proprietor brought my bill, I said, "You have forgotten to set down the refreshments just served to my Bedouin guests." He dug in his pocket and showed me a small gold coin. "You are already the rich sheik's guest," he said; "Mansour has paid generously."

Thrill of adventure surged high in my heart—not to mention a deplorable vanity—when I mounted my gayly betasseled mare and rode out of Amman with resplendent Mansour at my side, his black face grinning, his gold-embroidered robe and jeweled sword-hilt flashing bravely in the sunlight, his eyes roving right and left, delighted when a group of street boys cried, "*Wellah*, Mitkhal's men! And a *farengi!*" Behind us rode the others, unconcerned, rather despising the town and its people.

Less than an hour out of Amman, we left the sown lands and green behind, and entered the real desert hills. I was happy as they closed in around us—alone with a strange people whom I trusted and admired at first sight, a people whom I was destined to love and admire more before we parted—and to whom, even now, I am planning, if Allah wills, before many seasons to return. I think my feeling was something more than mere exuberant adventurous joy. The desert is a strange place. I think it is still filled with jinn and invisible influences. I think I was in the grip of a kind of mystical premonition. I was proud to be riding with Mitkhal's men. . . .

It was not yet twilight, and an enormous moon, pure

silver in the cloudless daylight sky, was just rising, like
the dome of a mosque in some holy city behind the hills,
as we came to a rise and looked down, in a little valley,
upon a group of fifty or sixty black tents, one set apart
from the others and much larger than the rest.   When

A BEDOUIN GIRL OF THE
BENI SAKHR TRIBE

Unveiled, Gay, and Free

I learned that it was Mitkhal's encampment, I was surprised, for I had expected to see many hundreds of tents.
I learned next morning that there were many hundreds
indeed, but scattered in groups of forty or fifty each, over
a radius of five miles or more among the surrounding hills.
The group we were approaching was that of Mitkhal,
his relatives, and the warriors who were his chosen bodyguard.

Dogs barked, and Mansour, putting his hand against his mouth, whooped like an Indian to announce our approach. There were answering shouts from the encampment. The moon was gradually changing from silver to pale gold, but daylight was still in the sky. Women, slender, bronzed like the men, with unveiled faces, all robed in dusty black garments so long that they trailed the sand, with stark-naked youngsters clinging to their skirts, stood in front of the smaller tents as we rode past. They were frankly curious, unashamed, not at all like the Moslem women of the towns. Several of them waved friendly hands, and one of the pretty younger ones shouted a laughing greeting—something I could not understand, but it made Mansour chuckle.

And then we were dismounting before the great tent— a ninety-foot pavilion which faced away from all the others, toward the rising moon.

Sheik Mitkhal himself was standing outside it and raised his hands in welcome. As I went to meet him, he ignored my outstretched hand, put both his arms around my shoulders, embraced me and kissed me on the forehead, saying, "*Khai el Amir Amin khuya* [the brother of Amir Amin is my brother]."

So this was the man of whom my princely friend had told me so many fascinating things, which now flashed through my mind in a jumble as I stood facing him— the overlord of fifty thousand flocks and twelve thousand fighting men—a multimillionaire even in terms of American dollars—the owner of six villages, many miles of cultivated land, and a palace, where he kept a retinue of slaves and the eldest of his wives, but which he never lived in and rarely visited except to entertain official guests of state—preferring to lead his tribes and share their life in the desert.

In any company in the world, Mitkhal would have stood out as a born aristocrat. He was a man of scarcely forty, medium height, slender, with beautifully formed hands, smooth olive tanned complexion, features of classic regularity, small pointed black beard and small mustache, with deep-brown eyes remarkable for their kindliness and intelligence—but which I learned later could turn black and flash fire.

He wore no gorgeous robes nor special insignia of rank. Save for the finer texture of his white *kafieh* [headcloth] and the long-sleeved *gumbaz* [under-robe] of fine muslin which he wore beneath the black *abba* [cloak] of camel's hair, he was dressed exactly as his warriors. The *agal* [head coil] which topped his *kafieh* was not the elaborate affair wound with gold thread usually worn by native princes and nobles, but the simple Bedouin double circle of black twisted horsehair, or glossy, twisted wool thread.

Luckily for me—since my Arabic was limited— Mitkhal had a smattering of French; and more luckily still, it turned out later that two warriors of his immediate household had an ungrammatical but adequate vocabulary in that universal language.

Mitkhal led me into the tent, where we reclined on a low divan, resting elbow and shoulder against camel saddles. Mansour, who had put away his peacock finery, approached with a long-spouted brass coffee pot in his left hand, and two tiny cups without handles in the palm of his right. Pouring a thimbleful of coffee into one of the cups, he dropped on one knee and offered it to Mitkhal. The Pasha motioned him to serve me first—

but I refused. There is more etiquette in the black tents than in any formal house of Fifth Avenue or Mayfair—and the guest who has not taken the trouble to inform himself at least of its simpler details, no matter how great his natural courtesy, is bound to commit blunders at every step. It was proper for me to accept any refreshment which Mitkhal offered with his own hand, but if another served it, Mitkhal must have precedence. Mitkhal, in motioning the black to serve me first, had simply been making a concession to what he thought might be *my* idea of the courtesy due a *farengi* from a Bedouin. When I refused it, Mansour grinned his pleasure and flashed the whites of his eyes at Mitkhal—who, I could see, was also not displeased. A trivial thing—but not to the subtle eastern mind. To them, it was an assurance that I came not to be treated as a condescending member of a race which regarded itself as superior, but with the desire to be accepted as a friend, and to respect their customs, great and small.

A British official from Baghdad had cautioned me, when he learned that I planned living with the native tribes, that the only way a "white man" could make himself respected was to maintain an uncompromising attitude and feeling of inherent racial superiority with all "natives" and at all times. A white man who "turned native," he told me, was always held in secret contempt and imposed on.

It was well-meant advice—and for all I know, such an attitude may be necessary when the "empire builders" mingle with members of "subject races," or races which they hope to bring under subjection—but as I sat in Mitkhal's tent, I am afraid I was not conscious of any feeling of "superiority," and I'm sure I hadn't the slight-est wish to make myself respected. I liked him. I hoped he would like me. I was his guest. And I had the simple notion that when a man accepts another's hospitality, whether in drawing-room or tent, it can do no harm to observe whatever rules of courtesy prevail there.

After the coffee, Mansour brought us two bubble-pipes, and we sat silently smoking.

Casual travelers in the Orient, who have seen only the filthy, wretched tents of the tribeless gypsy Bedouins, along the roadside or on the outskirts of some town, would be surprised, perhaps, at the spaciousness and sim-ple luxury in the tent of a great desert sheik.

The roof of Mitkhal's tent was a rectangular canopy or awning of black, woven goat's hair, stretched on poles, with long guy ropes, and all the walls, of the same ma-terial, were detachable, like curtains. Its dimensions were ninety feet by thirty.

A central curtain, or partition, usually hung with rugs and tapestries, divided the *hareem* from the *mukaad* [men's quarters].

The tent is always pitched facing the east. At night, in fair summer weather, all the wall curtains of the *mukaad* are removed or lifted, so that one sleeps in the open, with only the canopy stretched overhead. In the morning, as soon as the sun becomes unpleasantly hot, the eastern curtains are drawn, so that the tent becomes a shaded pavilion, wide open toward the west. Later, while the sun is overhead, the tent is thrown open on all sides, to catch whatever little breeze may blow. In afternoon, the morning process is reversed. The *hareem* end usually remains curtained.

On the evening when I arrived, and sat for the first time smoking with Mitkhal, a profusion of bright-colored rugs had been laid in the sand, near the *hareemlik* wall. On these rugs was placed an ordinary bed mattress (which I discovered later had been made in Germany); over this, softer rugs were spread, and camel saddles were placed at each end, against which we reclined.

Mansour had disappeared. We sat watching *el-gamar*, the rising moon. Under the far southeast corner of the canopy, two black slaves sat hunched beside the coffee pit, where a smoldering fire glowed.

Out of the east, and silhouetted for a moment against the sky, came a procession of camels—a part of Mitkhal's flocks, returning from pasture.

Warriors of his bodyguard, from neighboring tents, by ones and twos and threes, came quietly, touching hand to forehead with a low *"Salaam Aleikum"* and seated themselves in the sand,[1] until some thirty or forty had formed a semicircle. Most of them lighted cigarettes with flint and tinder (the Bedouins, like western cowboys, habitually "roll their own"); a few of them engaged in low-toned conversation, but for the most part they were silent.

The moon, now golden red, was mounting high, and flooded the hills with a bright, warm light. A slave moved about the semicircle, with coffee pot and two little clinking cups, from which all drank in turn. Mansour

---

[1] The Arabian desert is not a "sea of sand" like the traditional desert of fiction. One may cross the northern desert from Syria to Irak without ever encountering sand; there are immense stretches of hard, baked clay, others of gravel and flint. Our first Beni Sakhr encampment was on a sandy hillside in territory where gravel and clay predominated in the surrounding topography. The only great sand waste which my own wayfaring touched was the edge of the Nefud, three hundred miles southeastward.

appeared with a wooden bowl of camel milk, fresh and foaming, dropped to one knee and presented it to Mitkhal, who took it in both hands, and offered it to me. I took a long draught, then handed it to him, and the bowl passed to and fro between us until we had drained it.

More than an hour later, two kerosene lanterns of the familiar type used on the American farm were hung from wooden pegs against the tent poles, and dinner was brought in—a great brass platter, fully five feet in diameter and six or eight inches deep, borne by five men who gripped it by iron rings. The entire carcasses of two sheep reposed on a mass of rice and gravy, with folds upon folds of soft, thin bread-flaps draped around the dish's rim.

On the top of each carcass was the severed head of the sheep, to show that it had been freshly killed, also to indicate the kind of meat it was.

Mitkhal called by name five or six men from the semicircle. With them we went outside the tent and scrubbed our hands with sand, after which a slave with a tin teakettle, a towel thrown over his shoulder, poured a little water for each of us, with which we completed our ablutions.

We squatted around the great dish, and ate with our right hands. Mitkhal selected pieces of the liver, which he handed me, and afterward tore off choice morsels from the carcass, and laid them in a little pile in front of me.

The rice and gravy were eaten by scooping a whole handful into the palm, then tossing it up and down in the air, over the dish, until a part of the gravy had trickled through the fingers, leaving a ball of rice. This was scooped out of the palm with the thumb of the same hand, then balanced on thumb and forefinger, and tossed into the mouth. It is impolite to lick one's fingers, or to put them in one's mouth.

When we had finished, we went outside the tent again, and scrubbed our hands thoroughly in the sand. The grease itself with which the right hand was covered to the wrist supplied a soapy moisture, and the process was completed without the need of water.

After we had eaten, the other warriors had their fill, in succeeding groups, and what remained was carried into the *hareem* for the women.

The nights are always chilly in the desert, and Mitkhal, thinking that my blanket might not be heavy enough, brought me a clean white cotton quilt. I was to sleep on the same mattress and rugs where we had been sitting. I had been told that even in the tents of the great sheiks I might encounter vermin, but I never did. The Bedouins are rarely troubled by lice; bedbugs are absolutely unknown; fleas, however, are legion.

I tossed about a bit, as one does in wholly new surroundings, and just as I was finally dropping off to sleep, came back to consciousness with a nervous start, opened my eyes, and saw in the darkness, silhouetted against the bright outside moonlight, a silent black-cloaked figure crouching over me.

I had an unpleasant half-second of unreasoning fear, and started to leap up. Then I recognized Mitkhal. He had come to see how I was resting. He bent down, carefully pulled up the quilt around my shoulder, then went stealthily away. It was the first time I had been "tucked into bed" since my mother had done it when I was a little boy.

I had arrived in Mitkhal's camp wearing knickers and pith helmet, but Amir Amin had insisted on my bringing along in the saddlebags a complete outfit of Bedouin clothes—not for disguise or masquerade, but because European garments, he told me, would be impractical and uncomfortable.

The sheik of sheiks was pleased and a bit amused next morning to see me rigged like one of his warriors and presented me with a rifle, cartridge belt, and pistol.

My breakfast, eaten without ceremony, consisted of cinnamon tea, steaming hot in a heavy glass, a handful of dried dates, and some bread-flaps.

Mansour, the black, capered with delight when he saw me turned *Bedawi*—made exaggerated pretense of failing to recognize me, stalked about asking, "*Wein el farengi?* [where is the foreigner]"—hugged me like a bear, and then subjected my get-up to a minute examination. He approved of everything except my *gumbaz*—the long white cotton garment, something like an old-fashioned nightshirt, which is worn beneath the *abba*. He called the Pasha to witness that it was not true *Bedawi*. It was town Arab. The sleeves were not sufficiently voluminous. Mitkhal agreed with him.

It turned out that our camp was pitched within an hour's ride from Mitkhal's chief village, Um-el-Akmid, and he invited me to ride over with him and see it. I hoped it would be by camel, but there wasn't a camel anywhere in sight. They had all left before dawn for the pastures. I rode at Mitkhal's right hand, on the white mare he had presented me. Mansour rode at his left, and five or six warriors followed behind us. We all had rifles slung across our shoulders. Mansour sang as we rode. The Bedouin horse is guided by a single halter rope. He wears a bit, with a supplementary short rope bridle, but it is used only for bringing him to a stop when in full gallop.

Ten minutes' canter to a hilltop brought the village into view. In the transparent morning glare it seemed only a few hundred yards distant, on the slope of another hill—but very tiny. It was really seven miles away. As we rode on, it seemed to get larger, but no closer. Finally we arrived.

Some hundred stone and clay houses, built square with flat roofs, were clustered irregularly around a larger structure that seemed like a fortress or barracks, which was Mitkhal's palace.

We entered the palace courtyard without dismounting, through the "needle's eye" gate of a heavy wall—thence through a bare, vaulted chamber like a guardroom, large enough to hold more than a hundred men, and through a rude, massive studded door, which Mansour unlocked and unbarred, into the reception hall of the sheik of sheiks.

The stone floor and walls were bare, but a slightly raised dais at the farther end of the hall was spread with rugs and piled with cushions. Low stone divans which ran the continuous length of both lateral walls, forty feet or more, were also rug-covered. The place seemed musty and unused. I doubt that Mitkhal entered it more than two or three times a year. It was like being shown the lodge-room of a Masonic hall at a time when there was no meeting.

Mitkhal and Mansour, who had been whispering, left me—I thought a little unceremoniously. At the end of some ten minutes, a servant came and conducted me to a smaller room, in which were several wooden chests, where Mitkhal stood smiling mysteriously like a sly boy with a secret, holding something behind his back.

Without a word of explanation, on a nod from Mitkhal, Mansour seized me with mock ferocity, and proceeded to strip me to the waist, leaving only my enormous baggy trousers and the slippers on my feet.

Mitkhal then produced a *gumbaz* of sheer white muslin, with sleeves so voluminous and long that they almost touched the ground. He pulled it over my head, stood off to view the effect critically, and announced that as soon as the sun gave my face a healthy color, I would be a true *Bedawi*.

THE SHEIKLY TENT OF MITKHAL PASHA

A Ninety-Foot Pavilion of Woven Goat's-Hair

Chapter II

BLACK TENTS AND WHITE CAMELS

My Bedouin friends of the Beni Sakhr were sons of Islam, true believers, sincere but not fanatical, easy-going in their observance of the rites.

The blessed Prophet himself had been a camel-driver and wild raider in his time. He knew the hardships of *rahla*, caravan, and *ghrazzu*. All Moslems engaged on long journeys, he had said, might be absolved from strict performance of the five daily ritual prayers. And since the Bedouin's life is more or less an endless "journey," he counts himself under a permanent special dispensation.

At least I found it so among the tribes I knew in the North Arabian desert.

Among the Beni Sakhr, it was the custom for only our sheik, Mitkhal Pasha, to do the praying, wholesale, as it were, for all his people. And occasionally even he neglected it. Was not Allah most merciful and prone to forgiveness?

I first saw him pray at a noon hour. He arose from the coffee circle, removed his *abba*, shook it, and spread it on the sand, a little apart from us, but still in the shadow of the great tent's open canopy. He owned beautiful prayer rugs, but I never saw him use them. The traditional prayer rug of the Bedouin is his cloak. For my arrival, and for special occasions, a wealth of luxurious carpets and tapestries had adorned the tent, but our common daily life was of Spartan simplicity.

The sheik of sheiks sat on the edge of his cloak and kicked off his shoes. A black slave brought a bowl of water, with which he rinsed his mouth, snuffed a little into his nostrils, expelled it with the aid of thumb and forefinger, then washed his hands and feet.

The invocation, with its alternate kneeling, rising, and prostration southward toward Mecca, was spoken in low tones, distinguishable at first, then blending to a whispered murmur:

"*Es salaat wes salaam aleik* [Peace be with thee and the glory]."

I was surprised to observe that while Mitkhal was praying, the dozen or more men in the coffee circle assumed no demeanor of silence or devotion. On the contrary, their conversations, cigarette-smoking and other little activities buzzed on—it seemed to me, even more briskly than usual. I learned that it is not polite to fall silent and watch a man intently while he is praying. If a slave is clattering the coffee pots; if a story teller is in the midst of a tale; if men gossip or bargain, it is polite for them to continue. And so they did while our sheik prayed.

Neither Mitkhal nor any one in the encampment had ever questioned me about my religious beliefs. It is a rule of the Bedouins not to inquire into the personal affairs of a man after he has been formally accepted as their guest. Never did they evince the slightest curiosity as to whether I was rich or poor in my own country, married or unmarried, or what might be my occupation. There is a story of an Austrian, who was *dackhile* [a protected guest] of the Annezy many years ago, and who arrived in the tent of a certain sheik to remain, presumably, for a day or a week. Instead, he settled down for life. Thirty years later, a boy of twelve said to his father, then sheik of the tribe, "This old man's hair and face and voice are different from ours, though he dresses as we do and uses our words. Who is he, and what is he doing among us?"

The sheik replied:

"My son, that man came to my grandfather's tent as a guest; he remained with my grandfather until my grandfather died, and with my father until my father died. Neither of them asked whence or why he came; I myself have no such discourteous curiosity—and it ill becomes you now to inquire into a matter which does not concern any of us."

And thus might I have dwelt with Mitkhal, for months or years, without discussion of personal affairs or beliefs. But chance willed it otherwise. One day a neighboring sheik who sat smoking with us remarked that he had been on a visit to el-Kuts [Jerusalem], and that among various holy places, he had seen the tomb of Jesus.

I gathered from the conversation that Jesus was known among the Bedouins and deemed a holy man; but in the course of it, this sheik said:

"Yet how can they be other than mad who imagine that a man of flesh and blood could become a god—when there is no god but God—Who is neither body nor spirit?"

So far as I was aware, I gave no sign of agreement or disagreement, but the discourse pleased me, and I think Mitkhal must have read it in my face, for after the visitor had ridden away, he was for a long time silent, and then said:

"There is a thing which I have perhaps misunderstood.

I have supposed that all *farengi* believed this Jewish holy man to be a god."

I replied, as carefully and as truthfully as I could:

"It is a matter which has been misunderstood. There are many among my people who believe that Jesus is indeed God—but there are also many good men, a few even among our priests, who do not believe it, and who feel,

CAPITALS AND ARCHITRAVE OF THE GRECO-ROMAN TEMPLE AT BAALBEK

with your wise friend, that he must be a little mad who can hold such a belief."

"What then is their belief?" asked Mitkhal.

"There are many," I said, "who believe that there is no god but God—Who is neither body nor spirit—"

"True believers!" exclaimed Mitkhal.

"True believers, perhaps," I replied, "but not Moslems, for they believe that this one God is truly worshiped under many names, and under many different forms and rituals, and that he has had many prophets—not only Moses, Jesus, and Mohamet—but Buddha, Confucius, Lâo-Tsze."

And I recounted to him a long conversation I had held with the Hodja el Vatan, under the trees in the courtyard of the Pigeon Mosque, at Stamboul, in which that venerable doctor of Islam and I had come to almost perfect agreement about the ineffable oneness of the final mystery.

Mitkhal smoked in silence for the better part of half an hour. There is time for reflection in the desert. Then he reached over and patted me on the shoulder.

"My friend," he said, "I believe myself to be a true Moslem; yet it seems to me that you and I worship the same God. It seems to me, therefore, that you must also be a Moslem in your heart, though you do not keep the observance, and have never made the pilgrimage to Mecca."

"That I know not," I replied; and added, not to please him, but because it was the fact, "At least it is certain that I am not a Christian, for I do not believe that Jesus was God or the son of God, or that he rose from the dead, or that I must worship him."

"Do you believe that there is no god but God?" asked Mitkhal.

"*Bissahi!* [truly!]" I replied.

"A little while ago," said Mitkhal, "I think I heard you speak the name of Mohamet, among the prophets of the one God."

"I did, indeed."

"But there is nothing more required to live as a true Moslem and enter paradise," said Mitkhal. "*La illaha illullah; Mohamet rassoul ullah.* Will you not repeat it after me?"

"Willingly," I replied, and did.

He was delighted, but there was no solemn unction or fervor in his pleasure. On the contrary! With a happy laugh, he shouted for Mansour, who was occupied with something outside the tent. The black and five or six others came to see what it was about.

"I have discovered that my brother is a true believer," cried Mitkhal, which was his sincere way of looking at it; nor had I any wish to gainsay him. He did not feel that he had "converted" me or that I had turned renegade to another faith. He simply felt that I was by nature a Moslem.

Then, for the rest of the evening, whenever one of the men who hadn't heard it entered the tent, Mitkhal had me repeat the simple formula, "There is no god but God, and Mohamet is his prophet."

Mansour, for his own amusement, I think, rather than with any idea of its value to my soul, was for having me immediately taught the prayers and ritual. Mitkhal seemed to think this was neither desirable nor necessary.

He carefully taught me to say, *"Bismillah el rahman el rahhim* [In the name of Allah, the Merciful, the Compassionate]" and recommended that I should repeat it when in danger or on the eve of any important action.

Next day Mitkhal presented me with a gift which I still keep—a hollow amulet of heavy silver, in shape and size like a lump of Domino sugar, containing an actual copy of the entire Koran, in Arabic characters so tiny that they can be distinguished only with the aid of a microscope. The lid was held in place with a thin streak of solder, which was cut open to show me the tiny, precious volume, and resealed with the end of a knife-blade used as a soldering-iron, before it was strung on a leather thong and hung around my neck.

Certain passages in the Koran, believed to have special efficacy in warding off illness, violence, and various misfortunes, are written on pieces of paper, enclosed in metal or leather amulets, and worn around the neck by nearly all Bedouins. To have the entire Koran in the amulet was as if a devout Catholic had the medals of all the saints strung around his neck—or like the "shot-gun" serums which physicians inject, for protection against germs of a dozen different sorts.

Mansour bethought himself also to present me with a gift, and returned presently with a dagger—not the curved and beautifully chased blade of ostentation—but what my friend Achmed Abdullah calls a "business knife" —a straight, thick, eight-inch blade, set deep in a solid metal hilt. The blade was coated with a film of blackish grease. On one side was stamped a rude crescent, with the maker's name, his seal, with the date and place of forging—Medina, in the year 1243 of the Moslem calendar (1825 in the Christian). On the other side, more lightly cut, and obscured by the film of oil, was an inscription.

The point to the gift became clear when Mitkhal read the inscription, the battle cry of the Jehad: *"Thibhahum bism er rassoul!* [Kill, in the name of the Prophet!]"

I doubt that Mansour had any idea of making me a member of his "church militant"—I am sure, indeed, that he himself had never cut a Christian's throat for purely theological reasons—but when I accepted the dagger and hooked it on my belt, he again became insistent that I be taught the prayers and genuflections, until

Mitkhal finally lost patience and abruptly told him to shut up.

Mansour retorted with the privileged Oriental impudence of his class:

"Is there a lame goat, then, in the tent of my uncle's new brother?"

A MUEZZIN CALLING THE FAITHFUL
TO PRAYER

This sally, greeted with laughter, was too deep for me until they explained it.

The tale was that a certain Bedouin who had not prayed for years, and who belonged to no tribe, but lived alone on the edge of the desert, tending his tiny flock of five goats, one camel, and two sheep, was visited one day by a wandering Dervish, zealous in observance of all the rituals.

The Dervish, by promising greater prosperity in this life and paradise in the next, persuaded him to resume the long-neglected prayers, and he began their scrupulous observance, five times a day.

At the end of a week, as it happened, wolves came and devoured his two sheep.

"Alas!" said the Bedouin to himself, "this is easily explainable. During the long years of my silence, Allah, whose ways are past knowing, has forgotten all about me; but now that I have recalled myself to his memory, he is punishing me a little for my neglect. Now that I have disturbed his Compassionate Indifference, there is nothing to do but keep on praying, until I gain his mercy."

So he went on praying five times a day. Presently his only camel was stolen, two of his goats became sick and died, two others ran away, and he was left alone with nothing but one little she-goat, who couldn't run away because she was lame.

Whereupon the Bedouin threw up his hands and cried:

"Evidently Allah in his divine wisdom does not wish to be disturbed by my supplications, and the best thing for me to do is to let him forget me again and leave me in peace."

So he ceased praying and was there alone in the desert, with his one little black she-goat, and nothing to live on but her milk.

Goats are violently gregarious, and when the little she-goat had lost all her fellows, she insistently sought the companionship of the Bedouin; she ran into his tent and would not be driven out; she upset the bowl; she tried to snuggle down beside him at night for warmth, so that the fleas feasted on him. One night after he had driven her out, she came stumbling in again and stepped on his face with her sharp little hoofs.

Whereupon he awoke and shouted angrily:

"Get out of my tent, or I will start praying again, and then Allah will send the wolves to eat you!" [1]

Good-natured humor is the strongest prophylaxis against fanaticism. Not only were these Bedouins always ready to make jokes against over-pious adherents of their own faith, but they seemed to have no special antagonism toward the *Nazara* [Christians].

The harsh Fundamentalism of the Wahabi Meccan group further south was totally foreign to them. Their friendliness toward me after I had willingly acknowledged Allah was no different from what it had been before. Their attitude toward native Christians, however, was tinged with a slight amiable contempt.

When four men of the Salib—an extraordinary and little-known tribe of Christian nomads whose territory is far southeastward of Damascus—arrived in our camp to barter donkeys in exchange for grain, they were treated politely, but as inferiors.

Water and coffee were given them freely in Mitkhal's *mukaad*, but I noticed that they sat apart from our own men. And when evening came, they pitched a little *hejra* (a kind of traveling pup-tent) of their own, where they prepared their separate meal, and slept.

My friend, Amir Amin Arslan, who knew the Salib when he was desert governor under Turkish rule, had a theory that they were of mixed blood, dating back possibly to the last Crusades.

They have no ritual, no contact with the Maronites or

---

[1] The literal Arabic ending of the story is *"Rouhi wallah sallalik thlatha.* [Get out! or, by God, I'll kick you three kneels.]"

other native Christian cults, no symbols except a wooden cross. They believe in the divinity of Christ. Blue eyes are frequent among them, though not unknown among the pure Semitic tribes; a few of them are blond; some of their men are freckled and sandy-haired.

Their status in the desert is peculiar. By the unwritten Bedouin laws, they are outside the pale, but inviolate. They are permitted arms, but only for hunting and protection against criminal marauders. They cannot engage in *ghrazzu*—the great Bedouin "game" of raiding other tribes to capture camels and flocks, rather than to make war or shed blood, though blood necessarily is often spilled. They have no allies, and no other Bedouin tribe is permitted to raid or attack them.

When raiding tribes pass through their territory and chance to stop where their tents are pitched, they can demand water of the Salib, and coffee, but not food.

Among the regular tribes, by desert law, if men come riding in pursuit of a fugitive, and ask whither he has fled, it is a point of honor to lie or to refuse the information.

But when a man is being pursued, and these Christian nomads are questioned, the point of honor is reversed, and they must tell the truth; they must give the information that may lead to the fugitive's capture, and they are not disgraced by doing so.

They speak Bedouin Arabic, but have certain special words which seem to be of French origin—or which at least trace back to Latin roots.

Many of them wear the skins of gazelles as shirts, beneath their *abbas*, whereas no other northern tribes dress in skins.

They have donkeys, goats, sheep, and camels, but no

horses. This custom dates back to the period, which ended scarcely forty years ago, when no native Christian or Jew in Arabia was permitted to appear on horseback. Under Turkish rule, even in Damascus and Jerusalem, the native Jew or Christian, no matter how rich, went about on a donkey or mule.

For the male Bedouin of any Moslem tribe to touch a donkey, much less ride one, is a shame and an uncleanness. There were many donkeys in Mitkhal's camp, but they were worked and ridden exclusively by the women, who can touch them without shame, or by pre-adolescent boys.

Unaware of this, I had made the mistake of patting a donkey foal one afternoon in Mitkhal's camp. Had I not given previous proof of desire to learn and respect their customs, they might have let me "lose face," without taking apparent notice. Instead, two men came running on the instant to stop me, explained with eager volubility, and took me to a tent where I might wash my hands thoroughly with soap—the first I had seen in camp.

They had a curious dislike also toward stallions. The stallion was not deemed unclean as was the donkey, but I noticed the men avoided touching or going near one when possible. Whether an obscure, primitive male jealousy was at the bottom of this, or mere natural precaution toward beasts that were occasionally dangerous, I could not guess. But their dislike was marked, and they never rode them. All their saddle horses were mares, for which they had great affection.

The spoiled pets of the camp, however—better loved even than the finest mares—were Mitkhal's white camels. I know this is contrary to the report of most observers, but there is a distinction and an explanation.

Almost every writer on life in the desert has given the camel a bad name—and indeed he richly deserves it, if by "camel" one chooses to mean only the ungainly, buff-brown beast of burden.

He has the combined malice and stupidity of the worst type of "jarhead" Georgia mule. He is ugly as sin, and he does not belie his appearance. His black heart is filled with a vicious and melancholy hatred. He frequently stinks, or rather his breath does, like ten thousand constipated devils. And one of his favorite tricks is to vomit his vile greenish cud explosively in the face of the man who may be seeking to do him a kindness. He will bite you, not in anger as high-tempered horses sometimes do, but in casual, cold contumacy. If you are lying asleep, he will walk out of his way to step on your face. A dying camel has been known to drag himself for miles to a spring, not to drink there—so the Arabs take oath—but so that his carcass might pollute the water and poison those who come to drink afterward. If there is a ditch or pit, he will seek it out and fall in, breaking his legs if need be, merely to inconvenience his master. He is lazy and treacherous. Nobody loves him—not even Allah, the Merciful, the Compassionate.

But there is another breed of camel in the Arabian desert, different from these sons of Shaitan, as a pure-bred greyhound is different from a hyena—the white *hejin*, or racing camels, the pride and glory of their owners.

On the first night of my stay in Mitkhal's camp, they

had come home at dark; I had seen them only silhouetted black against the moon, and when morning came, they were gone again to the pastures.

On a subsequent evening, however, they arrived at sunset—a procession of five hundred superbly beautiful animals, pure white, long and clean of limb, with graceful necks, and small, well-formed heads. They were in charge of one old man and a little camel-boy.

Mitkhal was tremendously proud of them, and pleased at my excited interest. I wanted to go immediately and get a closer view, where they were grouping together, in the shelter of a knoll, some hundred yards to the left of the tent, preparatory to settling down for the night.

Instead, he held me back, and standing in front of his tent cried out, *"I-ee, i-ee, i-ee!"* I could see the entire drove craning their necks to listen. Then he called, *"Mazir! Mazir! Mazir!"*—repeating it perhaps a dozen times, until one camel disengaged itself from the others and came ambling toward us. It was his own favorite steed—a male. The name meant "Little Whirlwind." Friendly and eager, Mazir nuzzled against Mitkhal's cheek, while he stroked the powerful, slender neck. He shouted for a bread-flap, which he fed the camel in little bits from the palm of his hand. Something struck me as particularly curious about its eyes. I couldn't make out what it was, until I realized that it had heavy eyelashes on both upper and lower lids, which made its eyes look queerly human. A zoölogist told me later that so far as he knew, the only animals with eyelashes were the *hejin* and the borzoi. I stroked Mazir, too, and fed him bits of bread. His hair was soft and silky, shaggy and thick on the hump, smooth on the other parts of the body, like finest sheep's wool. His nose was soft, and his breath was sweet like a cow's. His belly was hard and tight, like a barrel or huge kettle-drum.

We walked over to the drove, with Mazir following Mitkhal like a dog. He assured me they were as intelligent, loyal, and affectionate as the finest horses. He stopped to pat one and another and speak to them by name as we walked among them.

We watched the baby camels sucking at their mother's teats. I tried to stroke one which had finished its dinner, but it was shy and jumped awkwardly away. A slave came with a wooden bowl and milked standing, holding the bowl in one hand and milking with the other.

Camel's milk when fresh tastes so nearly like good cow's milk that I do not believe any one could tell the difference. When it is fermented, however, in which condition it is usually drunk, it has a strong characteristic taste and odor.

For use around the camp, it is put in a goatskin hung against one of the tent-poles. It ferments almost immediately from the bacteria already in the skin (which is used over and over again without being cleaned out) and remains drinkable for days without turning sour.

Before going to bed that night, I went out again in the moonlight to look at the camels and found that most of them slept kneeling like cows, with their legs doubled under the bellies, but that some were sprawled sidewise with their long necks and heads flat in the sand, twisted in weird fantastic postures that suggested their prehistoric ancestors.

The actual ancestry of the *hejin* is disputed. Academic authorities believe that they are descended from the Indian *suwaree*, brought through Persia into Arabia centuries ago for breeding purposes, but the Arab himself insists they are indigenous.

When Mitkhal gathered that I was at least as eager to go riding on a real racing camel as a Dervish is to be carried on angel wings to paradise, he offered me in princely fashion the choice of his entire flock. With his help, I selected a female named Chrallah, gentle, he told me, and smooth of gait, but almost as swift as his own "Little Whirlwind." She was mine in reality. It was not Mitkhal's fault that I couldn't bring her home with me. But I still keep, for memory's sake, Chrallah's bright-colored and betasseled saddlebag, the dagger presented me by black Mansour, and for the sake of other memories, certain silver anklets with tiny tinkling bells, and a pair of silver armlets that make the heaviest of the fashionable "slave-bracelets" on the Avenue seem like fragile, masquerading toys.

I had once or twice suffered the usual unpleasant experiences of the unhappy amateur camel-rider. But now, with a finely trained, gaited racer and the benefit of Mitkhal's careful instruction, it was a wholly different story.

I learned that the long wooden saddle-pommels, front and back, like heavy, sawed-off broomsticks, were not designed primarily for piercing the stomachs and breaking the backbones of unbelievers, but had more reasonable uses. The correct seat, as Mitkhal instructed me, was "side-saddle," on the broad, rug-covered wooden frame, with front pommel held firmly in the bend of right leg, and right instep locked loosely under the left heel. The rear pommel, which never jabbed into the back if one sat properly, was useful as a peg for rifle, water-skins and other accoutrements that couldn't be carried conveniently in the saddlebags.

Chrallah knelt, amiably chewing her cud, while Mitkhal got me properly seated and showed me how to swathe the folds of the *abba* around my legs. Hung to my wrist by a leather thong was the light, knobbed bamboo camel-stick, about four feet long. Chrallah had no bit or bridle, only a halter, with a rope tied loosely to the saddle pommel.

Mitkhal had taught me two or three guttural words of command—*ikh* [kneel], *dhai* [rise], *yahh* [go].

I said briskly *"Dhai!"*—braced myself, and expected some great thing to happen. But nothing whatever occurred. I repeated it, in various intonations, but Chrallah continued placidly chewing her cud. She was friendly enough from the first, but never learned to understand my Arabic. It mattered little, for the Arab himself seldom directs his steed verbally. It is more easily done with taps of the stick.

Following instructions, I tapped Chrallah gently and most respectfully under her chin. Her front part heaved upward several feet while her back part remained stationary as the Sphinx, and I clung to the pommel at an angle of forty-five degrees. She had merely straightened her upper forelegs, with her knees still in the sand. Then her back heaved with a double movement to its full height, and I pitched forward, with the forty-five-degree angle reversed. Her front legs opened like a jack-knife, and I was restored to horizontal. The sense of elevation was prodigious, though she was a comparatively small camel.

And then we started. She was easily guided by light taps of the camel-stick on the sides of the neck. The gait is regulated by kicking inward with the heel. A light kick means walk, a sharper kick produces a trot, and a quick, light tattoo means run. The walk is the gait which occasionally produces seasickness. There is a steady backward and forward lurch, like the pitching of a ship. The transition into the trot was rough weather indeed, but the long trot of the gaited camel when she had struck her stride seemed to me easier than that of the average horse. The full run, which I did not undertake until the third or fourth day, was sheer marvel. It was like flying with the wind.

For the next week Chrallah went no more to the pastures. Every morning, usually accompanied by Mansour, also camel-mounted, I rode for hours, circling among the hills around our camp, racing when we came to level stretches.

Having heard contradictory stories, I wanted to learn for myself what a racing camel could do against a horse, and one morning Mansour rode the white mare. At a walk, the camel drew slowly but steadily ahead, as a long-legged man gains on a short-legged one without quickening his stride. At a trot, the camel definitely had the advantage, and the mare had to break into a canter every minute or two to keep abreast.

At a dead run, much to my disappointment, the mare slipped forward as a stripped racing-car slides away from a powerful limousine with both their throttles wide open. At the end of a mile, good going over firm, level earth and sand, the mare was fully three hundred yards ahead and apparently still gaining. Then Mansour doubled back.

"I thought you told me the *hejin* could outrun any horse," I called to him.

"More distance is needful," he replied.

"How much?"

"Five miles—perhaps ten."

He was reluctant to try it that morning, for fear, I imagine, the Mitkhal might scold him if the white mare were too badly winded. Another day we raced my *hujun* against one of Mitkhal's prize bay mares, which Mitkhal himself rode, over the eight miles to a neighboring encampment. At three miles, Mitkhal seemed almost half a mile ahead but was no longer gaining. From that point on, the gap between us lessened slowly. At six miles, as nearly as we could guess, I came abreast him, and the race was practically over. The mare was terribly winded, though still going bravely, while my camel was at the top of her stride and breathing steadily.

One thing, however, worried me about Chrallah. She had learned to know me, and we seemed to be on terms of affectionate friendship; yet from time to time, and under the most varied circumstances, she gave utterance to heart-breaking and melancholy groans. They were loud, prolonged, half-human, full of infinite sadness and reproach. She would sometimes moan when I climbed on her back, as if an insufferable burden had been laid on her white hump. But she was just as likely to lift her voice in lamentation when I dismounted. I came to the conclusion that she had either a dreadful belly-ache, or a secret personal sorrow.

When I made Mitkhal party to my fears, he assured

me that all camels groaned, and that whatever pains or sorrows weighed on Chrallah's soul were shared equally by the entire camel tribe. There was a story about it, he said.

A caravan was crossing the desert, strung out in single file, led, as is nearly always the case in Arabia, by a little boy riding a donkey. The first camel of the caravan was groaning at every step, and the second camel said, "O brother, why do you groan?"

"I groan," the first camel replied, "because it is our fate, though the largest and noblest of Allah's creatures, to be always led by that shameful little one, the ass."

I had been told of a harsh, angry snarl that all camels are said to emit when enraged, but the only sound I actually heard them make, in addition to their groaning, was the shrill, piercing noise they produce by rasping their teeth together, which carries for hundreds of yards, and which they seem to use in calling one another.

It is true, by the way, that the camel can, and often does, go seven days without water. But when in camp or pasture he is taken to the wells every third or fourth day. We watered Chrallah every three days at a well near Mitkhal's village, and she habitually drank from eight to ten bucketfuls.

Since she was not going to pasture with the others, we fed Chrallah on hay taken from the store for the horses, which I supplemented with many bread scraps, of which she was inordinately fond. I used to stuff them into my belt, and if they weren't forthcoming, she would nose for them inside the folds of my *abba*.

One night as I lay asleep beneath the open tent canopy, I woke to see dimly an enormous flat white head and long

THE MOSQUE OF MERDJAN AT BAGHDAD

curved neck wavering over me, like some gigantic serpent. It was Chrallah poking around for a hand-out. She had left her hump outside, which was fortunate for the canopy and tent-poles. I didn't want her to be contracting midnight supper habits; so I slapped her sharply on the nose, and she withdrew, groaning.

Chapter III

A VAMPIRE OF THE DESERT

ONE morning, Sheik Mitkhal sat in divan, like a sultan, to administer justice by the patriarchal desert laws.

The dispute was an intimate family matter, involving the domestic relations of his own nephew and niece, yet all who had "ears to hear" were summoned to gather at the great tent.

The nephew, Jerid, a boy of twenty, but already an important minor sheik in the tribe-group with his own encampment and fifty warriors, had married a girl of the El Khour, by name Thirya, two years before. She had borne him one child, and was now again pregnant.

Thirya, I was told, had been insisting that her husband take a second wife, and Jerid had persistently refused. They had quarreled and threatened to separate, but had agreed to submit their difference to Mitkhal for adjustment.

The party arrived soon after eight o'clock, Jerid with twenty of his men on horseback; Thirya in a curtained litter on a white camel, with an old, black serving-woman on a donkey.

The young wife wore a mantle of heavy, crimson Baghdad silk (the first Bedouin woman I had ever seen in other than the trailing robes of rusty black). Broad silver bracelets circled her arms, and gold coins were braided in her hair. Her boots were of red Damascus leather, with silk tassels of peacock blue. She was un-veiled, as Arab Bedouin women always are. She was rather pretty, but she was no raving beauty such as the gorgeous damsel—a veritable "desert vampire"—whom Mitkhal took me miles to see, a few days later.

Thirya and her black woman disappeared into the *hareem*, while Jerid and his men joined us. The young sheik sat with Mitkhal and me on the piled-up rugs, but no word did they mention of the dispute. Their talk was of camels, pastures, and the autumn *rahla*.

The warriors sat cross-legged, in a great open circle, shoulder to shoulder, four or five deep, beneath the wide-spreading canopy, and other rows stood just outside be-hind them.

Mansour, black major-domo, brought from the *hareem* a small rug, cushions, and an incongruous pink silk counterpane with which he arranged a small couch, near the center of the circle facing Mitkhal. Then he placed another rug beside it, for Jerid.

The men did not rise when Thirya came from the *hareem* and disposed herself on the pink couch, but when Jerid left his place beside Mitkhal, they all arose with him and remained standing until he was again seated. He ignored the rug that had been laid for him, and squat-ted apart in the sand.

When I arose with the others, I noticed that thirty or forty women stood grouped outside the tent. They couldn't see over the heads of the men, but were close enough to hear. A whispering and rustling came from the other side of the *hareem* curtain wall behind us where other eager ears were listening.

Mansour, squatting at Mitkhal's feet, tapped sharply

three times on the sand with a camel-stick, and the divan was opened.

"*T'fadal bil awal, ya Jerid?* [Wilt thou speak first, O Jerid?]" asked the sheik of sheiks.

"*La, wellah* [No, by God]," replied the youth, "for I am content" (meaning that his wife was the one who had made all the trouble and who demanded changes)—and he began sulkily rolling a cigarette.

"Wilt thou speak then, O Thirya, or wilt thou have another to speak for thee?"

"I will speak, O my uncle," she answered, and began fairly, but soon became excited and poured out such a stream of words that I could not follow them. What I missed, together with its implication, was explained to me later.

Thirya was insisting that Jerid add a second wife to his household, for three reasons:

The first was the matter of child-bearing. The wealth and strength of a Bedouin tribe lie in its man-power, even more than in its flocks, and every Bedouin father wants to have as many children as he can—particularly males. A man can beget twenty—forty, children, with joy in the begetting and no subsequent burden, but a woman who is compelled to bear many children "carries an endless burden," loses her youth and beauty, grows quickly old. The women of the poorer warriors are content to become broodmares, because their life in any event is one of continual work and hardship, so that it makes little difference. But the wife of a young sheik, particularly if she is proud and beautiful, prefers to bear two or three children, and no more, retaining her figure and youth, and letting other wives in turn take up the burden of child-bearing.

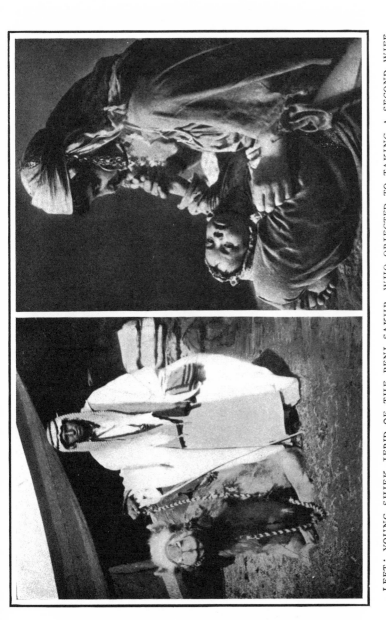

LEFT: YOUNG SHIEK JERID OF THE BENI SAKHR, WHO OBJECTED TO TAKING A SECOND WIFE.
RIGHT: THE YOUNG WIFE WORE A MANTLE OF HEAVY CRIMSON BAGHDAD SILK

The second reason was the question of companionship. The unmarried Bedouin girl may have beaux, suitors, visitors to her heart's content; in this respect she is astonishingly more free than other Islamic women; but once married, her social contacts are more limited. Even her husband spends nine-tenths of his idle time in the coffee circle, from which women are excluded. Thirya complained that life was stupid with only serving-women and inferiors in her *hareem*. She wanted the companionship of a second wife, an equal.

She contended, furthermore, that it was "undignified" and "unnatural" for one wife to be saddled with all the domestic responsibilities of a sheikly tent. A prosperous sheik keeps continual open house. Eight, ten, frequently twenty guests may "drop in" unexpectedly for dinner. No matter how many servants there may be, certain household duties devolve on the wife in the desert just as in London or New York, except that she hasn't the compensation of dining with her guests—and Thirya, with one baby to care for and another soon coming, insisted it was high time for her husband to show decent consideration and install a second wife.

She pleaded at great length, being the aggrieved party. Jerid replied in few words. He proposed to take a second wife in due time, but he was sick and tired of being nagged about it, and he didn't want to be hurried.

Mitkhal puffed placidly his *nargheela*, pondered, and gave judgment:

"Every man wants many sons, if it is the will of Allah, but it is not good for a sheik's wife to bear burdens, like a camel, all her life. Yet a complaining and discontented wife is also a heavy burden, and if one wife fill the *hareem* with discordant quarreling, how shall the husband wish to take another? Let Jerid and Thirya return to their *beit-shaar* in peace, and let her reproaches cease. And at the end of Ramadan (the following spring) when we are returned again from the south, Jerid shall take a second wife. I have spoken."

Mansour tapped thrice with the camel-stick to announce that the divan was adjourned. Thirya, pretend-

RUINS OF THE OLD QARA SERAIL AT MOSUL

ing she had triumphed, but really piqued, retired to the *hareem*.

And presently all was tranquil again in the coffee circle. Only a tapestried goat's-hair partition separated the women from us, yet we were again in a world of men, removed and apart from all feminine disturbances.

Bedouin women enjoy a liberty unknown in Moslem cities, but in desert as in town, the man remains lord and master. The male Arab of a tribe like the Beni Sakhr is an aristocrat of a type which ardent feminists would scarcely find sympathetic—though his favorite motto is "let the women do the work." He would be even less sympathetic to the pacifists. He is too proud to—do anything but—fight.

My host Sheik Mitkhal owned, on the desert edge and in neighboring oases, many thousand acres of cultivated land, yet not a man of his own tribe ever deigned to touch plow or sickle. He employed *fellaheen*, native peasants, mostly women, Moslem and Christian, for all farm labor. His warriors despised them and called them the "people of the earth-gray faces." Old men, little boys and girls, tended the flocks, camels, black goats and sheep. The women did all the household and camp work—while the only concern of the warrior was his own mount and his weapons.

His was a life of indolent, primitive luxury and ease—it must be remembered that I was visiting one of the wealthiest tribal groups in all Arabia—alternated by periods of violent activity and unbelievable hardship.

On *ghrazzu*, as I was to learn later from personal experience, they go for many days, pursuing or pursued, with no food except balls of dried, crusted camel cheese, insufficient water, snatching an hour's sleep on the hard ground, shivering with cold, for the desert nights are bitter even in summer, suffering the mid-day heat often without halt, riding day and night to the point of exhaustion.

But in camp, we lolled indolently on the rich rugs, gossiping idly, listening to tales and songs, rolling cigarettes or puffing the *nargheela*, and drinking innumerable thimblefuls of black, unsweetened coffee.

The food in Mitkhal's tent was wholesome, abundant,

but without variety. Breakfast was casual. Cinnamon tea, sweetened with molasses, a flap of bread from last night's baking. Toward noon dried dates, more of the same bread, and fermented camel's milk. The one cooked meal of the day might come any time from four in the afternoon to late at night, but its form and substance never changed—the whole carcass of a sheep or goat, on a great mess of rice and gravy, and freshly baked bread-flaps. All cooking was done by the women, behind their end of the tent and twenty paces distant, so that neither sight nor smell reached us. Two great iron cauldrons are set on stones, above a shallow pit in which are camel-dung embers. One cauldron is for the flesh and one for the rice. The bread flaps, unsalted and unleavened, made from wheat ground by hand between two flat stones, are baked on dome-shaped iron skillets, like shallow, inverted bowls.

Sun-dried camel dung is an ideal, clean fuel. The women gather it in their skirts. The pellets are round, hard, odorless, black, acorn-sized, with a smooth shell like lacquer or enamel. Bedouins use them to play a game similar to jackstones.

Coffee-making is the exclusive province of the men. Its paraphernalia for a sheik's household fills two great camel hampers. We had five pelican-beaked brass pots, of graduated sizes, up to the great-grandfather of all the coffee pots, which held at least ten gallons; a heavy iron ladle, with a long handle inlaid with brass and silver, for roasting the beans; wooden mortar and pestle, elaborately carved, for pounding them; and a brass-inlaid box containing the tiny cups without handles.

Occasionally we rode abroad to visit the *menzil* of some

neighboring friend or vassal sheik, but more frequently they visited us.

Despite our lazy indolence, a certain formality prevailed. When a person of importance entered or departed, all arose and returned his *"salaam aleikum,"* touching fingers to forehead. If the guest were friend and equal, Mitkhal embraced and kissed him; humbler men in their escort dropped to one knee and kissed Mitkhal's hand.

The visiting sheik Barokat had a Turkish scimitar, which I admired and asked to examine. He arose and presented it to me "as a gift in friendship," but because it was his personal weapon, I could decline without violating the rules of etiquette. Among the Bedouins, one must be careful in declining a gift, however extravagant, and must always assign some special reason, lest it be inferred you think the man is not rich enough to offer it. To decline on the ground that the gift is of too great value is gross discourtesy.

Among the gifts which Mitkhal himself had presented me was a brass bowl from Mecca, elaborately inlaid with gold and silver, almost a museum piece, and of considerable money value. I felt that I had no right to keep it, for I had nothing nearly commensurate to offer him in return. Yet he had insisted, and I was anxious not to offend. Later, on the morning of my final departure, I asked him, in the name of brotherhood and friendship, to give me in its stead the carved wooden bowl from which he and I had first drunk camel milk together, which I declared was more precious to me than silver or gold, and which I would keep all my life in remembrance. He looked at me keenly, patted me on the shoulder, and was content.

I never discovered to a certainty whether or not Mitkhal knew how to read and write. These desert princes, like kings and feudal lords of medieval time, disdain pen or pencil. One of Mitkhal's warriors was also his scribe, who could write both Arabic and bad French. In a little leather bag, Mitkhal carried a small brass seal on which was inscribed his family name "El Fayiz," with the *wasm* or symbol of the Beni Sakhr—a bar and circle joined. When he wished to dispatch a letter or written order, which occurred only two or three times a month, he dictated it, and the scribe read it back to him. He handed the seal to the scribe, who rubbed a bit of the ink on it with his forefinger. Mitkhal laid the sheet in the palm of his left hand, and pressed down the seal with his thumb.

The Bible story of how Jesus wrote in the sand had always seemed to me picturesque, unusual. Instead, it was the common, universal habit. As the Bedouins sat idling, they would scribble words or meaningless arabesques, with finger or camel-wand. Once, when Mitkhal wanted to describe the posting of certain men in ambush, he drew the plan in the sand, and on another occasion, when there was a dispute between two men about the number and value of some sheep, all the computations were made by writing in the sand.

All-over bathing is unknown in the desert, and the Bedouin lives his entire life without tub, shower or swim. Is life in the black tents dirty? The truest answer is that there is any amount of healthy dirt, even in the tent of a great sheik, but no germ-breeding filth. We lived next to the earth, sand, gravel or sunbaked clay, and the earth itself is a purifier, as are the wind and sun. Our water, brought in goatskins from distant wells, was muddy with sediment of sand and clay, not to mention goat hairs and other extraneous matter which made it occasionally resemble a defunct aquarium—yet I drank it without boiling and suffered no ill effects.

We all used the same cups and drank from the same wooden bowls without ever washing them, and dipped our hands to the wrist in the same great trencher of rice and grease—yet these Bedouins in their bodily habits were clean, as animals are clean. Every evening around sundown, and oftener if he has been perspiring and can find opportunity, the Bedouin rubs sand under his armpits, and on the other parts of the body where perspiration gathers. If he is camped in a part of the desert where there is no sand—and there are enormous desert stretches in Arabia where one never encounters sand at all—he uses the hard, gravelly clay. He has an odor but it is not sour,—it is dry and pungent, like the smell of a squirrel or bear. They pick their teeth after eating meat, and scrub them occasionally with a short thorn stick, chewed and fibrous at the end. Their loose boots or slippers, worn without stockings, are kicked off at every opportunity, so that their feet are as clean as their hands.

A man living their life for a month with western clothes would be in a disgusting and unpleasant state. But with the loose Bedouin garments, through which the air circulates freely, and adopting their "dry cleaning" methods, I found it possible to be quite comfortable. To tell the truth, I remembered maternal tyranny in childhood, and rejoiced in my unwashed freedom.

Some of the Beni Sakhr warriors had their hair cut short, but the majority wore it in numerous braids; their skins were naturally as white as ours, but bronzed and

weather-beaten; a few of them had blue eyes, but I saw
no blond hair among them; their beards were usually
sparse. Many had taken a fancy to European coats,
which they wore under, or as a substitute for, the *abba*.
The sheiks fancied a coat of bright blue serge, made in
Germany, with wide sleeves and heavy black braid, like
the hussar's coat in operetta. I frequently saw poorer
warriors with khaki U. S. Army coats, bronze eagle buttons and all. An enterprising firm of Syrian Jews had
bought more than a hundred thousand of these, after the
war, and put them on sale in the bazaars of Damascus and
Baghdad. But the coat was not a substitute for native
garb, and I think can never replace it in the desert life.
It was good only for a bit of swank, or for added warmth
against chilly nights.

I found a curious male modesty among them—unknown in our own civilization, recalling the old Semitic
story of Ham's punishment when he looked upon drunken
Noah's nakedness and drew no cloak over him. When a
Bedouin scrubbed his body, or retired for his other private
occasions, he always withdrew several hundred yards, and
if there were any depression which made it possible, he
managed to get out of sight.

It was not improper for me to be stripped to the waist
in the presence only of Sheik Mitkhal and Mansour when
they presented me with a new robe, but one day in the
coffee circle, when it chanced that some buttons of my
gumbaz were missing, so that it gaped and left part of
my chest and upper body exposed, Mitkhal, immediately
on noting it, motioned me to draw up the folds of my
abba until the damage could be repaired.

Casual group nakedness among men, such as is commonly seen in the locker rooms of American country clubs, would have been shocking and unthinkable to these sons of the desert.

A few years ago, the Sirdieh attacked an enemy tribe, not in *ghrazzu*, but in blood feud. It was a night attack on the *menzil*, with hand-to-hand fighting in the darkness, and in order that the Sirdieh might know each other from the enemy, they stripped off everything, wound their *kafiehs* around their loins, and attacked with cartridge belts, pistols, and knives strapped on their naked bodies. It was good strategy and they won the fight, but were severely criticized by neutral tribes for having resorted to shameless and unmanly tactics.

Bedouin frankness about certain intimate relations, on the other hand, is much greater than ours. One afternoon, as a score of us sat chatting in Mitkhal's coffee circle, he arose quietly, motioning the rest to remain seated, stretched himself, and said simply:

"*An'rayah li hormti* [I go in to my wife]."

"*Bismillah yjyk gowwa.* [Praise be to Allah, and may power go with thee]," replied the company casually, and resumed their talking. Mitkhal had three wives—one in the palace at Um-el-Akmit with his mother, and two here in the tent *hareem*.

He was gone perhaps an hour, and reappeared outside the pavilion, shouted to a slave for kettle, soap and towel. Presently he returned and quietly rejoined our gossiping circle.

I never entered the *hareem* of Mitkhal's tent or engaged in conversation with his wives because I thought it wiser not, but had I done so it would have been no violation of decorum.

On a number of occasions I visited other *hareemlik* of
the encampment, taking care, however, that I was always
accompanied by Mitkhal or Mansour, since, after all, I
was not of their own people.

A feminine custom of tattooing the chin was far from
universal with the women of the Beni Sakhr. Less than a

THE WIFE OF A COMMON
BENI SAKHR WARRIOR

third of them were tattooed, and very few wore the nose-
ring, which is common among the gypsy Bedouins.

Among the women, I never saw any apparel or trinkets
of European origin or design. Their jewelry was always
the heavy, handwrought native type from the bazaars of
Baghdad, Medina, or Damascus, usually silver.

It is true that the Bedouin women, even in the highly
raced tribes, break early, in the sense that they lose their
bloom and freshness, but they preserve their splendid,

free carriage, often remain straight as lances, and do not run to fat. I saw more than one woman past forty, lean, straight, and with thin, finely chiseled features.

The common dress of the women was a voluminous black woolen robe, even in midsummer, with black head-dresses of the same material, wound turban-wise. All of the well-to-do, however, had at least one robe of heavy red silk for special occasions, like that worn by Thirya when she came to Mitkhal for judgment.

Her visit, by the way, was the only occasion when I ever saw a woman in the *mukhaad*. Though wide open as all outdoors, always free of access to every man of the tribe and to passing strangers, it was a sort of "club" from which women and children were excluded by custom rather than rigid law.

A few women of the camp were pretty, one or two were real desert beauties, as full of flirtation as any New York flapper. And when I chanced to encounter them they delighted in kidding the *farengi*. They would ask how many wives I had left at home, and whether it wasn't high time for me to be choosing a Bedawi bride. Their wit was sparkling and equivocal.

Their freedom of word and gesture is based on the fact that among the highly raced Bedouins who adhere to the old desert law, all responsibility in pre-marriage contact between the sexes rests on the shoulders of the male. If an unmarried Bedouin girl is seduced, she is not punished; but the guilty man, and his two closest male relatives— if they can be found—so harsh is the code—are slain without recourse. Consequently flirtation and "petting" are common, and carried to lengths that no western girl would risk or dream of.

If a married woman is guilty of infidelity, however, the law is different. She is divorced, and sent under escort, a virtual prisoner, to the male head of her own family—usually father or brother. The men of her family sit in judgment, the rôle of the husband being that of accuser rather than judge, and if she is found guilty, she is immediately dragged outside the tent and her throat cut.

Another ancient law still actually enforced is that if a man spread evil report about a woman's virtue, and the report is found untrue, he is slain by the tribe.

Marriage, as in all Islam, is a civil contract rather than a sacrament. After signing the agreement, before witnesses, in the tent of the bride's parents, she mounts on the rump of the bridegroom's horse or camel, decked out in a red robe with silver bracelets and anklets—with gold coins braided in her hair, if she is rich—and he rides with her, in and out among the tents, until he has passed before them all, so that the whole tribe may be formally advised of the marriage.

If they are of sheikly condition, a small closed booth, its inner and outer walls gayly hung with rugs and tapestries, is pitched, either against the *hareem* wall of the husband's tent, or separately a few yards from it, and this is their bridal chamber for a month.

The marriage price, which may be much or little, is paid by the bridegroom to the bride's father, and she comes to her husband without dower or dot. He may divorce her at any time, but she has the like privilege of leaving him and going back to her parents if she is illtreated, and the husband has no power to compel her to return. If he can show, however, that she left him without just cause, he may demand that the marriage price be restored to him.

Love matches and freedom of choice on the girl's part are common among the Bedouins. It was told of Mitkhal's rich old father that after his beard was whitening, he sought in marriage the pretty fifteen-year-old daughter of one of his poorest warriors. The chit, already in love with a youth of twenty, replied:

"The honor is too great for an humble girl like me. You are asking me to wear a robe in which are woven too many silver threads." (A reference to his white beard.) The sheik of sheiks was chagrined but not angry, and the girl's father did not coerce her, although the marriage would have brought him many camels.

The thing I liked best about the Bedouin women, from the personal contacts I had with them, was their good-humored impudence and wit.

One day I rode over the hills with Mitkhal to see a noted beauty of the Beni Hassan, Furja by name, who was, like Scheherazade, a famous narrator of tales. She had refused many offers of marriage, and on that very day there was in camp a rich young Moslem farmer-merchant of the Hauran, who had been vainly courting her.

He was a tall, hulking, and it seemed to me rather slow-witted Arab, who sat gloomily silent for a few moments after our arrival in the lady's rug-strewn *hareem*, and then betook himself to the *mukhaad*.

She was a real beauty, and a cruel flirt—a veritable "vampire" of the desert, aware of her powers, and skilfully bent on destroying the tranquillity of every man who came within range of her charms. She wore a robe of black Damascus silk shot with gold. Broad silver bracelets encircled her forearms halfway to the elbow, and silver anklets with little bells and turquoise pendants tinkled when she wiggled her henna-pinkened toes.

Mitkhal had told me that she was "virtuous," lest I should misinterpret our reception, and she turned out indeed to be an outrageous comédienne. While we sat talking, a tottering old man, blear-eyed, bent and feeble—possibly a poor relation—came in and asked for food. To his evident astonishment, she **leaped up**, made much of him, and brought him a bowl of rice and meat with her own hands. As he sat in a corner mumbling it with his toothless gums, she said to Mitkhal, "How old would you suppose this man to be?" and he replied at a venture, "Eighty."

Whereupon she assumed a most doleful expression, and cried:

"Alas, alas, I meant only to give him happiness, but my beauty is accursed. This man, broken and bent, is younger in actual years than either of you! Only one year ago, he was straight as a lance, tall, strong and beautiful, the swiftest of our riders, and in his prime. May Allah, the Merciful, the Compassionate, forgive me."

And with a brazen flash of her eyes, and a serpentine undulation worthy of Gilda Gray or the Queen of Sheba, she lay back among her cushions and wiggled her tinkling, shameless toes.

Hearing her voice raised, and our laughter, the young Hauran farmer returned, awkward and doubtful of his welcome, but unable to stay away from the cruel beauty. She made him miserable by refusing to look at him or include him in the conversation, and presently said to us:

"I will tell you the strange story of an adventure which befell me. But, no, for if I told my story, it might be misunderstood by the 'people of the earth-gray faces' [farmers]. They have no imagination, and they would think it a history of *heeaki winietche*" (an untranslatable phrase).

The unhappy suitor protested that he would not misunderstand. "Take care that you do not!" she cried, and this was her story, which she extemporized, I think, solely to plague him:

"One day, as we were moving camp, I suddenly recalled that I had left behind, under a stone near my tent, a ball of camel wool which I had been spinning into thread. We had only gone a short distance, so I took a donkey, and went back for it. I found the wool and spindle, so presently, there I was, riding alone through the desert, following the tribe. I was content to be alone, and as there was no hurry, I spun as I rode." [1]

The bedeviled farmer began to look already restless and uncomfortable, while she continued with a mocking gleam in her eyes:

"As I was riding along, I heard groans, and suddenly saw outstretched on the ground a man who lay on his face, and moaned and twisted, and seemed unable to rise —but how dare I continue? The 'earth-gray face' will surely misunderstand and think it a history of *heeaki winietche*."

---

[1] One frequently sees Bedouin women, when the tribes are moving slowly, spinning thread as they ride. They sit side-saddle, on the donkey, and lift their skirts, so that the end of the spindle rests and turns against the inside of the leg, just above the knee. To say that she rode spinning was, therefore, equivalent to saying that she rode with her skirts pulled up.

Again the unhappy suitor protested that he could not possibly think ill of her, and she continued:

"I lifted the man, and put him on the donkey's back behind me, but he could not keep his seat. He fell like a bag of meal, first to one side and then the other. I want to tell you all that happened, but how can I tell it in the presence of one who will misunderstand?"

I began to observe that she was a superb actress, and that every gesture and intonation as she went on was deliberately designed to increase his distress and make him "misunderstand."

"Finally, as he kept falling off, I lifted him up a last time, and took both his arms and put them around my body, and then he managed to hold on with a grip that was like the grip of death. He had been writhing on the ground, and was covered with dirt and sand. I was wearing a fine new garment which had just been sewn on me the day before, and I pulled it out of the way as much as I could so that he wouldn't dirty it. And as we rode, his arms kept getting tighter and tighter—but surely I can't go on, for the 'earth-gray face' is already thinking this is a history of *heeaki winietche!* No, I cannot tell you more, for suddenly I felt that the man, who had been groaning and half dead, was very much alive again, and was tearing at the threads of my robe! I fought with all my might, but he was strong and terrible, and we fell from the donkey. In his hands I was like a bird in the claws of a falcon. I was alone, at his mercy in the desert, my tribe was far—"

At this point the Hauranese suitor, goaded and miserable beyond endurance, leaped to his feet, threw out his arms in protest and shouted:

"Now, in the name of Allah, if this be not a history of *heeaki winietche*, I cannot comprehend that it is a history at all!"

TOMB OF ZOBEIDE

Here the Wife of Haroun El Reshid, Legendary Narrator of the "Arabian Nights," Is Buried

And he rushed out of the tent, followed by her cruel laughter. But Furja was more than a sharp-tongued comédienne, and proved it later when she sang for us, to the twanging of her one-stringed *rabeyba*, a modern recitative ballad, which celebrated the heroism of a certain beautiful Bedouin girl, Gutne [Cotton Flower], daughter of Sheik Ibn el Ghanj, of the Sirdieh, in a battle which that tribe fought with a branch of the Annezy.

Pitched battles still occur occasionally among the prouder Bedouin tribes, conducted as they once were in Europe, in the old days of chivalry. The time and place are appointed. The opposing forces arrive panoplied, with all their tents and women, and set up their camps in full view of each other. Personal combats like the tournaments of old often precede the battle.

It was of such an event that Furja dramatically sang.

Instead of a flag or banner, each tribe has for its standard a sort of human oriflamme—an enormous throne, fitted to a camel's back, a big square litter with a canopy, completely covered with ostrich plumes dyed in brilliant colors. On the day of battle, this throne is placed on a giant camel, with three or four of the most beautiful marriageable virgins of the tribe, dressed in crimson silks and adorned with all their jewels.

A small camel boy, perched in front of the throne, guides the beast, and they ride backward and forward, on the actual edge of the battle, screaming encouragement to their warriors.

If a tribe goes down to absolute defeat, these chosen beauties become captive to the conquerors, but are treated with the greatest honor, and are even permitted to choose whom they will marry, though the most beautiful usually becomes a wife in the *hareem* of the sheik.

Furja's song told how on the day of the battle between the Sirdieh and Annezy, Gutne rode with three other Sirdieh beauties, and kept screaming to the camel boy to push in closer. At a moment when the battle seemed to be going against her tribe, she leaned forward, seized the bamboo wand from the little camel boy's hand, then knocked him off his precarious perch, and drove the camel forward into the thick of the battle, crying at the top of her lungs the prolonged "ooo!—ooo!—ooo!—ooo!—" which is like the war cry of the American Indians—with the other girls screeching and clawing at her in terror.

The song told how in the midst of the confusion and excitement, the Sirdiehs rallied, and won the battle.

I wanted to present our fair entertainer with a couple of English gold-pieces, which she could pierce and string on her necklace, but Mitkhal thought she might be offended—so instead, after she had served us with sweetmeats and cinnamon tea, I bent over, European fashion, in thanking her, and kissed her hand. It was a gesture entirely new to her, for in the desert, hand-kissing is an homage paid only to men—powerful sheiks or potentates. She giggled and demanded to know what I meant—and I explained that it was a usual *farengi* custom in taking leave of a very beautiful lady.

Chapter IV

MANSOUR, THE SLAVE

RIDING southeast from Um-el-Akmit one day with Sheik Mitkhal and twenty of his men, to visit the ruins of an old Omayid fortress, we came upon a bamboo wand, the height of a man, planted on a desert hilltop, with a black rag fluttering in the wind.

Beneath the hill on lower ground, a half mile farther south, were the tents of a Beni Hassan encampment. We drew rein where the wand stood, and with his binoculars Mitkhal showed me several other signal wands, planted on distant hilltops, circling right and left, so that no rider could approach the camp without noting them.

"There will be six, in a wide circle," he said, "with yet a seventh in the *menzil*, and presently you will see a rare thing, lamentable."

Ordinarily, on entering an encampment, we rode decorously to the sheik's tent, dismounted, and were silent until the sheik came forth to greet us.

But now, as we approached, Mitkhal began shouting and the men who rode with him, all except myself, joined in the clamor:

"*Ilmin hasswad?* [For whom is the blackening?]" they yelled, again and again.

Tribesmen of the friendly Beni Hassan, emerging from their tents and gathering before their sheik's, shouted back to us in chorus:

"*Il Furtak ibn Klaib.* [For Furtak Ben Klaib.]"

We did not dismount when we reached them, but remained in our saddles. The general yelling stopped, and Mitkhal demanded again in a loud voice:

"*Ilmin hasswad?*"

One man stood out from the group and replied:

"*Furtak ibn Klaib sswad houahlu weayalu.* [Furtak Ben Klaib is blackened, and his parents, and his family.]"

"For what is he blackened?" cried Mitkhal.

"For that he treacherously sought the dishonor of his cousin's wife—and he is not slain because he laid not hands upon her body, but sought her only with crooked words."

"*Aiee! Aiee! Aiee!*" cried Mitkhal and all his men. "May Furtak's face be blackened, and his parents and his family!"

Then with the men of Beni Hassan leading us, we rode among the tents to one with drawn curtains, and in front of it, planted in the sand, was another wand with its black, fluttering rag like a sign of death or pestilence.

And there, again, all shouted, "May Furtak's face be blackened!"

This accomplished, we returned to the sheik's tent; he embraced Mitkhal, and embraced me when Mitkhal presented me as "brother," and we sat for coffee, and no one spoke another word of Furtak and the blackening.

But afterward when we had taken our leave, Mitkhal explained the harsh, immemorial desert law. When a Bedouin treacherously wrongs another of his tribe, and when the wrong is great, yet not so great that it calls for shedding blood, the aggrieved individual must give fair notice of *"ukhutru bisswad* [intent to blacken]"; and if the wrong is one which the accused man can correct, he must be given an opportunity to do so, or to prove his innocence.

When he can do neither, after a period of three days, the blackening takes place. The aggrieved one first plants the wand in front of the guilty man's tent, then rides a wide circle around the encampment, and plants six others on conspicuous rises.

For the space of three days the black signals flutter in the wind and whenever strangers visit the *menzil*, whether a single rider, or a company, the ritual sentences are repeated.

It is the same whether the blackened one is secluded within his tent, or whether he has already fled from the disgrace, with his goods and family—which he is permitted to do, but in that case he can never return, and the tent itself he is not allowed to strike or take with him.

If the blackened one remains, he is permitted to bear arms, ride in *ghrazzu* or war, hold property, but is in a state of disgrace, excluded from coffee circle and councils.

Usually he does remain, and after a suitable lapse of time, seeks by some form of expiation or apology, accompanied by a peace offering to the wronged man of a camel or a few goats, to obtain pardon and reinstatement. If the wrong is a private one, power lies in the wronged man to grant or withhold forgiveness.

Only when the wrong is uncondonable or irreparable, does the blackened one leave his tribe, and then he becomes a wandering pariah—for not even a blood-feud enemy tribe will accept him. The only new alliance he can make is with one of the sneaking, cut-purse, tribeless

THE OLDEST AND YOUNGEST WARRIORS OF THE BENI
SAKHR

The Boy, though only Thirteen, Already Rides in Raids and
Battles.

Bedouin gypsy bands which infest the roadsides and town outskirts of Syria and Irak.

This Furtak, whom I did not see, had chosen to remain. When anger had cooled, in a month or so, probably, he would make overtures to the husband, offering apologies and a peace gift, confessing his fault, and quoting Koran passages which extol forgiveness. And since no ultimate harm had been done, he would probably be reinstated,

THE ARCH OF CTESIPHON, ON THE LOWER TIGRIS

though, as Mitkhal said, because of the nature of his offense, he would still have a "little bad name."

In generations past, the blackening weighed as heavily on the man's immediate family, sons, father, brothers, as upon himself. Today, the old ritual formula, "and his family," is preserved and is in that measure a disgrace to them all, but the subsequent ostracism is usually inflicted upon the guilty individual alone.

There remain certain death offenses, however, including rape, seduction and murder by stealth, for which the offender's father and brothers, though innocent, are slain with him—the male family wiped out at the root.

I had noticed curiously that Mansour, whose own African face was black through no fault but by the will of Allah, had cried "May he be blackened," as lustily as the rest.

Black, among the Bedouins, is a symbol of calamity, guilt, grief, and evil fortune—but the evil is in the symbol, not in the intrinsic blackness. Black holds no magic quality or inherent shame. A man has a black (wicked) heart. His face is blackened (disgraced). Yet the very tents in which the Bedouins dwell are black, the *abbas* of the men are more often black than not, the *agal* is black, the common garb of all their women is black from head to foot.

Likewise, though a swarthy countenance is regarded as a defect in womanly or manly beauty, the negroes among them, whether free or slaves, suffer no scorn.

No man of Mitkhal's household was more popular than Mansour. Indeed, the status of a slave like Mansour was a thing not easy for the western mind to grasp.

Mansour took delight in teaching me new Arabic words, while I helped increase his knowledge of pigeon French; we liked each other from the start, and as the days passed, he became confidential.

One morning, back in our own encampment, he seemed depressed. His gay exuberance was missing. I asked him if he had a headache. "Nay," he replied, "it is my shoulders which ache and smart as if they had been trampled on by ten thousand djinn."

Seeing I was puzzled, he suddenly grinned a rueful, childish grin, and said, like a bad boy caught in a not-too-wicked prank:

"You see, last evening, I shot my brother."

This news surprised me, and what it might have to do with his aching back was not altogether clear.

"Last month, before you came," he continued, "we made a little *ghrazzu* against the Sirdieh, and I enriched myself with a mare and a colt.

"My brother (also a slave of Mitkhal's) rides not in *ghrazzu*, for being occupied at the palace. He deals generously by me, and I by him, and what I take in *ghrazzu*, we often share. This time he demanded the colt, but for a whim I refused him. Indeed I wished to keep both for myself, may Allah forgive my greediness! But yesterday I learned that my brother, for spite, had sent the colt to Amman, and sold it and kept the gold. So that I went to require it of him, but when I came upon him, the colt jumped up in my throat, and made me shoot him—but only through the arm, praise be to the All-Merciful, for I did not wish his death.

"Then came the Pasha"—this was one of the rare times when Mansour used any other term than "my uncle" for Mitkhal—"who beat us both most terribly, so that we howled, but my brother howled loudest because the blows spared not even his wounded arm—but though he beat us equally, he gave me a new colt." And Mansour grinned again like a bad boy.

I have recounted this in detail for the sake of contrasts with later facts which I learned about Mansour. On a westward excursion to Mitkhal's cultivated lands, back on the edge of the "sown," we rode through the fields in which wheat had just been harvested. Scattered in every direction as far as the eye could see, there were little groups of *fellaheen*, men, women, girls, native peasants,

Christian and Moslem, toiling, sweating, in the sun, while we rode like lords among them.

Mansour, the black slave who had been beaten like a dog, now superbly mounted on a white mare, with his gold-embroidered *abba* and the jewels of his scimitar gleaming, stretched out his great black paw and a long arm from which flowed pointed voluminous sleeves of

A GUARDIAN OF CROPS ON THE DESERT
FRINGE

finest muslin, and made a sweeping gesture to indicate a stretch of fields which must have comprised at least three hundred acres.

"All this is mine," he said proudly, "and all these people of the earth-gray faces toil for my increment."

"How did you get it?"

"My uncle gave it me, after I had warded a sword-thrust from him when the Wahabi came against us in the south."

I glanced at Mitkhal for confirmation, and he nodded that it was true.

But when I returned to America and said to friends, without explaining the circumstances: "I have seen on the desert edge a black Moslem slave riding bejeweled, in gold-embroidered robes, among white Christian girls and women who toiled for him barefooted in the fields," my friends replied: "Stuff and nonsense! You are stringing us, for there was nothing like that even in the days of Haroun el Reshid, and now it is a modernized country, where the French and English have abolished slavery itself—certainly slaves who wear curved swords and are masters over Christian women."

Yet there are stranger things than this in desert tent and palace, where *farengi* law has never reached, and perhaps never will.

Mansour, though a slave, was one of the richest members of the tribe, after Mitkhal's own family. He could have ridden a couple of days' journey to any British post and become automatically a freed man, but he would have been a fool to do it. In fact, I heard of no slave who had invoked the *farengi* law, and of only one who had ever run away. And that was a generation back.

Mitkhal's father had a powerful Sudanese, mighty in battle but evil-tempered. One night he fell in a rage with his master, tore the sheik's weapons from him, and mauled him like a savage beast. Death would have been the penalty, so the Sudanese fled, and with rage still in his heart, sought sanctuary with the great Roualla tribe, hereditary enemies of the Beni Sakhr.

By stealth, he entered the Roualla camp, laid hold of the sheik's tent rope, and then cried, *"Dakhilak! Ana khadmak.* [Protection! I am now your slave.]"

But the sheik, a rude and lawless man, recognized him, had him dragged into the tent, and shouted,

"Nay, thou hast slain the Roualla in blood feud and now thou shalt surely die."

The slave invoked desert law in vain. He seized a boiling coffee pot and sought to drink from the spout, but it was knocked from his hands, he was dragged outside, and his throat cut.

When this came later to the ears of the Beni Sakhr, though they themselves would have slain the Sudanese, they rode against the Roualla, and fought until five Roualla deaths were exacted in vengeance.

The Roualla, a great tribe, are the rudest and most warlike of the northern desert. They are not as skillful horsemen as the smaller Sirdieh, nor are they as rich as the Beni Sakhr, but in hand-to-hand fighting they are unequaled.

At another time, and under wholly different circumstances, with Amir Amin Arslan and a Damascus banker, —myself and they in motor car and European clothes,—I visited a Roualla camp. We were received with a proud, rough, lavish hospitality, but not in friendship. Amir Amin is *"dakhile"* to all Bedouins north of Medain Salih, because he ruled them justly as desert governor under the Turks, but here was no embracing or talk of brotherhood. I felt in them—particularly toward myself and the Damascene—a savage, disdainful contempt.

When we entered the *mukhaad*, rugs and camel saddles were placed for us, but the sheik sat apart with his men on the ground. However, a big deal in flocks was pending, and though unwilling to be friendly, I think he wanted to impress the banker with the fact that the tribe was prosperous enough to hold out for its own terms. At any rate, when dinner time came, a gigantic iron pan, at least nine feet in diameter, carried by more than a dozen staggering men, was brought in, with the carcass of an entire camel roasted whole. We were invited to sit around it and eat our fill; no member of the tribe, not even the Roualla sheik, ate with us.

When we had finished, the sheik and some twelve of his warriors squatted around the enormous feast.

Amir Amin had told me to watch closely for unusual happenings. I observed that the sheik picked up a small piece of the liver and ate it; but that afterward he scooped up a handful of rice and gravy, prepared a ball as if to put it in his mouth, but kissed it, dropped it to the ground, and ate no more. The Roualla warriors each tore off from the carcass a strip of meat, wiped it across their lips, dropped it to the ground, sat back with every sign of having finished a satisfactory meal, squatted perhaps five minutes more, whispering and conversing like people who had enjoyed a good dinner, and then all saying, "We have eaten," arose and went out wiping their hands on their *abbas* or in their hair.

New groups of warriors came into the tent to see the strange guests; they were invited by the sheik to partake of the feast; some of them had been riding hard all day and I am sure not a mouthful had passed their lips since morning. In every case it was "Thanks, O sheik, in the name of Allah, but we have eaten."

A half hour later, the enormous pan was carried out and put on the ground some ten feet away from the tent and within the light of the lantern; a slave waved the long sleeves of his *gumbaz*, and I have never seen a sight to equal that which followed. There were perhaps a hundred or a hundred and fifty naked brats, boys and girls, browned little savages, from three years of age to seven or eight. They came rushing to the camel carcass, climbed over each other in their haste and joy, fought for places; some of them finally fell like little pigs, into the enormous dish.

After these children had eaten their fill, the women came with wicker baskets and wooden bowls and picked the carcass clean to the skeleton.

While the children were stuffing themselves, I had noticed a group of other children, perhaps a dozen or more, naked, and in appearance exactly like the rest, who stood at a distance of some twenty feet and took no part in the infantile orgies. I noticed one of these, a little boy of about five who, approaching closer than the others, stood disconsolately sucking his thumb. I asked Amir Amin, "What about this second group of children?" He said, "These are little Rouallas; the ones you saw running to the carcass are not Rouallas at all but members of a tributary tribe camped with them."

The Rouallas have the old Spartan idea of discipline and hardship, and teach their men and male children to abstain at will from meat. But I thought there was a strong element of surly ostentation and pride in this extraordinary exhibition.

Life and customs among the Beni Sakhr I found far less rude, yet at times astonishingly primitive. One morning, a man of our tribe appeared at Mitkhal's tent bareheaded, his *kafieh* bound round his shoulder, and soaked with blood. He had an ugly knife-wound, the result of a private quarrel.

The antisepsis was quick, crude, and, I imagine, fairly efficient—but it must have been damnably painful. Mansour boiled a cup of molasses, pulled off the bandage, pried open the wound with his fingers until it gaped, poured in the stuff, still boiling, and tied it up tightly with a clean *kafieh* which had been brought from a chest in the *hareem*.

The man's shoulder and arm quivered like the flank of a horse being stung by flies, but he made no sound. When the job was finished, somebody handed him a lighted cigarette.

I was a bit surprised, for in Mitkhal's tent, and in those of many other sheiks I later visited, it was a common thing to see modern appliances and utensils, Zeiss binoculars, "Ever Ready" flashlights, automatic pistols, and other products of western science—not to mention mattresses, stuffs and tinware from England or Germany. It seemed to me strange that a sheik as progressive as Mitkhal hadn't learned that there were better things than boiling molasses to sterilize wounds. I had a small "first-aid" kit which contained, among other drugs, a bottle of iodine and a tube of permanganate crystals. I showed them to him, and explained their use. He wanted to know in what respect they were better than the boiling molasses, and I suggested that they were at any rate less painful. That made little difference, he assured me, for the pain was bearable and quickly over. And he added, with a certain practical common sense, that molasses could be found in every desert camp, while a man might die of his wounds before he found *farengi* medicine, even if a few scattered sheiks did keep a supply of it.

I inquired if he had no *farengi* medicine of any sort,

and he replied that he believed his younger wife once had a box of aspirin tablets, but that they had all been used. "It is a pity too," he said, "for one of her women has been suffering from headaches and it is more powerful than our own *dawwa* [drugs]."

I gave him three tablets for the woman, and we resumed our conversation about medicine. I discovered that, of European remedies, he knew the uses only of aspirin, quinine, and laxative pills, which he called "*purga*."

The commonest Bedouin medicine, he informed me, was horse's urine, which acted both as a purgative and emetic, and was also valuable in fever.

He went again into the *hareem* and presently returned with a little wooden chest which contained all the *dawwa* of his household. There were small boxes in it, two or three bottles and several leather pouches. With a courage stimulated by curiosity, I smelt and tasted the contents of them all. One lump of gum which stank to high heaven was easily identifiable as asafœtida. He called it *haltita*. There were also camphor, garlic, coarse black pepper, and an odorless, tasteless brown-gray powder which he told me was pulverized sheep dung. The actual medical value of various excrements is known to savage and primitive tribes the world over. There were two or three aromatic herbs which I could not identify, and I have forgotten their Arabic names. The black pepper, he told me, was made into a drink for fever; the *thum* [garlic] was given in sour milk for the belly-ache, and the camphor was good for chills. About the other remedies, he was vague.

He also showed me a black goat's horn, wide open at

the base, with a smaller opening at the filed-off tip, used for "cupping" or blood-letting. Here again, I found a sound, rudimentary knowledge of antisepsis, for he explained that the skin was first scratched with "a knife-point blackened in flame." After the cup was pressed down, the air was sucked out with the lips, and a piece of leather slipped between the lips and horn's tip and tied down to preserve the vacuum.

Searing with hot irons or cauterizing with boiling molasses were common for all sores or wounds of man or beast. I saw them efficiently sear a running sore on the cheek of a mare, and within eight days it had healed with a clean scar.

If a member of the tribe, man or woman, became seriously ill, I was told, and if their simple medicines proved of no avail, he was isolated in a little tent set far off from the others—they have a definite idea of contagion—with sufficient food to last for weeks, and left alone, to recover or die, "*ilram tallah* [as Allah willed]."

In treatment of serous wounds which require drainage, they use clean straw beneath the bandages, not as tubes, but wisps of it loosely inserted, so that the drainage trickles or seeps out.

The belief in charms and magic, particularly the efficacy of certain verses from the Koran to ward off or cure disease, is still widespread.

Occasionally, but not often, they seek *farengi* aid in Amman, Jerusalem, or Damascus.

A sheik of the Annezy had a badly infected eye, and was persuaded to seek aid from a German doctor in Amman.

It developed that the sheik expected him to perform

the cure, not by treating the eye, but by supplying him with a *hijab* [amulet or charm] to drive out the evil spirit.

The doctor lost patience. "I am a scientist, a medical man. If you want to be cured, perhaps I can cure you, but if you want charms, you can go to one of your own witch-doctors."

"No," the sheik replied, "I have greater confidence in you."

"In that case, you must do what I tell you."

The doctor washed out the eye, prepared a bottle of boracic acid in solution, with an eye-cup which he taught the sheik to use, and made him swear by Allah and the Prophet that he would use it exactly as instructed, three times a day, until the bottle was finished, and then return to him.

The sheik, who was rich, paid the fee of a gold pound willingly, and then hesitated.

"It is finished?" he asked. "It is finished," the doctor replied. But the patient was not satisfied.

"*Btunti*," he began—meaning "You will give?"—and repeated a special Bedouin formula of request which cannot be refused except with grave discourtesy if the favor is reasonable and within one's power. "I have promised to use your medicine," the sheik continued—"and now it can do no harm if you will also give me a *hijab*."

"Very well," shouted the doctor, exploding with impatience, "I will give you a *hijab* indeed!

"Send your servant to the bazaar, and have him fetch me a piece of leather and a thong." While the servant was fetching them, he wrote on a sheet of his prescription pad, in Arabic:

"In the name of the Prophet, and by the Ninety-Nine Names of Allah, and by the Hundredth Name,—as one of your eyes is now afflicted, may you become totally blind in both!"

A VILLAGE STREET IN TRANSJORDANIA, ON THE
EDGE OF THE DESERT

He wadded this mighty incantation into a ball, sewed it up tightly in the piece of leather, and the sheik departed, well content, with the amulet strung round his neck.

A month later, he returned, cured and grateful, still wearing the *hijab*, and said:

"It is all clear to me now, O powerful friend; the water which you gave me in the bottle was but a test to try my faith—and I was faithful. The charm you hung around my neck has cured me."

"O wise and perspicacious sheik," replied the doctor, "if you are grateful, go now into the bazaar and return to me with witnesses."

Ten minutes later, the sheik returned with three friends —the *hijab* was opened in their presence, and its contents read—to the terror and astonishment of them all.

The sheik was angry, and insisted on having the paper immediately burned, but a year later when a son fell seriously ill, he brought him to the same doctor for treatment.

And while my Bedouin friends never bothered to supply themselves with even the simplest *farengi* medicines, which they could have procured easily from Damascus or Amman, they were willing enough to try mine.

News that I had aspirin soon spread through the camp, and presently came a man who said:

"My wife is afflicted here," tapping his forehead.

I gave him two tablets. In less than an hour came another, and then they kept coming. It seemed there was a headache epidemic in all the *hareems* of the Beni Sakhr —though I had never heard neuralgia was contagious. The tube had held at least a hundred tablets, and scarcely a dozen remained.

Then came Mansour, who had constituted himself my guardian in emergencies great or small, and whispered:

"The pills enter not the bellies of their wives, but repose against a future time tied in the folds of their own *kafiehs.*"

"No matter," I replied, "but I shall guard the small remainder for such as really have need of them." So it was announced the aspirin was "*ma fi* [all gone]."

I thought then and still believe, that an interesting and useful career—with possibly large material rewards—is awaiting any competent doctor with a taste for excitement and rough outdoor life who would attach himself permanently to one of these rich, powerful tribe-groups. Many camels and a great name might be his, in time, particularly if he kept a record of his experiences.

Chapter V

THE ROBBER-SAINT

"WE ride," said Mitkhal, "to visit the *menzil* of a saint."

And as we rode, he told me briefly the history of Haditha Pasha, sheik of the El Khour. He had inherited wealth and the leadership of a powerful tribe, but his possessions and the number of his warriors had dwindled, because of his extraordinary generosity, which had become famous throughout the desert.

It had made him universally honored and beloved, but it was "poor business," Mitkhal pointed out, for men to spend their lives following a chief who habitually gave away three-fourths of the tribal flocks they bred or stole in *ghrazzu.* Therefore, many of the tribe had "loved him and left him," to join some more practical leader.

"We would not see him actually abandoned or in poverty," said Mitkhal. He still had six hundred loyal warriors and ample flocks to maintain his honorable estate. But he was "poor" compared with Mitkhal himself and other rich sheiks who counted their men by thousands and their flocks by tens of thousands.

When we reached the El Khour *menzil*, I found Haditha Pasha—who welcomed us with courtly dignity —a tall, elderly man, of grave and noble countenance, seldom smiling, with whitening beard, and the far-away look of a dreamer in his eyes.

His tent, in which we sat, was large, but scantily furnished, almost bare. Three weeks before, a neighboring friend, the Sheik Sirhan, had ventured south for honey-dates of El Ally, and the Wahabi had plundered his caravan. When Sirhan returned, stripped, Haditha had made a division of all his own personal belongings, piled them into equal stacks, and given one to Sirhan, with several camels.

Sirhan was gone now, to mend his fortunes by doing unto others as the Wahabi had done unto him, but one of his cousins, Dirdar, who had been with him in the adventure, recounted these things to us, while Haditha was beyond earshot.

Dirdar was mild-voiced, gentle, with hands as delicate as a woman's. I remarked them for contrast with his scimitar, which seemed heavier than most. I asked to see the blade and discovered the difference was in width rather than weight. It was an old blade, ground to razor sharpness, without ornament or inlay, but only the maker's mark, rudely stamped, like a sun and crescent. My request to see the blade pleased him, for Dirdar was a famed swordsman. He had cut a Wahabi in two, clean through the waist, in recent fighting, and with this same sword, in his lifetime, had slain more than thirty men.

As we sat talking, a diversion occurred outside. A merchant arrived, with his stock loaded on four mules, and set up a gayly striped and colored *Engleysi* tent, in which he sold cotton prints from Manchester, tin cooking utensils, small iron gear, salt in hunks big as a fist, and coarse sugar. We went to watch the trading. I found in the merchant's tent a half dozen ripe tomatoes, and wished to buy them. The price was only a few copper piastres, but he insisted on giving them to me and would take no pay because I was Haditha's guest. I offered some of them to Haditha, Mitkhal, and other sheiks, but only one accepted. I had been without fruit or vegetables for several weeks and had an intense craving for green stuff. The habituated Bedouins cared nothing about it. I think it must be the fermented camel milk that saves them from constipation and scurvy.

In Haditha's tent was less formality than at Mitkhal's great *beit-shaar*, but a beautiful courtesy. A worn and ragged Bedouin of unpleasing, evil features, who had evidently ridden far, stood outside, holding his horse's halter, and ventured a *"Salaam Aleikum,"* uncertain of his welcome. He was of a tribe unfriendly to Haditha's, but not a blood-enemy. It was plain in his attitude. He stood as one who would say:

"I know that I am a man of no importance, also that you have no reason to be friendly with me or my tribe, and that I have no right to claim your hospitality; but I am weary and hungry."

There was a moment's hesitation; then Haditha rose to his full height, and replied, *"Aleikum salaam."* Water, milk, cheese, and bread were given him freely, and a rug was thrown in a distant corner of the tent, where he lay on his belly like a dog and slept.

The big coffee-pot was awkwardly upset by a man stirring the embers, when all exclaimed *"Khair Inshallah!* [A good omen!]" I asked why they said it. "Because it has always been the custom," said one. Mitkhal suggested that perhaps it was "so that the awkward one should not lose face." I wondered if it really traced back to pagan libations poured out on the sand in pre-Moslem times.

Haditha had a falcon, chained to a short wooden perch. He tossed it shreds of goat-flesh which it ate greedily, but it stared with unblinking eyes. Presently he unchained the bird and threw it into the air. It flew in widening circles, mounting. I tried to follow it with Mitkhal's glasses. When it was only a faint speck in the sky, Haditha stripped off his *abba* and waved it. The bird caught his signal from that great distance, and returning, came to rest on his wrist. The falcon is used

A HIMYARITE INSCRIPTION ON AN ANCIENT STONE IN
THE ARABIAN DESERT

for hunting gazelle and the dove, pigeon, and other edible birds which abound on the edge of the desert; also, farther in the great desert, the bustard, a bird twice as big as a turkey, the same mentioned by Xenophon. They hunt also with a small greyhound, fleet, but scarce half the size of Europe's breed. They carry the falcon hooded, on wrist or saddle pommel, as did lords and ladies in times of chivalry.

When darkness fell, a lantern was hung on the tentpole, after we had eaten, and a man sang to the twanging of the *rabeyba*. In the after pause, our ragged, villainous-featured guest rolled over and grunted in his sleep. I said a word in praise of Bedouin hospitality, which included even such as he.

"It is a small thing," replied Haditha, "but it is true that hospitality is of the desert rather than the town.

"Two years ago, I crossed to the *Engleysi* border [Irak] on a *ghrazzu*, which went ill with us, and we took no cattle, and were worsted. We were three hundred horsemen, returning, and were ninety-six hours without food or water, save a little for our horses, which cannot bear thirst as a man or a camel. We came to an encampment of no more tents than my fingers, where dwelt an improverished sheik, Sahr Assarah, may Allah grant him better prosperity; for his sole wealth then was two camels and fifteen black goats.

"My name he knew, though he had never looked on my face. And while my men rode to the well from which he drew, he gave me to drink in his tent, but called another to make coffee, and was gone.

"Somewhat distant I heard a great, shrill bleating. Sahr Assarah, with his sons, had gone among the goats and broken of each goat a leg."

Haditha ceased, as if the tale were finished—and indeed it was. *"Aiee!"* cried Mansour; and *"Wellah* [by God]! Here is a thing to be remembered," exclaimed Mitkhal; and the others said, "May Allah grant that sheik prosperity."

A goat with a broken leg must be immediately killed. Sahr Assarah knew that if he began to slay his flock, Haditha would hear and forbid it ere three throats had been slit. With the goats' legs broken, it was useless to stop the slaughter, and there was flesh for Haditha and all his famished warriors.

Then followed other tales of memorable hospitality, and Sirhan told this, which he had from his father:

A rich sheik died without sons, and his widow became gradually poor. Where the tribe pastured, she followed, but always pitched her tent alone, far distant from the rest. Had she dwelt in their midst, it would have been the duty of every important stranger to visit the sheik's widow, and hers to provide refreshment. She lived on the milk of her one camel, taking it to pasture, riding it home in the evening.

One dark winter night came a wandering merchant to buy camels, and stumbled on her tent before he found the main encampment. By her words and bearing, he knew her to be a personage; shadows concealed the poverty of her dwelling. He asked if she had camels for the market. She replied:

"No, I have but one camel here. My flocks are in far pastures."

And having no beans for making coffee, she set milk before him. Said the merchant: "I have come a weary way. If there is a second tent, I would rest and sleep."

By Bedouin law, a wanderer who comes in peace may demand shelter at any tent, but it would not have been seemly to share the same tent with a woman, even an old one.

"I have another tent," she replied, "where I will lie, while you remain here."

In a couple of hours she returned with a big bowl of steaming hot meat, rich with gravy. The merchant said: "I have eaten like a Sultan, O Mother of Bounty!"

She had no other tent, and slept *bithelje wil bard*

brah'm tallaah [with cold and snow, under the mercy of God].

When she returned at morning, the merchant saw her soaked garments, and wondered. She explained that the second tent was with relatives, "beyond the hill," and that coming back she had passed through a heavy gust of rain.

Looking about him in daylight, the stranger suspected her poverty. Without injury to her pride—because he was not a desert dweller whose tent must also be open to all wanderers—he had the right to offer a gift in return for hospitality, and asked for the loan of her camel, so that he might send her a load of wheat.

"Alas!" she said. "Last night my camel died."

A woman of lesser station would not have felt obligated to so great a sacrifice, but she, for her sheikly family honor, and having no other meat to set before the stranger, had slain her one camel for his food.

When Sirhan had finished, I said:

"I ask answer and pardon for a graceless question, but I come from a country where one part of this tale would be ill taken."

"Ask," replied Sirhan, "in the name of Allah."

"We would deem it a great shame that so noble an old woman, the widow of a former sheik, should be allowed by her own tribe to remain apart like a dog outside the *menzil*, in poverty and want. How, when the *Beduw*, in their pride of hospitality, grant shelter and entertainment to all strangers—even to that one of evil countenance who grunts there in his sleep—do they yet succor not their own?"

And I told of our proverb that "charity begins at home."

"It is a good question," they replied, and Sirhan said: "All of the woman's relatives had died. She was too old to marry again, and her great pride was such that she refused to accept their alms, because there could never be requital."

They were not displeased that I had raised the question. But perhaps in friendly malice, they asked if I could match their tales with one of *farengi* generosity. With Haditha's bird perched near, I told them Boccaccio's story of the man who had slain his pet falcon to set meat before his lady. It was a proper tale, they said, but Mitkhal keenly added that it was "not the same," since it was done for romantic love, rather than hospitality.

Another of their stories that night struck me as being fabulous or at least embroidered with exaggerations.

Sheik Hatim of the Beni Tai had a son named Zjeyd. The child had no sense of property value, and from the age of eight he would give to any passing stranger goats and sheep from the flocks entrusted to his care. Finally his father sent him with the herdsmen, into the far desert, where strangers seldom passed.

One day the boy was riding with a herdsman, leading a hundred camels. They chanced to meet three *mnashid* [Bedouin troubadours] who sang for him. He was enchanted and said: "I will make you a gift." He divided the flock into three parts and gave one to each of the singers. The herdsman could not forbid it, because Zjeyd was the sheik's son, but he sent word to Hatim, saying: "Your son is smitten by Allah. He is a saint, but if he remains with us you will soon have no camels left."

Hatim sent for Zjeyd and said sternly: "Where are my hundred camels?"

The son replied: "I have made for you and for our tribe a name from this day on until the day of judgment" —meaning that the *mnashid* would make a song about the gift, and that the song would be immortal.

The father died. The son succeeded as the head of the little tribe and soon reduced them all to poverty. One night four guests came to their tent. He said to his mother: "What have we to offer them?" and she replied: "Alas, the last goat has been slain!" He said: "An hour distant are camped some of the Annezy. I will stain my face black, and you will sell me to them as a slave, taking in payment goats which you can slay for our guests, so that my father's tent will not be dishonored." She refused. He then took a dagger and threatened to kill himself; so she did as he had commanded.

The son who had become a slave toiled with his new masters for five years. Then it chanced, as he was tending the flocks, that one of the same troubadours passed by in his wanderings, and said: "If your face were not dark, I could believe you were that one," and sang him the song which he had made about the gift of a hundred camels. The boy said: "It was not I," and stayed tending the sheep.

On a later day, after our visit to Haditha, I asked Mitkhal, who was a man of great common sense, which among these stories might be true fact and which fables. He said the tale of the sheik's widow seemed to him true —for its like must have happened many times. About Haditha's story of Sahr Assarah and the goats, there could be no question. The tale of the hundred camels for a song, on the other hand, seemed to him *"fantasia"* —one of the many European expressions the Arabs have incorporated into their own language.

Bedouin truthfulness—or lack of it—is a subtly complicated matter. They consider lying a shameful, unpardonable sin, and men of honor adhere to the code, but it takes a born *Bedawi* to understand the hair-splitting distinctions of what is a lie, *a priori*, and what is not. Nor

A DESERT CAMP AND COFFEE FIRE

Sheik Mitkhal Pasha in the Center, the Author at His Right.
(*From a Photograph*)

is it, strangely enough, a matter of the oath. A man can come in from the desert and swear by the beard of the Prophet that he met a caravan of a thousand green camels with wings—and it is not a lie. If a man has been robbed on the road, he can declare that fifty warriors despoiled him, though they may have been but three. After a battle, he may swear by Allah that he has slain ten of the enemy, though perhaps he slew only one or two; for such a falsehood, he might be "ragged" as a braggart, or even despised—but he would not be blackened and dishonored as a liar. None of these lies, theoretically at least, can do injury to another, or affect subsequent events.

On the other hand, there are astounding cases in which an Englishman or American would be tempted to lie— or at least to maintain a strict silence—when the Bedouin of honor must speak the truth.

Amir Amin Arslan was in a small Bedouin *menzil*, having coffee with the sheik, when he saw a woman pass in front of the tent two or three times, glance at him significantly, and make a motion toward an adjoining tent. He could not believe that she was flirting with him, and was mystified. When she had done it a third time, he got up and went to the tent she had indicated. He found there two men of a neighboring enemy tribe, bound hand and foot, and a group over them preparing to cut their throats. Amir Amin, who was at that time governor of the territory, stopped the procedure. The sheik said the men were being justly executed because they had come as spies and in disguise to assassinate him in his own camp. They had committed no overt act, but he said he had been reliably informed of their purpose. Amir Amin said: "You cannot murder two men on hearsay." The sheik lifted his eyes in surprise and said: "Ask them." Amir Amin had the two men unbound and brought before him into another tent. He said: "Why did you come to this camp?" They replied: "We came to slay the sheik." He said: "Don't you know that if you say that, even if I do not permit them to kill you here, I will have to turn you over to the Turkish authorities, and you will be put in prison for life?" They said: "That is in the hands of Allah, but we came for the purpose we have stated."

It would take many volumes, and they would be as

technical as those of our own courts, to codify the unwritten laws of the Arabian desert.

The Bedouin may steal by guile, he may rob and kill
by violence, he may strike from behind in cold blood—
but only under certain circumstances. The identical deed,
under different conditions, may be a hideous crime.

His code of honor, in some respects, is as quixotic and
fantastic as that of King Arthur's knights. Haditha
embodied it, perhaps, more than any other Bedouin I met.
My friend Mitkhal was rich, prosperous, and worldly-
wise, cynical, too, in an amiable way; yet he revered
Haditha as a sort of saint. Among the many stories
which Mitkhal told me of him, the following is most
typical.

Haditha had a white mare which he loved. A neighboring sheik named Goren, on friendly but not intimate
terms with Haditha, admired the mare and was very
anxious to buy it. He offered Haditha three hundred
gold pounds, and when he found that Haditha would not
sell the mare at any price, he offered in exchange one of
his daughters noted for her beauty. Haditha refused to
part with the mare. Goren then called on him formally
and said: "As we are not enemies, honor and the desert
law compel me to warn you that I am going to any lengths
to get your mare even if I have to steal it." Haditha
replied: "I am warned."

Goren bided his time in long patience. When more
than a year had passed—this event occurred in 1920, according to Mitkhal—Goren learned that Haditha was
planning to ride into Damascus to make arrangements
about the sale of some camels.

The Bedouins usually trim their beards to a short point.

Goren had kept out of Haditha's sight and had let his
beard grow rough and long. He stained his face with
streaks of henna and rubbed it with the ashes of camel
dung; next he took a dagger and inflicted on his right foot
a painful but not dangerous wound, which would cause
him to limp; he bound it up with an old rag so that the
blood seeped through and made a spot; he then dressed
himself in the garments of a beggar and took a staff.

On the morning when Haditha was to ride into Damascus, Goren took the road before him, and walked with his
lame foot for miles until he was actually worn out,
covered with perspiration, and in great pain. These pre-
cautions might seem theatrical and unnecessary, but the
eyes of the Bedouin are keen as a hawk to penetrate disguise or sham. Goren had therefore produced in himself
a condition, even down to the details of exhaustion and
pain, which was not sham but real.

Presently Haditha, cantering along on his white mare,
overtook Goren, and as he came abreast, Goren sank into
the road almost under the mare's feet. Haditha, observ-
ing the bloody bandage and the exhaustion, failed to
recognize Goren because of the beard, the henna and dirt
on his face, and the *kafieh* which partly covered it; he
halted and dismounted to help the wayfarer in distress.

Goren moaned that he was on his way to Damascus
and had become exhausted because of his wound.
Haditha did the thing that any Bedouin sheik might do,
under the circumstances; he lifted Goren to the back of his
mare, held him in the saddle, and set out toward Damascus, himself on foot, letting the beggar ride. Goren kept
silent for more than a half hour, giving his strength time
to return; then he said: "Noble sheik, your gun is heavy

on your shoulders; do, therefore, hang it here on the pommel." It was a hot day and a long road, and Haditha, suspecting nothing, acquiesced. Two or three minutes later Goren dug his heels violently into the mare, and in three bounds was out of Haditha's reach. He then wheeled the horse, unslung the rifle, and returned to where Haditha stood.

"Oh! Haditha, I gave you honorable warning."

Haditha recognized Goren and replied, greatly chagrined: "O Goren, you did give warning!"

As Goren turned to ride away triumphantly, Haditha suddenly shouted. Goren wheeled again and returned to him. Haditha said: "I have reflected. The mare is yours, and I will promise not to seek its return either by violence or guile, if you will promise what I ask of you."

"I promise," replied Goren.

It is the custom among Bedouin sheiks to demand a promise and to acquiesce in it without saying what the bargain is—depending on each other's honor. Haditha said: "You will promise on the name of the Prophet, and I will promise likewise, that we will tell no living soul the manner in which you obtained my mare."

"I promise, O sheik! But why?" replied Goren.

"Because," said Haditha, "if this tale spread from mouth to mouth in our desert, no rider would ever dare to stop and give aid to a wounded man or a beggar again, and this would be a shame greater than the loss of a thousand white mares." Goren reflected, got down from the horse's back, put the bridle in the hands of Haditha, and said: "I cannot steal, even after honorable warning, from such a man."

Haditha, because of Goren's wound, helped him back

into the saddle, they went together into Damascus—and remained fast friends.

Of course such a story depicts only one side of the true Bedouin character. His code of honor is higher in many respects than that of any European race; yet he remains essentially a professional robber. Raiding and cattle-stealing—next only to the breeding of cattle—are his chief occupations.

Nor does he always confine his robbery to the plundering of other native tribes. He still regards the European traveler as his lawful prey, and though he is wary of *farengi* vengeance on the borders of Syria, Transjordania, and Irak, the stranger who ventures far into the desert risks his property and his life.

Despite airplanes and camel corps, even the Nairn transport company, which sends its Cadillac convoys straight across the desert from Damascus to Baghdad, and return, three times a week, pays regular gold tribute to certain tribes—and even so is occasionally robbed, though rarely, because of some "misunderstanding." Such a hold-up involves serious consequences, reprisals, dispatches to the newspapers—and for this reason the Nairn convoy is by far the safest, as well as the quickest and most comfortable, way of crossing Arabia. If their price of twenty-five pounds sterling ($125) per person seems high, it is because a part of it goes as tribute to keep the route comparatively safe.

The traveler who ventures alone, or in private convoy, is taking an unhealthy risk. One morning I saw a German archeologist, his wife, and five native servants, in two cars loaded with baggage, set out from the Hotel Victoria, in Damascus, for Palmyra, only six hours distant. They

ENTRANCE TO THE GREAT BAZAAR AT DAMASCUS

Where Northern Desert Bedouins Trade

felt they had nothing to fear, for Palmyra is the head-quarters of the *Mehari*, the French desert camel corps. They returned unexpectedly that same day, in time for late luncheon. The angry gentleman came afoot, bare-foot at that, and naked as a jaybird, except for his linen duster. His lady rode a donkey which they had bor-rowed on the edge of the city. She had been permitted to retain her skirt and blouse. They only returned at all because they had had the good sense to offer no resistance.

It was hard for me to remember things of this sort, however, when I was guest of the Bedouins, bound to them by the friendliest ties. But occasionally some little thing occurred or a word was spoken which made me realize that I would be painting an untrue picture if I recounted only their wonderful hospitality, their honor among themselves, and their loyal friendship.

For instance, there was talk of the Zionists in Haditha's tent, and I was amazed at the bitterness of the words. I have life-long friends among Jews, and I relate now simply as a part of my attempt at a true record that the Bedouins whom I knew held all Jews in hatred and con-tempt. I had asked the gentle, saintly sheik Haditha what he thought of the actual Zionist movement. He had replied, with the mildness of a lamb, and no intention of irony, that he considered it a most admirable arrange-ment; when the British had brought them all in, and then withdrew armed protection, it would be easy and con-venient to massacre them all and take their flocks and crops!

These tribes with whom I dwelt in peaceful security—and other tribes like them—were held in as great terror by small Jewish agricultural colonies on the desert fringe as ever the redskins were by isolated prairie settlers—and, I fear, for equally good cause.

Only three months before, a tribe less than a hundred miles to the south had raided, burned, and massacred a Jewish "fenced farm" of some thirty persons. There was no survivor. The women and children were found outside the charred ruins, with their throats cut like sheep. Nor was this regarded as a "shame" to the tribe which had done it, for between the men of the desert and the *Yahoud* colonists, there is declared blood feud. This death proscription is not against Jews in general, but against all colonists who have been allotted lands which the Arabs regard as their own. "This land was ours," they say, "before Moses and his thieving horde of runaway slaves ever came ravaging it out of Egypt. It returned to us under caliph and sultan, and it shall yet be ours again."

So, naturally, the Jew on the edge of Palestine regards the Bedouin as a cruel and ruthless savage who gives no quarter. The only good they will grudgingly admit of him is that he does not torture and does not rape. He has no habits, like the Sahara Tuaregs, of mutilating captives or slitting off their eyelids and pegging them out in the sun. He brings massacre, but "clean," quick death. So far as I could learn, the Arab Bedouin does not practice torture. The only physical punishment ever inflicted in the black tents is plain old-fashioned beating with anything that comes to hand, usually a rope halter or camel-stick. The only torture of which I ever had knowledge in modern Arabia was that undergone voluntarily by Dervishes and fakirs in the name of religion, and that occasionally still inflicted in palace *hareems* on unfaithful wives and concubines.

In *ghrazzu* among the Bedouin tribes themselves, quarter is freely given, prisoners are honorably treated, and usually the casualties are small. Wars of blood vengeance, wars of extermination between tribe and tribe, still occur, but with increasing rarity.

Mitkhal told me a few of their simpler laws in intertribal *ghrazzu*.[1]

If a man fell from his horse, he could not be attacked. If a mounted enemy cut him down or shot him, that enemy would be "blackened" by his own tribe.

And because of this, an unhorsed man who fires against a mounted enemy would be a murderer.

In attacking a *menzil*, it is a crime to shoot into the tents, for risk of hitting women and children.

A man who is taken prisoner must be permitted to sit in the coffee-circle with his captors and must be permitted to eat his fill from the common dish. When the *ghrazzu* is over, he is allowed to return to his own tribe, and a horse or camel is lent him for that purpose (often his own captured mount). But his tribe is in honor bound to return it later to the captors. The Bedouin has no place or use for prisoners. The humblest warrior would die rather than soil his hands with any physical labor. So general exchange, with no count kept, is universal.

If a ruling sheik is taken captive, he is entertained with sheikly honor and goes free later without ransom. A certain one was taken prisoner in a raid in which fifty

---

[1] *Ghrazzu,* I want to repeat, is merely a wild, rough game, with stolen flocks as the prizes. In *ghrazzu* the Bedouins never kill for the sake of killing.

of his camels were also captured. Sitting that night in
his captor's tent, he bargained to buy back his own camels,
agreed upon a price in gold, and was allowed to ride
away with them on the morrow, with no security but his
word that the gold would be sent later.

Captives are "guests," Mitkhal told me.

Another set of unwritten laws cover the personal feud
—more honorable than those which prevail in the Ken-
tucky hills. If a Bedouin has a death feud with another,
he cannot slay from ambush or take him unaware. He
must not only send formal word, if the man does not
already know it, that there is blood between them, but
when they do meet it must be *"Bissot* [with shouting],"
so that neither has the advantage of surprise.

In the few cases where a man's death is decreed in
tribal council, he is slain without opportunity to defend
himself, but certain rules must also be observed. Under
no circumstances, for instance, can a man be slain in his
sleep. If they go to the tent where a man is asleep, for
the purpose of slaying him, they must first awaken him
and give him opportunity to speak, eat, drink, and smoke.

Once a Sirdieh slave, deputized to do a throat-cutting
of this sort, neglected, perhaps through fear, to awaken
his victim, and for years after that, when the Sirdieh
went into battle, their enemies taunted them by crying:
"Ya thebbahin ennwaum [oh, slayers of those who
sleep]!"

Chapter VI

WE RIDE IN GHRAZZU

ALLAH, eternal dramatist, whose plots are *kismet*, iron-ically set the stage one night with tranquil beauty for what turned out to be my wildest adventure among the Beni Sakhr.

Our eastern tent-wall was lifted, toward hills flooded with light by the red-gold moon of Araby. I lay on a pile of rugs, awake, but half dreaming. How silent and peaceful the desert was, and how weirdly beautiful was Mitkhal's flock of white camels, asleep before the *menzil*. The bubbling of the sheik's pipe at my elbow was the only sound, except for the occasional click of flint on steel when a cigarette was lighted by one of those who sat late in the coffee-circle, like a row of squat, triangular statues, cloaked, mysterious.

Suddenly there was a shout in the distance, a long-drawn *"Oo-oo-oo!"* and a camel rider appeared, first sil-houetted against the sky on a hilltop, then down the slope toward us, riding at breakneck speed.

A lantern was hastily lighted and hung on a pole. Two men hurried out to take charge of his mount, as he rushed into the tent.

There was no *"Salaam aleikum"* now. He dropped quickly to one knee, kissed Mitkhal's hand, stalked into the open semicircle, and squatted down, facing the sheik, without removing either his cartridge-belt or the rifle slung across his shoulders. Neither coffee nor water was offered him, though he seemed in need of both. He was a little, wiry, dried-up *Bedawi*, oldish, ragged, haggard under his dried sweat and dirt.

Lifting his camel-stick, he brought it down against the sand with a sharp impact almost like the crack of a pistol, and began talking in a harsh, rough voice that rose at times almost to a shout. What he said in his rude dialect was more than I could follow. He harangued rapidly, but at the end of every sentence he paused and banged the sand with his stick. His words and manner were so rough and noisy that I suspected, despite his first obeisance, that he had brought some angry message of defiance. But in that I was wholly wrong.

For when he had finished, Mitkhal, who had listened in thoughtful silence, cried: "*Wellah* [by God]! This is good hearing. Ask later, and I will give a reward."

Two men sprang to the courier, lifted him to his feet —he was, as a matter of fact, close to exhaustion—took his heavy cartridge-belt and rifle, while another brought a tea-kettle of water. He filled his mouth without touching the spout to his lips, spat, gulped as if to ease his parched throat muscles, and then drank. He took only a few drops of coffee, but presently ate ravenously from the wooden bowl of rice and meat scraps, the best they could find for him at that hour of the night, and lay down to sleep. He lay on the bare sand, but some one brought an *abba* and threw it over him, in addition to his own.

Meanwhile Mitkhal had called sharply to five men in turn, by name, who hurried out with his whispered instructions and were off in various directions, bareback, at a gallop on their mares.

During this excitement, Mitkhal had not let the coal on his water-pipe die, and now he smoked placidly, like a man musing and well content with his thoughts.

Presently he asked if I had understood, and when I told him "No," he explained.

The Sirdieh, a small but daring tribe east of the Djebel Druse, famed for their skill in *ghrazzu*, were on their way to seize Mitkhal's flock when it went to the pastures —the same five hundred white *hejin* which now lay sleeping outside our tents—a tempting prize.

For weeks Mitkhal had been sending them out every morning before dawn, with no guard save the little camel boy and one old man, to graze all day on the thorn bushes, not supposing that any one would dare to raid them, since it was common knowledge that more than a thousand of his warriors were camped in these close-by hills.

The Sirdieh had learned the situation and hoped to strike by surprise and be off northward with the entire flock to the Leja without firing a shot, before Mitkhal could raise his men.

And they might easily have succeeded, except that the courier—a man of the Beni Hassan—had chanced to see them circling eastward, then south, had guessed out their intention, and had ridden for thirty hours at a pace no horse could follow, to warn us.

The news had come in ample time, for it was now only midnight, and the Sirdieh could hardly reach the pastures before sunrise. It would have been simple enough for Mitkhal not to send his flocks out at all that morning, or to send them under a guard so strong that the Sirdieh would not dare to attack, for the *ghrazzu* numbered only about a hundred men. But Mitkhal's plan was otherwise.

He hoped to catch them in a trap, since the advantage now, both in strategy and numbers, was on his side.

He proposed to send the camels to pasture as usual, guarded only by the boy and the old camel master, but four hundred of his own warriors would be posted in ambush, taking advantage of the rolling ground, to protect his *hejin*, and capture some of the enemy's mares as well.

It promised to be an exciting game, and Mitkhal offered not the slightest objection when I begged permission to take part in it.

While we talked, there was a sudden rhythmic shouting of many voices, surging closer like a chant, cadenced to the beat and pounding of horses' hoofs, and some eighty warriors of the Beni Sakhr, waving their rifles and howling like Dervishes, came galloping to the tent of their sheik. Their howls were not fanatic rage or thirst for Sirdieh gore—but mere exuberant joy at the prospect of a fracas. In answer to their noise, the women of our camp, from inside their tents, replied with long-drawn Indian war-whoops. I have never heard Indians in real battle, but the noise these women made was identical with that which Buffalo Bill's redskins made when they "attacked" the stage-coach in his Wild West circus. The Bedouin women always shout so to hearten their men riding to *ghrazzu* or battle.

It was a wild, glorious noise, and I thrilled to it. So did some of the horses, snorting, pawing the earth. None of them said "Aha!" but it is asking too much to expect that a Bedouin's horse shall have read the book of Job.

The warriors crowded in and around the tent, while Mitkhal addressed them and issued his instructions; then leaped to their saddles and were gone, still shouting their wild song.

Several times within the next hour the scene was repeated, new parties rode up, took their orders, and galloped away.

The camp lay again in comparative silence when the *hejin* flock, superb bait for our trap, ambled off to the pastures, led by the little boy perched without saddle on a camel's rump, and followed only by the old driver, high-mounted on a saddled beast, beneath the waning stars, with his cloak swathed around him, like one of the Three Magi.

Mitkhal and I, accompanied only by Mansour and the twenty men of our sheik's body-guard, galloped after the camels a half hour later, then detoured south, to come in at the rear of one of our already ambushed bands.

I rode a small bay mare, swift but less high-spirited than my white, and easier to control. At my belt were short dagger and automatic, in addition to the rifle slung on my back, but Mitkhal had made me promise to keep absolutely out of any hand-to-hand fighting that might occur. Many Bedouins still use the long, curved scimitar in mounted combat, with pistol in the left hand, controlling their horses by swaying of the body and pressure of the knees, a game which no unskilled novice like myself could play. The best fighters among our own men, about a third, including Mitkhal himself, carried swords. To save anticlimax, I had better say now that there was no hand-to-hand work in this foray, though we had some gun-fighting and more than a bellyful of other adventure before it ended.

At dawn, which came quickly, we were screened behind hills. Mitkhal, Mansour, and I dismounted and crawled to a ridge. From there we could look down into the oblong valley where the white camels grazed among scrubby thorn bushes. My heart beat fast with excitement, though there wasn't a sign of the Sirdieh, or of our own bands either, so skilfully were they disposed.

But presently Mitkhal, with his glass, picked up one moving speck, then another. Soon after, I could see, but only for a moment at a time, three mounted men, edging warily closer from the north, to reconnoiter. Perhaps the Sirdieh suspected the trap, or had been warned in turn. At any rate, their main band was riding into no traps that morning. The three scouts continued to come closer. Then they disappeared for a time, and to my utter surprise, reappeared riding full tilt in the open, less than a quarter mile away, directly into the pasture. It was their plan to secure the herdsman and his boy, then start the camels northward to where their own force waited.

"Now!" cried Mitkhal, and I began pumping my rifle, while the others cracked beside me. I couldn't have hit such flying targets with a shotgun, but I hoped Mitkhal didn't know it. The three riders swerved sharply, scattered, and were off to the northeast, zigzagging, bent low in their saddles. I thought they were going to get clean away, and I don't believe we hit any of them, but a crossfire from another hilltop brought one horse crashing down as the other two disappeared over a rise, with a handful of our own pursuing.

As we galloped to the man who was down, he scrambled to his feet unhurt and shook himself, not troubling even to throw up his hands in token of surrender. And I thought it one of the strangest things I ever saw in the

desert when this captive Sirdieh, whom we had been try
ing to kill a moment before, now stood nonchalantly,
with impudent good humor, his hand dangling not six
inches from the butt of his loaded automatic—and, so
help me God, they didn't even bother to disarm him.
Except for the mare that lay shuddering, it might have
been polo or cricket.

This was a "game," not a war—a game with camels
for prizes—a rough game in which lives were a part of
the score, but there could be no killing except within the
rules. We lost only a minute or two before following
our men in pursuit of the main Sirdieh band, but the
extraordinary dialogue that occurred in those few moments is worth recounting.

"*Wein sokkr il pasha?* [Where is the pasha's falcon?]"
inquired our prisoner with cheerful impudence. Mitkhal
himself smiled, and Mansour roared with savage laughter.
It was a true *Bedawi* quip, twisted and indirect, but
crammed with malicious meaning: So you are coursing
birds this morning, Mitkhal! But Sirdieh are not partridges to walk into your net—and now they are off with
such speed that it would take wings to catch them.

"Nay, slayer of those who sleep," retorted Mitkhal;
"we course a wolf-pack, and our horses will be trampling
them before sunset."

Indeed the main body of Mitkhal's band was already
in hot pursuit. I wondered how he would dispose of the
prisoner.

"You can bide with my herdsman and return tonight
with him to my *menzil*," said Mitkhal, "or go now with
one of my men, who will ask your rifle in payment for
the escort."

I could hardly believe my ears: "I bide, under the law, O sheik!" said the prisoner simply, and it was finished. We left him standing there, still armed, with only the old man and little boy left to guard the flock which he had come to steal—and were off like the wind. Here was "honor among thieves" with a vengeance! Or, rather, pure, fantastic chivalry such as I do not believe survives anywhere else on earth.

We rode for two hours and finally came up with our men, who were following like hounds on the Sirdieh trail, at a steady but unforced gallop. We were about four hundred, and from their tracks, plainly marked in some places, invisible for stretches of miles in others, they numbered, as we had been informed, about a hundred.

But they had a good start, and despite the fact that our horses were fresh and theirs not, since we frequently lost the trail and had to scout right and left to pick it up again, Mitkhal judged at sunset we had gained little on them. Bright moonlight helped us, and we rode on. I was sick, sore, tired out, damnably thirsty, and hungry, too, for a while in the late afternoon; but as the night wore on, my hunger passed. Of course, no horse could stand a continued gallop for this long time, and there were short stops, but it was hard, forced riding. When the moon set, we camped. In one side of my saddlebag was a water-skin, in the other a few crusted balls of dried camel cheese, rancid but concentrated nourishment, with a peck or so of grain for the mare. Mansour came with a leather bag and helped me water and feed her. I drank about a pint of water, managed to eat two of the cheese shards, and lay down, shivering with cold, too worn out for sleep. Mitkhal brought me a lighted cigarette, asked how I was feeling, and I told him "all right," but he knew I was dead tired. Two hours later, at crack of dawn, we were off again.

As the morning wore on, intolerably long toward noon, with the increasing heat and glare, I got the feeling that something was going wrong. Everything was wrong with me personally by that time—I was wondering whether any amount of will-power could make me stick it out— but I don't mean that. Mitkhal was worried over some new element in the game, and so were his men. The trail had been swerving from north to northeast, and now we were following it almost due east, which was not the route the Sirdieh should have taken to get back to their own hills and safety.

As the uneasiness increased, we proceeded more and more slowly, and finally halted.

The terrain looked flat—a seemingly uninterrupted eye-sweep of pebbly, baked clay to the skyline—but there were treacherous depressions and gullies big enough to have concealed a sultan's army. The unexplained swerve eastward had been suspicious, but I think also the Bedouins have a sort of sixth sense that advises them of lurking danger.

Mitkhal sent six men forward, spreading fan-shape, alternately hidden by the terrain and then reappearing; and only after he had followed them for a mile or more with his glasses, did we dismount, hastily water and feed our horses, and drink from our depleted water-skins.

A half-hour later we heard the popping of distant rifles—then descried two men, evidently of our scouts, riding back toward us for their lives, followed by a band of about thirty, firing as they galloped after.

Though we were four hundred, we leaped into our saddles at Mitkhal's shout of command, turned tail, and fled.

The pursued men and their pursuers followed, gaining, as we hung back to let the scouts rejoin us, and the enemy began firing into us at long range.

We spread out, still running, and returned the fire. I blazed away with the rest, but did not distinguish myself except by nearly hitting one of our own men, after which I deemed it safer merely to wave my rifle and shout bravely, though I was really pretty thoroughly scared. I'm more or less a coward under any sort of fire, but the sing of bullets has always made me more nervous than any amount of shelling.

Two of our men went down, though I didn't see them hit, for presently I noticed two riderless horses galloping with us. Then a Beni Sakhr horse and rider crashed in a heap as we swept on. I saw only one of the Sirdieh shot from his saddle. They had gained on us steadily, but now hung back, following, but keeping almost out of range, still firing; and then, all of a sudden, they were simply not there any more. They had ceased the pursuit.

The reader may be wondering (as I did at the time) why four hundred able warriors were fleeing for their lives from thirty.

What had happened was this.

In the first place, Mitkhal knew that thirty men wouldn't have attacked us unless there was a "trick" in it. Furthermore, rused fox that he was in *ghrazzu*, he had "guessed out" the trick with uncanny accuracy. The Sirdieh had known that the Roualla (a big tribe to which they were allied) had gone east on a great *ghrazzu* of their own and would be returning in force. They had led us eastward hoping to effect a junction with the Roualla, and turn on us. They had effected this junction with the Roualla advance guard, and it had been sent against us as a "bait" to hold us engaged, if we were stupid enough to stand, until their main force came up.

Mitkhal believed that the Sirdieh, having led us nicely into this counter-trap, would swing homeward, but that the Roualla main force would give us a hard run, not merely to kill (the Bedouin avoids useless bloodshed in *ghrazzu*), but with the hope of taking many of our horses.

I don't know to this day whether the Roualla were close on our heels or not, during that (to me) hellish thirty-hour forced ride that brought us back to the border of Transjordania. Not another shot was fired, not a sign of a pursuer ever appeared behind us. An exhilarating mixture of fear, excitement, and curiosity had kept me fairly up to scratch, but now I was too far gone to care much about anything. I discovered that my thumb was worn raw from the rope rein and that I was clinging with both hands to the wooden saddle pommel. I wasn't dying of hunger or thirst, but my mouth and throat were drier than I had ever imagined they could be. Fortunately Mitkhal recognized my plight and at our first short stop insisted that I get "aboard" one of the five *hejin* which had been brought along with extra water and fodder. (The *hejin* are more than a match for horses in long going, but are not ridden in *ghrazzu* because they are not so good as horses in quick maneuvering.) It was a blessed relief, and I managed to hang on, half asleep during a good deal of the time. I think we made several more brief stops, and I remember, after the heat and glare, an endless night in which the bitter cold was even worse; and then it was bright day again—and after more hours of misery, without much remembering how I got there, except that I didn't actually "pass out" and have to be carried, I was inside a tent, and Mansour was pouring water over my head, and I was drinking water out of a tin pan and spitting it out and then swallowing a lot of it—and I went to sleep sucking at a hunk of goat-meat I was too tired to chew.

How delicious was idleness the next two or three days, as the soreness went out of me. I was a little ashamed that I hadn't shown more stamina and feared I had "lost face," but fortunately they liked me well enough to be lenient and took an amiable interest in my quick recovery. Mansour swore shamelessly by Allah that a bullet of mine had brought down one of the Sirdieh, and the others acquiesced in this flattering fiction.

We were destined to hear more of the modest part I had taken in the *ghrazzu*—and from a most unexpected high source. Riders came from Amman a few days later to announce that His Royal Highness, Amir Abdullah, ruler of Transjordania, brother to King Faisal of Irak and son of former King Hussein of the Hejaz, was coming out next day to visit his friend Mitkhal. He would arrive at Mitkhal's seat, the palace at Um el-Akmit, next morning around ten or eleven o'clock.

This native shereefian ruler, who holds his power under the British, is not popular among Arab nationalists, because they feel he has played too much into British hands; but he is a prime favorite with the Bedouin tribes in his

territory, because he never interferes in their tribal affairs
and allows them their old-time freedom.

The Bedouins of the northern desert have little nation-
alistic feeling, in a political sense. They would like well
enough to see all *farengi* expelled from the peninsula—
just as they wanted the Turks expelled during the World
War—but their only real allegiance is to the only thing
they know—their individual tribes. Another drawback
to nationalist sentiment among them is that they are
hereditary enemies of Ibn Saud and the Wahabi, the
great, fanatical, unconquered nationalist group further
south, around Mecca.

The Amir's proposed visit to Mitkhal had nothing to
do with politics, big or little. It was merely for friendship's sake and private business affairs of their own.
Mansour rode over immediately to get things ready at
the palace, but Mitkhal remained with us and spent the
night in camp. I got the impression that Mitkhal never
went near his palace if he could avoid it, and I think he
would have preferred to lie in the sand with his goats
rather than sleep under its roof.

Next morning, he rode away early. I was to follow
with some of the others when I pleased. When I reached
the palace, soon after ten, I was told that the Amir had
already arrived. There was nothing in the courtyard to
indicate it, except a battered Ford, newer than most, its
steering-post festooned with patched tubes, as desert-
going flivvers invariably are, and a big canvas-covered
water-bag slung from a bolt near the windshield. The
flivvers boil from Damascus to Baghdad, but they get
there just the same. And this battered Lizzie, for that
day at least, was the royal carriage of His Royal High-

ness, the ruler of Transjordania. The going is rough and
rocky in spots between Amman and Mitkhal's village,
with no road at all, and the Amir had wisely left his
Rolls-Royce limousine at home.

In the big, bare guardroom, some scores of Bedouins
had piled their weapons and stood whispering, anxious to
enter the assembly hall, but hanging timidly back from
its door. As three men mustered up their courage and
went in, I peeped after them.

The low platform at the far end of the hall was piled
with gorgeous rugs and cushions, and in their center sat
the Amir, cross-legged like a Turk, with a bubble-pipe at
his side. Mitkhal sat similarly at his right hand. A
hundred or more of the Beni Sakhr squatted in rows on
the stone floor, right and left, leaving a broad open lane
from the door to the divan.

The three newcomers who had conquered their first
timidity now strode proudly down the hall, even swag-
gering a bit for the benefit of those who might, like me,
be peeping after them, dropped to one knee before the
Amir, kissed his hand, then rose and joined the circle of
their fellows.

I was in some doubt what course would be proper for
me to pursue on entering the hall. As a man in rough
Bedouin garb like the common warriors, and certainly pretending to no sheikly state, it might be simplest to do
obeisance like the rest, and truly I had no stiff-spined
objection—as some English have—to participating in
that harmless courtesy toward a native potentate. But
I reflected it might be construed as undignified by their
own customs, since I was the special friend and guest of
Mitkhal. So I pursued a middle course.

I walked down the hall some two thirds of the distance to the divan, stopped, made a profound bow followed by a military salute, and continued to stand.

The Amir whispered a question to Mitkhal, then arose, came to meet me, shook hands, and said in English: "Oh, hello, how do you do!"

"It is a great honor," I replied, "to meet the ruler of this country where I have found true hospitality and friendship."

He motioned me to sit by him, at his left on the divan, and said nothing more while other groups came in to kneel before him.

The Amir Abdullah is a stocky man of medium height, with beard and complexion sandy rather than bronzed— an unusual type for an Arab—yet his appearance belies him, for he is of the purest Mecca shereefian blood, and his slightly bulging forehead holds a shrewd and cunning brain. He knows the psychology of the desert tribes more intimately than any other politician in Arabia, for he was sent by the old family custom to live among the black tents in his youth and fought for the Allies at the head of Bedouin troops in the World War. He still affects the Bedouin style of dress rather than town Arab. Except for his *agal* [head coil], which was wide and glittered with gold thread, his costume was no different from Mitkhal's. And at his belt, instead of the elaborate high-hilted and gold-sheathed shereefian dagger which appears in his formal photographs, was a heavy automatic in plain leather holster.

He presently said to me good-humoredly: "My cousin Mitkhal tells me you have been riding with them in *ghrazzu.* I wish you wouldn't do it any more, for you might get hurt."

I replied that since I was eating Mitkhal's food I had thought it my duty to ride with the rest in defense of his flocks, and because that sounded silly and self-righteous, I added impulsively: "Besides, there was a camel of my own in the pasture."

This seemed to amuse him. He chuckled and said: "Ho, little Bedawi! And I suppose you hoped to come back from the *ghrazzu* with four!"

Later he said to me privately: "I think you misunderstood me about the *ghrazzu.* It isn't that I care anything about saving your skin; that is your own affair. It is simply that if you were killed out here, there might be an investigation injurious to Mitkhal."

He made no reference to my unpleasant previous encounter with his prime minister, and I came to the conclusion that Rakaby Pasha had not mentioned it.

The Amir's courier had announced the day before that his master would not remain to dinner, and after transacting his private business with Mitkhal, he embraced and kissed him and departed.

He had none of his palace guard or uniformed gendarmerie with him. He replaced the glittering *agal* on his forehead with a common black coil, climbed into the front seat of the flivver beside the driver, with a rifle between his knees, and two other Bedouins with rifles in the seat behind.

As it rattled away, there was nothing to indicate that it carried royalty—and I thought of the great Caliph Haroun el Reshid, who would surely have owned a battered tin Lizzie for such informal excursions, if they had been available in his glorious day.

Chapter VII

"FOR THE EYES OF GUTNE"

THERE are no flowers in the Arabian desert, and none in the mountain of the Druses.

When Ibn el Ghanj, sheik of the Sirdieh, rode raiding into the valley of the Euphrates for forage one dry autumn and found cotton fields in bloom, their beauty moved his fierce soul.

Two years later, when a baby girl was born to his youngest wife, he said: "We shall name the *bint* Gutne [Cotton Flower]."

This was but one generation ago, so that among the tribesmen of the Beni Sakhr, the Sirdieh, and the Beni Hassan, from whom I learned piecemeal, at intervals of months, the complete tale of Gutne's Odyssey, there are many who had known and talked with her and many whose fathers and brothers died "for the eyes of Gutne" when her girlhood beauty burst into the flame that drenched the desert with blood from Palmyra eastward to the Baghdad Gardens.

No one, I learned, had ever photographed her. The Bedouins use the language of poetry to describe her, so that the image does not emerge clearly—the same old phrases—hair like the blue-black winter sky when Algamar, the moon, has sunk beneath the sand; eyes like pools in the oasis; breasts like ripening apples; waist like a young palm tree; feet like the gazelle. Phrases so familiar that they convey no picture. Only by the faces of the men who tried to tell me, old men whose eyes were miraculously made youthful by gleaming memories, could I almost see her.

Amir Amin Arslan, Arab of the Arabs, but citizen of the world, who knows beautiful women in every European capital—and who saw Gutne twice in Amman—tried to

A BEDOUIN FESTIVAL

The Principal Beauties of the Tribe Adorned and Standing on the Backs of Camels

describe her for me, and talked eloquently over the coffee and Benedictine, at the Army and Navy Club in Beirut, but he too failed, except that I remember this:

". . . She was like no other woman I have ever seen —she was female—female as a she-animal is—yet there was nothing soft or voluptuous in her beauty—there was something sharp and painful about it, like the edge of a sword."

Out in the desert, beneath the black tents, when the riders sit in a circle around the coffee fires, they sing songs of Gutne, to the twanging of the one-stringed Bedouin lute, but the best song of Gutne is Gutne's own song, which she made and sang, when her younger brother, Ali, lay slain by the Annezy.

And it is with this song that Gutne's story properly begins, as it was unfolded to me gradually, on many nights when I sat in the coffee circle, as Sheik Mitkhal's friend and brother, dwelling as no stranger among the Beni Sakhr.

Old Ibn el Ghanj, sheik and father of Gutne, died when she was thirteen, just budding into young womanhood. She had two brothers who adored her: Ali, a year younger than herself; and Meteb, a taciturn, strange, violent man of thirty, who ruled as sheik of the Sirdieh in his father's stead.

One night when Meteb and some hundred of his chosen men were riding far, the Annezy smashed into the Sirdieh encampment, killed young Ali and a dozen other warriors, and were off again to the east.

The Sirdieh should have been swift on their heels for vengeance—but their sheik was absent with more than a third of their best horsemen, for they were a small tribe, and those who remained sat cursing the Annezy, awaiting Meteb's return.

The mothers, wives, and sisters of the slain put on their oldest garments, let down their hair, streaked their faces with the black ashes of camel dung, and walked among the tents, wailing and moaning.

Thus the women walked and bewailed their slain, as dawn rose over the tents of the Sirdieh—but though young Ali lay among the dead, his sister Gutne walked not among the wailing women.

Therefore, the men raised their voices and said: "Who

is Gutne?" And others replied: "She is the sister of Ali who lies among the slain, but she walks not with those who mourn."

And they said: "May the shame be upon Gutne, and not upon her dead brother's face."

But as they murmured, a woman appeared, gorgeous in a robe of crimson silk, with gold coins twined in her hair, and her breasts gleaming with gold, appareled like a bride in her glory, riding upon the back of a white camel, decked with all its bright-colored trappings.

The woman was Gutne, and all who beheld her marveled.

Behind her, on a second white camel, rode her serving-maid, around whose wrists, and neck, and waist, and ankles Gutne had hung all the jewels and treasures from her casket—bracelets of broad silver, anklets with pendant turquoises and little tinkling bells—so many necklaces of gold coins that the girl's body gleamed as if in armor.

Thus Gutne rode among the tents of the dead, where the men sat disconsolate and the disheveled women walked with blackened faces, wailing.

"Are you crazy, Gutne," they cried, "with your brother Ali's blood scarce dried in the sand? Has madness come upon you?"

But as they cried upon her and stared in their amazement, Gutne rode slowly among the tents, weaving back and forth among them, and as she rode, she sang the song that she had made:

Shame on those whose breasts gleam with brass cartridges—
Shame upon those who wear curved swords—
Shame on those who ride swift horses.

Let them take the white mare which has never known a stallion—
Let them take her decked with gifts and trappings—
Let them walk humbly on foot, leading the white mare—
Leading her as a gift, to the sheik of the Annezy!

The gift of a white virgin mare, led by men on foot, is made among Bedouins only when they are forced to sue for a humiliating peace, or to ask for mercy.

But in Gutne's song, the white mare was a symbol, meaning herself, and her song meant:

"Shame on you, warriors of the Sirdieh. My brother, the brother of your sheik, lies slain by the Annezy, and instead of following them for vengeance, you sit here like cowards.

"Behold me dressed and ready to make your shame complete—to be led as a gift, as a slave, to the sheik of the Annezy, who will spare your lives for the sake of my body."

Thus Gutne inflamed them with her taunts and with her beauty—and they remembered that they were Sirdieh, and leaped into their saddles, shouting, "For the eyes of Gutne!" and rode to take their vengeance. . . .

But the few then slain were as naught to those who later died, when her eyes began to flash with the fatal fire of love.

As the fame of her courage and of her flamelike beauty spread through the desert, scores of young Bedouin warriors, proud sons of sheiks, the flower of all the northern tribes, hawk-faced and lean, with sharp, sparse beards, and their black hair plaited in short braids, came by ones and twos and threes, in their gold-embroidered robes of camel's hair, to sit in the *hareem* of Sheik Meteb's tent, and play with Gutne the hazardous game of *nasr'b hbal*, which means a snare, or net.

And this is the law of *nasr'b hbal:* the maiden may adorn herself and dance with tinkling bells, to delight some favored suitor, alone with him behind drawn *hareem* curtains—or may walk far with him alone beneath the desert stars; and she is safe from harm, for shameful death is the penalty if he forces or betrays her.

Be therefore sure that those who later died for the sake of Gutne, died otherwise, and cleanly without shame.

Among the proud young sheiks who first sought Gutne's favor, she chose not the youth whose beauty matched her own, and not the minstrel who made songs of love, and not him who bore the richest gifts. Her heart was drawn fatally to the lean, rude Trad Ben Zaban—he who had the body of a half-starved panther and the face of an eagle thirsting for prey—Trad Ben Zaban, minor sheik of the powerful Beni Sakhr, silent and aloof in the council circle, but their glory in the day of battle.

Cruel was the manner of his wooing. On the first day when Gutne danced alone before him, he looked on her with hard and mocking eyes, and bent down to trace idle arabesques with his finger in the sand; and once alone with her, upon another day, when she was trembling, he laughed in her face, and arose and went away.

And it would have been better far if he had never returned, for the eyes of Gutne had pierced his soul, and her beauty was in his veins like a fever—and when he sought the Sheik Meteb, Gutne's brother, to ask her hand in marriage, Meteb refused with violent words, and swore, by Allah, that his sister would marry no man, save by his own choosing.

And this he had the power to compel, by desert law, for he was master of both household and tribe since the old sheik's death.

Meteb liked not Trad Ben Zaban in any case, but the root of his refusal was nourished from the poisoned waters of a deeper, darker spring.

Meteb was a man accursed by fate—seared by the forbidden flame of his own sister's beauty. No brother has mated with sister in Arab lands since the ancient days of the kings who were idolaters from Egypt, and for Meteb's wound there was no healing. The laws of Allah and Mohamet were adamant, and he dared not confess the truth by word or deed—either then or ever—but his heart was filled with jealous rage at the thought of yielding Gutne to another.

So that now he said to Trad Ben Zaban, whose face was clouded and whose eyes were black with pain: "Go thou, and return not!"

And as Trad rode away, Meteb, as the Bedouin law required, lifted his pistol and fired three shots toward the sky, as a warning that if Trad ever returned, there would be blood.

Trad neither turned nor looked back, but reflected deeply as he rode. And arriving at the encampment of the Beni Sakhr, he went not to his own tent, but straight to the tent of Talaha, the venerable sheik of sheiks, who reclined on a great pile of rugs, leaning against his silver-bossed camel saddle, puffing a water-pipe, attended by two black slaves.

"*Salaam aleikum,*" he said, and Talaha replied: "*Aleikum salaam.*"

Trad sat with the venerable Talaha and spoke long and

earnestly, keeping nothing back, and finally saying: "It is a weakness and a certain shame, but it is as Allah wills. I must have this woman, or my life will be no longer of any use to me, or to you, or to our tribe, O my sheik and uncle!"

And Talaha arose and called to council the sheiks and warriors, and they came and heard and answered: "We will do all that can be done in honor, for Trad is our glory in the day of battle."

And when the next sun arose, one hundred of the proudest among them mounted their finest mares, bedecked with their gayest trappings, and rode in cavalcade, led by the sheik of sheiks himself, to the camp of the Sirdieh, and the tent of the young Sheik Meteb.

When Meteb saw that Trad was not among them, he greeted the Beni Sakhr with honor, sending slaves to slay the fattest camel, and invited them to enter.

But the venerable Talaha said: "May your hospitality be blessed, O Meteb! But we cannot enter your tent and share your food, unless you promise."

"Promise what, O sheik of sheiks?"

"We have come in peace—and may peace endure between our tribes—to ask the hand of Gutne for Trad Ben Zaban in honorable marriage."

Meteb perceived that the affair was now too grave for blunt refusal, so he replied: "Enter, then, freely. Drink and eat. And afterward we will discuss the marriage price."

When they had drunk and eaten, Meteb said with proud insolence: "For Gutne's marriage price, you will give me five hundred white camels."

The Beni Sakhr replied, "So be it. We will give."

But it was a great price, transcending custom even as Gutne's beauty was transcendent, and they were amazed when Meteb cried: "You will give also thirty rifles."

They were angry, but replied: "We will give."

And Meteb, smiling a crafty smile, spoke on, making fabulous demands, three-score camel-loads of grain, so

A CORNER OF BASRAH

Through Basrah Pass the Gypsy Bedouins Wandering into Persia

many saddles, so many rugs—half the wealth of a little tribe.

But Talaha, too, was crafty, and the Beni Sakhr were a rich and mighty tribe. If they paid, indeed, this monstrous wedding portion, the Sirdieh would perforce be bounden to them in alliance—and Meteb's men, though few in number, were warriors of renown. So Talaha persuaded his followers until all were in accord, and cried: "We will give—but it is finished."

And Meteb was silent as Talaha rose with all his men, saying: "We go, and on the morrow we will send to you five hundred camels, loaded with all else that we have promised. Therefore, let the bride be ready."

But Meteb leaped to his feet and stayed them: "Are we Basrah Gypsies, O Talaha! and are you a king, that you would buy my sister Gutne with a royal dowry, yet ask her to leave her own *hareem* in an old ragged cloak thrown hastily around her shoulders? Think you that Gutne's wedding garments can be made ready in an hour, or a day? Return, rather, when seven days have passed, and she will be arrayed in robes of crimson silk, embroidered with silver and gold."

Talaha and all who listened in amazement knew that these were vain, crooked words—for the bridal raiment of a sheikly Bedouin maiden is ready from her fourteenth year. But rather than enter into disputation, they chose to be content, and so it was agreed, and they mounted their horses and rode away.

When seven days had passed, the Beni Sakhr returned with their rich caravan for Gutne's purchase price, and with a great dais mounted on a camel's back, as for a queen, to carry thence the bride in glory.

But when they came to the Sirdieh *menzil*, they found it all confusion, and they too were confounded, for Meteb had fled in the night, with his tent, his slaves, six camels, and his sister Gutne. The Sheik of the Sirdieh had abandoned his own tribe and disappeared, no man knew whither.

When these strange tidings came to Trad Ben Zaban, he cursed Meteb's name and swore a bitter oath of vengeance against all who dared to harbor Meteb; and that same night he sent swift riders north and south. The word came in three days that Meteb had fled to an encampment of the Beni Hassan, pitched in the hills against the Leja, and Trad led a bloody raid against them, shouting, *"Mun shan ayoon Gutne!* [For the eyes of Gutne!]"

But Meteb with Gutne and his household had fled farther westward the night before, to find surer sanctuary in the Mountain of the Druses.

The Druse lords gave Meteb hospitality, and he dwelt there with his sister for a little while, inviolate from pursuit.

But the Druses were a people apart, dwellers within stone walls, worshipers of the golden calf, and Meteb was a stranger among them.

He was an exiled sheik without a tribe, and his heart was sick with longing for the black tents of the desert.

But he dared not return to his own of the Sirdieh lest he bring death among them by Trad Ben Zaban's vengeance. And he bethought him to seek alliance with the Roualla—a rude and powerful tribe, who were lords of the desert far north of the Beni Sakhr marches.

So he sent messengers to Sultan Pasha Shalan, ruler of the Roualla, and he, who feared no man's vengeance, bade Meteb come, together with Gutne and his household. But whether he remained would be determined in the council circle.

So Meteb came to the Roualla *menzil* and pitched his tent against that of Shalan, and when Gutne stood by the uplifted *hareem* curtains, all marveled at her great beauty.

And Shalan, who had thus far pondered only what selfish advantage he might gain, whether in war or peace, by accepting or refusing sanctuary to Meteb, looked now on Gutne's face. And when he beheld Gutne, that happened which fate decreed.

So that when Meteb presently sat before him in the council circle Shalan said: "I bid you summon Gutne." So Gutne came and sat also among them.

And Shalan said: "Hear now plain words, O Meteb! You have come asking sanctuary and alliance, but there can be none till this turmoil concerning your sister, Gutne, cease. And the fault is yours. So long as she remains unwedded, and in your keeping, vengeance will follow you, and you will be outlawed by Trad's curse. But with Gutne wedded to another man and in her own husband's keeping, the matter will be ended, for no man follows an empty vengeance, and Trad, in time, will find another wife.

"Hear me now, O Meteb! and take heed how you answer. I, Sultan Pasha Shalan, sheik of the Roualla, ask Gutne's hand in honorable marriage!"

And Meteb knew the hour of surrender and answered: "Hearing is obedience," and bowed his head.

And Gutne also knew the hour of surrender—and on the third day her slaves arrayed her as a bride in crimson silk and gold, with gold coins gleaming on her breast and forehead; and camels with many sheep and goats were slain for the great marriage feast; and when all the tribe had feasted, Shalan rode on a white mare to Meteb's tent, and a scribe witnessed the needful contract so that all was done in keeping with the Koran law; then by the more ancient desert law, Shalan lifted Gutne to the white mare's saddle pommel and rode with her thrice round about the encampment, with a naked scimitar held aloft, and all stood before their tents and shouted: "Behold Shalan's bride!"

Against the *hareem* wall of Shalan's great *beit-shaar* was raised the bridal bower, a small tent hung with colored tapestries, and brightest among them at the morrow's dawn hung the white, red-stained fleece from Gutne's bridal bed.

And if Gutne loved not Shalan, she held him in honor as her lord and husband, but her secret thoughts were of Trad Ben Zaban, and her heart foreboded evil.

So Gutne dwelt in her bower, as the wife of Shalan, and Meteb became a sheik of the Roualla horsemen until such a time as he might command his own.

And presently that came to pass which Gutne had foreboded. The evil news was from the southward marches, where Trad Ben Zaban, riding with a thousand men, had fallen upon and slain a *ghrazzu* of the Roualla. And it was told that Trad had cried amid the slaughter: "*Mun shan ayoon Gutne!*"

So there was war in the desert, and the summer moon was red, and the sands were wet with blood as warriors rode to die "for the eyes of Gutne."

And when the Roualla women began to count the number of their husbands, sons, and brothers slain, they cursed the day of Gutne's birth. They cursed Gutne's beauty, and they called her *Hormat Dima*, "Woman of Blood" —*Hormat Hamra*, "Red Woman."

And when she walked abroad from the *hareem* of Shalan's tent, the women, not daring to cry out openly against her, would gather and walk close, and whisper: "My brother's blood is in your eyes!" "My father's blood is in your face!" "My son, too young to have known what a woman is, has yet died because of thee, O thrice-accursed!"

But Gutne replied not to their taunts and curses. Neither did she flee, nor hide herself, nor make complaint to Shalan. She went among them proud and silent, unhappy, yet walking with her head unbowed, for she was Gutne.

Until, upon a day when the bitterness of her pride required a sign, she put aside the black robes which all women wear by desert custom except in time of joyful feasting, and arrayed herself in crimson.

Thus she walked among the wives and daughters of the Roualla, who were amazed, and she said: "You have called me *Hormat Hamra*, the Red Woman—and behold, I am she! My robe is gloriously dyed with the blood of many warriors. It is stained with the lifeblood of your husbands, sons, and brothers. Look you, does it not become me well? Is *Hormat Hamra* not beautiful?"

In their agony and grief, the moaning women would have slain Gutne as she taunted them, but they dared not. And from that day forth she moved in the encampment as a blood-red flame.

When Shalan returned from battle and saw her thus arrayed, he wondered and questioned her, and she answered: "My lord has paid a heavy price, and in gratitude I would keep myself always beautiful, that I may be in his heart when he rides forth, and waiting arrayed always as a bride, against each unknown hour of his return."

Meantime, week after week, the bitter war continued. And one night Trad Ben Zaban, with many horsemen, pushed far into the Roualla marches, and drove before him, southward, eight hundred of the Roualla camels.

When these tidings came, a force of the Roualla rode swiftly in pursuit, but Shalan, their sheik of sheiks, remained somber and disconsolate in his tent, for he had parried the blow of a scimitar with his rifle, and the blade had glanced downward, wounding his right hand.

Out in the desert, Trad and his men had driven the great camel herd of the Roualla through a narrow pass where the full body of his own forces lay in ambush. When the Roualla rode in between the hills, the narrow entrances were closed by Trad's men massed and lying, and their mares lying with them, behind ramparts of kneeling camels.

And the Roualla, trapped, between the hills, without cover, and without escape, were at the mercy of Trad.

But four men of the Roualla, riding far behind as is the custom in the strategy of desert warfare, saw the trap close, and turned back, not through cowardice, but because it was their duty.

And pushing their mares, to the death if need be, they rode back to Shalan's *menzil* with the evil tidings.

But there was naught Shalan could do in that evil hour save dispatch other messengers with little hope, for the warriors who remained to him were in *ghrazzu* far distant from the *menzil*.

The ill news spread in the encampment, and the women, foreseeing new slaughter, came to the great tent, daring the anger of Shalan, screaming curses and cruel insults.

Shalan would have defended Gutne and driven them

away, but as he arose, Gutne herself tore wide the *hareem* curtains and faced the screaming women like a fury: "You sows, you starving, weak-loined female cattle! You dare to reproach me, Gutne! Reproach yourselves, O women with little wombs! O women who breed not men but sheep! who let themselves be butchered like sheep. If you cannot bear infants that are men, go you to Trad and the Beni Sakhr and throw yourselves on your backs, and you will know what it is to breed men-children, though it burst your bowels!"

The women fell back, huddled together in silence and horror—which lasted a long moment—but was finally broken by a hushed, eager whispering. For they knew that the reckless words of Gutne had flouted Shalan's honor, and the male honor of the tribe, beyond forgiveness.

Shalan indeed had heard, and anger surged within him so that he thought to slay Gutne with his sword forthwith. She neither fled nor asked for mercy, but knelt before him and lifted her throat for the edge of the blade. But because of her great beauty he could not strike. And he said: "I cannot do it." And Gutne arose from her knees and entered the *hareem* and drew the curtains.

But the women stood at a little distance and waited patiently, for they knew, and Shalan knew, that Gutne's words had touched his honor and were beyond forgiving.

Yet because of her great beauty and the love he bore her, which was a weakness, he could not find it in his heart to slay her or put her from him. So he sat taking council with his thoughts—and all was waiting silence, save for the light thud of his camel-wand as he sat tapping, tapping in the sand.

Now presently the tapping ceased, for Shalan was transferring the wand from his left hand to his right, which had been wounded by the scimitar's glancing blow. His fingers closed upon it, but the bandage cramped them, and he stripped the bandage off.

He gripped the wand with his fingers, caked and stained with blood, and arose, and drew apart the *hareem* curtains, and entered, and closed them behind him.

There was no struggle, and no word was spoken—only the sound of ripping, tearing silk—and then a whistling, hissing in the air, and the thud of the bamboo wand on naked flesh. And it continued long, broken by never a plaint or scream.

At last the torture ceased, and Shalan came forth, bent and trembling like a drunken man, with the shreds of the camel-wand still clutched in his blood-smeared hand.

But now, in a little while, there was a commotion and shouting from the far edge of the encampment. And a messenger galloped toward Shalan's tent, crying as he came: "News! Good news! Good tidings from the field of battle!"

As he leaped from his mare and rushed into Shalan's presence, he cried again: "Good tidings!"—but he was a man whom Shalan trusted not, and Shalan frowned and wondered, for the man's face seemed crooked and evil.

And it still seemed evil to Shalan, and his heart foreboded evil, when the gray-bearded old men had gathered in the council circle beneath the great tent canopy, as he sat in their open midst upon a heap of rugs, while the messenger bent knee before him and kissed his hand.

The messenger cried yet again: "I bring good news, O sheik of sheiks! and I pray you to summon Gutne, for this news concerns her closely, and for her this is a day that will be remembered until the last day."

And Shalan replied: "I will not call her," for he saw that there was hatred on the man's face when he spoke the name of Gutne. And outside among the women who stood to listen, there was whispering of how Gutne could not come because she, the proud and beautiful, wife to the sheik of sheiks, had been whipped like a Christian woman, like a slave.

But Gutne had heard, and scorned to hide her shame. Proudly she came, proudly in her torn crimson robe, wound in folds about her from neck to heel, concealing the great rents where Shalan had ripped it from her body, and the cruel stripes beneath.

Thus she came and stood beside her lord, and held up her head and kept her pride.

And the messenger, turning toward her with fair words, cried: "This is a great day for us, O Gutne! a day of days for the Roualla; and we owe it not to our own strength and not to strategy—we owe it, Gutne, to your eyes!"

Then fell a deep silence. And even Shalan, sheik of sheiks, was silent, for until the tale unfolded, there was naught that he could say.

In this deep silence, the messenger lifted his camel-wand, and smote the sand, and spoke: "We were caught in 'Trad Ben Zaban's net between the hills, and his men were massed and covered on all sides, and we prepared to ride our horses up against the rocks that only goats could climb, to die at least attacking, rather than be shot like quail.

"But at that moment Trad arose before us, standing

upon the edge of a great rock, with both his arms outstretched so that none would fire upon him, and shouted
with a deep shout: 'Come into my face!'

"And his men withheld their shots, and we dismounted
from our horses and clambered up the rocks and were in
his face. And he spoke not to us but to his men, who
now also gathered among the rocks, in a great circle
around us.

"As we stood there, in Trad's face, wondering, he cried
out to his warriors: 'Tuntuni! [You will give me!]'

"And they replied, shouting: 'Nuntik! [We will
give!]'

"And Trad cried in a great voice: 'You will spare all
their lives—for the sake of the eyes of Gutne!'"

The messenger paused, while the old men in the council circle and the women who stood beyond them, listening, marveled, and believed him and were glad. Even
Gutne dared in that instant to hope that his words were
true, knowing that one who is mad for love will do mad
things. But when she looked into the messenger's face,
she saw black hatred, and her soul shuddered.

Again he lifted the camel-wand and smote the sand,
and each blow was as if it fell again on Gutne's naked
flesh, for now there was open mockery and treachery in
his words.

"Trad cried again: 'Tuntuni! You will give back to
them, for the sake of Gutne's eyes, all the camels and
gear we have taken on this day! . . . You will give
back to them, for the sake of Gutne's eyes, all the flocks
which you have taken in ghrazzu since the first day of
war! Also, for the sake of Gutne's eyes, we will give
them, from our own flocks, ten thousand white she-camels!

And doubtless, Allah, matching our generosity, for the sake of Gutne's eyes, will raise again to life their sons and brothers slain!'

"Now have you heard, O sheik of sheiks, and understood my message?"

And Shalan knew that in the desert, Trad had wrought fresh death upon the Roualla, and that those who had escaped, revolting against further slaughter, would ride no more for the eyes of Gutne.

"So be it," said Shalan, "but it needed not to be accomplished through lying mockery."

Suddenly there was the flash of long, curved steel that eye could scarcely follow, and Shalan's scimitar clove the messenger's skull, and clove through his shoulders, and bit down through ribs and lungs to his deep bowels, which spilled out in the sand.

But that night Shalan divorced Gutne. . . .

Desert law required that on the morrow, Gutne be sent to her own tribe and kindred, the Sirdieh; but on that same night she took secretly a little bread and water and laid a saddle upon the back of a kneeling camel, and mounted it while all in the Roualla encampment slept, and rode southward alone, guided by the stars.

When the sun rose, she changed her course toward the east and the path between the hills—for her heart was leading her to Trad Ben Zaban.

A long day and a long night she rode, and her lips were parched, and her stomach was empty. With another dawn she came to the ravine between the hills, where lay the bodies of the men whom Trad had slain. Vultures and jackals stopped their feasting to see her pass in her blood-red robe.

Now she followed the hoofprints of Trad's horsemen, and after midnight of the third night, she came to the outskirts of his encampment, for they had no pursuers to fear.

She was worn and hungry and suffering great thirst, and she stopped at the first tent on the edge of the dark encampment, the tent of one Hassan, a man of no importance, who was greatly astonished to see a woman come alone, riding a camel, out of the darkness of the desert.

He helped her to dismount and hobbled the camel, and when she entered his tent, he was amazed by the beauty of her gaunt, wan face, in which her eyes shone larger than the eyes of any mortal woman he had ever seen.

And he stared, and he believed that it was Gutne, but he choked the question in his throat, for it is a gross discourtesy to demand the name of any who comes seeking hospitality or refuge.

But he was eager to gain profit for himself, and when she had drunk water from the wooden bowl, he said, without naming names, for he could not be wholly sure that is was Gutne:

"O thou beautiful one, may I go and tell him that you are here?"

And she was utterly weary, and bowed her head as if to say, "Do what seems best to you." And he knew that it was indeed Gutne. And he leaped up joyfully, and rushed out and slew a little goat and put it in the pot, and addressed her by name, and said: "O Gutne! the tent of Trad is away behind the second hill, and if I have not returned before the food is ready, take and eat freely,

for all that I have is yours; and may you be blessed in
the name of Allah, for I go as a messenger of good news."

And Hassan, in his eagerness, stopped not to find his
mare, but ran on foot over the two hills to the tent of
Trad, and awakened him, shouting in his joy: "*Bsharti,*
O Trad! [A gift of good news.]"

And Trad replied, as is the custom: "I will give."

Now Trad supposed that Hassan had brought news of
some small flock seized in *ghrazzu* or other matter of
slight importance and pitied Hassan for his greed to
receive a little gift.

But Hassan said: "You will give me, for the news I
bring, three camels; and you will give me a mare, and
you will gladly give me ten goats and twenty sheep."

And Trad was taken aback and reflected deeply and
made no reply, for it is not the custom in such cases to
use further words until the matter is pondered.

When he had pondered, Trad knew that Gutne had
come to him at last, and he said to Hassan: "If she has
left Shalan of her own free will, and come to me wholly
of her own free will, I will give you three times three
camels, and thrice all that you asked—but if she left
not Shalan's tent of her own free will, may Allah blind
me if I ever look upon her face."

When the messenger returned to his tent, he found that
Gutne had taken the flesh of the young goat from the
pot and had put it decently upon a great dish, though she
had fasted for two days and nights, and as he entered the
tent, she was lifting the first morsel of flesh to her mouth.

And he was so eager in his hope of enrichment by
Trad's gifts that he cried out: "O Gutne! tell me that
you left Shalan of your own free will."

And by the question, Gutne knew fatally all that had been said, as clearly as if she had heard Trad's own voice.

And she made answer, but not in words. She kissed the morsel of cooked flesh, in obedience to the law, and dropped it to the sand.

Without speaking, she arose and went out into the darkness to the kneeling camel on whose back was neither water-skin nor food-bag, caused it to rise, and rode with her face uplifted proudly to the stars, eastward into the trackless waste of the great desert. . . .

I ask belief for this tale of Gutne's Odyssey, for it is a true tale, and I have faithfully set it down, as it was told to me in the black tents of the Beni Sakhr, by men whose bodies still bore the wounds of those unforgotten battles.

Among the Druses

Chapter VIII

AT THE CASTLE OF SULTAN PASHA ATRASH

WHEN Daoud Izzedin said to Katie and me, as the Mountain of the Druses began to loom in the far distance across the Hauran plains: "We will probably sleep tomorrow night in the castle of Sultan Pasha Atrash at Kurieh," it seemed as queer as if he had said: "We're week-ending with the Prophet Mohamet," or "We'll be dropping in for luncheon with Saladin."

Few men become legendary figures within their own lifetime, but the tales I had heard of this man—the war lord of the Druses—in the European clubs of Beirut and the tents of the desert, were fabulous beyond belief. Miracles of ferocity and meekness were equally attributed to him. He fought with the savageness of an insane tiger, and returned from battle to weep and pray for the souls of the men he had hacked to pieces with his scimitar. His old mother had to restrain him from giving away all their goods to the poor. He was a devil, mad with bloodlust. He was a holy saint. He was a sort of Mad Mullah. He was a sort of Christ.

And now we were on our way to be the guests of this incredible Sultan Pasha Atrash, and of his people, the Druses of the Mountain.

We were following the old Roman road which disappears southeastward from Damascus, into the wild volcanic region of the Djebel, on the edge of the great desert. The camels which Daoud had promised were thus far unnecessary. We were traveling in a big open Cadillac, and intended to reach Souieda, the Druse capital, late that afternoon.

Our first glimpse of Souieda, rising miles away beyond the level plain, showed that it was no typical Arab city of any sort which I had previously seen. It was more like a feudal hill-town in Brittany, with its massive gray stone walls, square parapets, and close-clustering houses

THE TEMPLE OF BACCHUS AT BAALBEK

as solid as if they had been hewn from the living rock. There was never a dome nor a minaret, for the Druses are not Moslem.

They are a separate race, held together by a secret religion and by their marriage laws, which inflict swift death on any Druse woman who seeks to marry outside her own people.

Some of them have become Europeanized city-dwellers, but they remain always Druses and are welcomed as brothers when occasion takes them to the Djebel.

Like all Arabia, the Djebel Druse was theoretically under the domination of the Ottoman Empire for centuries, and since the establishment of the French mandate in Syria, the Druses have been theoretically under the domination of France. But they have never accepted either in fact, and their history has been one long series of revolts and wars.

Even as we were entering the Djebel, another revolt was brewing, though we did not dream it would come so quickly—the revolt in the late summer of 1925 which spread like wildfire throughout the whole of Syria.

As we came to the edge of Souieda, we crossed a wide esplanade in front of the government house and citadel, erected by the Turks in 1886, and now occupied by the French garrison. This was the citadel in which, less than a month later, the only Frenchmen left alive in the Djebel Druse were barricaded and standing siege.

But on the afternoon of our arrival, and for many days thereafter, all was peace. We managed to drive a short distance into the town, but soon the streets became so narrow and winding that no car could pass, and we walked the last few hundred yards to the house of Ali bey Obeyid, the old Druse civil judge of Souieda, who was to be our host for the first night.

Through an arched gate in a high stone wall we entered the lower courtyard. At the left, four small Arabian horses were eating from stone-hewn mangers. A camel knelt, chewing its cud, and eyed us with disfavor. In a corner were huddled a number of black, long-haired goats; the females had their udders enclosed in cotton bags. At the right, stone steps led to an elevated porch and doorway flanked by long stone benches. At the head of the steps stood Ali bey—a little gray-bearded man with kindly eyes, wearing the garb of a

Druse *akil*, or elder—high white turban closely wound, and voluminous black *abba* of camel's hair. The court-yard beasts and the man were patriarchal. Thus might Job have stood four thousand years ago to welcome the wayfaring guest, and thus might he have spoken:

"*Salaam aleikum*," said Ali bey—with the simple Islamic greeting that is older far than Islam—"Peace be unto you." To which we answered, "*Aleikum salaam* [and upon you, peace]." He kissed Daoud on both cheeks, shook hands, first with me and then with Katie, and whispered to Daoud, asking whether my wife pre-ferred to come with us into the *mukhaad* or to go into the *hareem* with the women. Daoud replied that she would first sit with the host, among the men, to do him honor, as was the custom of American ladies.

The *mukhaad* was a square room large enough to hold twenty or thirty persons. There were no furnishings ex-cept grass mats and cushions on the stone divans. Piled near the glowing charcoal fire in a depression in the stone floor lay the complicated implements for making coffee. When we entered the room, eight or ten Druse elders garbed like Ali bey stood gravely to welcome us.

Afterward Ali bey introduced us to his four sons, ranging in age from Fouad, twenty-four, to young Adham, fourteen, all of them full-fledged Druse warriors, or *jahils*, and all of them wearing the Bedouin *kafiyeh* in-stead of the turban. The elders sat, but the four sons remained standing during the entire half-hour of the coffee ceremony. To do us honor, Ali bey himself made the coffee, sitting cross-legged on the floor before the charcoal fire. As we drank in turn from the same two tiny cups passed round and round the circle, Ali bey told us of a curious custom in the Djebel. If a Druse ever shows cowardice in battle, he is not reproached, but the next time the warriors sit in a circle and coffee is served, the host stands before him, pours exactly as for the others, but in handing him the cup, deliberately spills the coffee on the coward's robe. This is equivalent to a sentence of death. In the next battle the man is forced not only to fight bravely but to offer himself to the bullets or swords of the enemy. No matter with how much courage he fights, he must not come out alive. If he fails, his whole family is disgraced.

Before dinner, we were invited into the courtyard, where Fouad poured water over our hands from a tall earthen jar and then dried them for us with an embroidered towel. We returned to a vaulted dining-hall and sat—five of us—in a semicircle on the floor. Presently the other sons, helped by a man-servant, brought in a whole sheep roasted, on a great brass charger. Another servant came in with an armful of bread-flaps, soft circular sheets as big as napkins and almost as thin as paper. We ate with the right hand, the arm bared to the elbow.

Katie and I slept comfortably on clean straw pallets laid flat on the floor. Ali bey apologized for not having bedsteads. They were not "practical" in the Djebel, he explained, because every six months or so for the past hundred years the Druses, fighting the Turks or Christians, had been forced temporarily to abandon Souieda, taking all their household goods camel-back and horse-back into the mountains.

Next morning, at breakfast in the *mukhaad*, I began to wonder if we were to take leave of Ali bey without having seen any of the female members of his household.

As a matter of fact, we had glimpsed one at the moment of our arrival, evidently an old serving-woman seated in a far corner of the courtyard, mixing dung and water into fuel-cakes, which she slapped against the wall to dry; but immediately she had pulled her veil over her head and scurried away.

Soon after breakfast, however, Ali bey said that his wife wished to meet us, and when we went to an upper terrace she emerged timidly from the *hareem* doorway and came toward us. I imagine she had bedecked herself for the occasion, for beneath the white veils which completely swathed her head and shoulders was a full skirt, elaborately embroidered with silk in brilliant colors.

When we spoke to her, she drew the veil aside, and we saw the sweet face of an old woman, wrinkled, gnarled, but eager and kindly. I think, perhaps, we were the first Westerners she had ever met. Katie kissed both her withered cheeks.

At that moment, Daoud discreetly nudged me, and I beheld, framed in the *hareem* doorway, a quite different sort of vision. It was the ten-year-old daughter of Ali bey, and she was a raving little beauty. She was dressed like a miniature Oriental queen, with full, long skirt, gay gold-embroidered bodice, wide silver bracelets, and white veil which she had withdrawn completely from her face. I caught one flash of pomegranate lips and bright blue eyes, a piquant oval face, half child, half woman, and then she darted back into the shadows like a scared rabbit.

Ali bey smiled, followed her, and dragged her by the hand toward us. She wanted to come, and she didn't. She wanted to be seen, and she didn't. By the way she held the veil across the lower part of her face and coquetted with her eyes, it was plain that she regarded herself as a grown-up young lady, ripe for romance and marriage.   But I scarcely think Ali bey shared that view,

A YOUNG DRUSE WARRIOR WITH BRAIDED
HAIR AND PAINTED EYELIDS

else he would not have let Daoud and me meet her at all. Despite her tender years, she was a dangerous and inflammatory little baggage, if I ever saw one.

It was our plan to push on immediately to the village of Kurieh, the stronghold of Sultan Pasha Atrash, further back in the mountain, but Ali bey told us that Sultan Pasha was coming that same day to Souieda for a con-

ference with the French military governor—then Captain
Renaud—so we postponed our departure.

Toward eleven o'clock, we heard shouts, and hurried,
along with half the populace of Souieda, toward the
citadel.

And presently they appeared, Sultan Pasha and his
bodyguard of more than a hundred warriors, splendidly
mounted, with modern rifles and cartridge bands crossed
gleaming on their breasts—yet to my eyes fantastic as if
they had come to life from the Assyrian paintings on the
walls of some old palace in Nineveh. It was not merely
their flowing robes and headgear—it was their braided
hair, their brilliantly dyed tunics, and their eyelids heavily
blackened with kohl. These were the fabled, fearful
"warriors with painted eyes." And as they rode through
the crowds, they sang a deep-voiced ancient chant, the
Song of Beni Maruf.

In their forefront rode, not proudly, but in a simple,
coarse black robe of camel's hair and common cotton ker-
chief, with bowed head, one of whom the people cried:
"*Hadha hoo* [it is he]."

And by this only I knew that it was Sultan Pasha
Atrash.

Always these flashing survivals of the ancient glory in
Arabia are accompanied by curious anachronisms. In this
case, it was, here and there, a pair of modern smoked
goggles worn by some older warrior to protect his eyes
from the sun.

Half an hour later, in the *mukhaad* of a private Druse
house opposite the citadel, where the sheiks and elders
had gathered for a preliminary conference, and where I

was taken, alone, by Ali bey, I first met Sultan Pasha face to face.

In the whole group, he was the last man I should have picked by guesswork as the legendary "Lion of the Druses."

He seemed to be about forty, of medium height and weight, clean-shaven except for a bristling mustache, and with no striking feature except his eyes. They were very pale blue, and in them was an expression of wistful, almost baffled sadness. The hand he offered me was soft, and his voice was gentle. We scarcely said ten words. That morning, to me, he was a complete mystery. He sat wrapped in introspective silence, while the others buzzed and disputed about the approaching conference.

I gathered that he had insisted on going alone into the citadel, and that the sheiks feared to risk their war-chief inside the walls. Real trouble was in the air, and they feared that he might be seized as a hostage. One of them finally protested loudly that it was madness "to enter the wolf's den naked [unarmed]." Patiently Sultan Pasha heard them, and at this he arose and approached the man who had cried out, smiled his queer, sad smile, and with his elbows pushed aside the folds of his black cloak. Beneath it, strapped close together on his stomach, were two heavy-caliber automatic pistols.

Later, I learned to know him a bit more intimately in his own home, meekly gentle as a lamb—and later still when he rode out to actual battle with the unmistakable gleam of the fanatical, born "killer" in his eyes. I came finally to the conclusion that he was of the abnormal "inspired mystic" type. It seemed to me that in private life

his character was little short of Christlike, as I had been
told, for though a rich man, even by American standards,
I found that his family had to guard continually against
his giving away all that they possessed, and that he de-
voted all his time, when not at war, to helping the poor
and praying.

Such was his mood that morning in Souieda. Neither
he nor the acting governor wanted war, and when he
came out of the citadel at the end of a half-hour, he said
to the great crowd of Druses that had gathered in the
square to hear the outcome: "Go home, my children, and
may peace go with you."

The next day Katie and I went by motor, accompanied by Daoud Izzedin and young Sheik Fouad, son
of Ali bey, to visit Sultan Pasha and his family in his
own village of Kurieh, about three hours away from
Souieda. We found the Atrash castle, a great mass of
ruins, in the center of the village. It had been dyna-
mited by the French two years before and was three-
fourths wrecked. The family lived in five rooms of
which the walls still stood, and, to replace the assembly-
hall and coffee-room, which had been destroyed, they had
erected of stone from the debris a sort of pavilion, having an open front and an arbored roof on high poles. It
was in this pavilion that all passing guests were received.
When we arrived, there were already a dozen or more
visitors from surrounding villages. We were welcomed
by the brothers of the Sultan Pasha—Ali, who was killed
in the first battle with the French less than a month
later, and Mustapha, who was badly wounded in the same
engagement.

There was a fountain in the courtyard, a big stone

basin into which water bubbled up through a pipe from a spring. As we sat in the pavilion, having coffee, six or eight Bedouin women with camels entered the courtyard. Two of the women came and stood in front of the pavilion. Ali, the elder brother, went out to speak to them, and they knelt and kissed his hands. Then they returned to the fountain and filled a number of goatskins with water, loaded them on the camels, and went away. An hour later a Druse peasant—a stranger—riding a donkey and leading one camel, came and sat with us and had coffee. His camel was piled high with empty five-gallon gasoline-tins. He subsequently filled them at the fountain and departed. Yet I saw no persons from the village taking water from the fountain. Ali explained to me with what seemed a mixture of exasperation and pride: "It is my brother, Sultan, you know. Since most of our wells are dry in the Mountain this summer, he has spread word that all nomads and travelers, and all Druses who come from other villages where there is no water, may take freely from this spring, while we, of his own family and village, must use water brought by caravan from another well, hard of access and four days' journey distant."

Sultan Pasha came later to the pavilion and greeted us gravely, apologizing for the humbleness of the entertainment. He said: "Forgive me that I was not present on your arrival. I was praying for the peace that the Druses have never known, that we have never had for a thousand years, and that some day must be sent. But I fear it will not be now."

When I asked him about the alleged tyranny of the French, with which the other Druses had begun to fill my ears, he answered only: "They could do nothing if it were not the will of God. Nothing happens outside God's will. What can I say?"

Luncheon was presently served us in one of the still intact rooms of the castle. The room was a jumble of chests and furniture and draperies piled pell-mell. The meal was simple; pieces of lamb broiled on spits, eggplant salad, and a great bowl of clabbered cream which was

A RUINED MOSQUE OF THE EIGHTH CENTURY
Built from the Stones of a Former Roman Temple

passed from hand to hand with one huge silver spoon which we all used in turn.

On the wall was the framed portrait of a powerful and dignified Druse elder. It was Thoukan Atrash, father of Sultan Pasha, who had been a sort of giant, a man of enormous physical strength, famous in both conference and battle. Sultan Pasha spoke of him with pride. "This I cannot remember," he said, "but my mother told me. When I was a baby only one year old, the Turks came, and my father, holding me in one hand

and his drawn sword in the other, leaped to the back of his horse and, guiding it with his knees, charged through them, slaying three as he escaped, so that the blood was spattered in my face."

When I asked how long Thoukan Atrash had been dead, it was Ali who responded: "He was captured through treachery and hanged in 1912 by the Turks, at the order of General Sami Pasha Feruki, in the public square of Damascus. They had an old rope, which broke three times, but by the third time he was already dead. Beforehand they had asked him if he had anything to say, and he had shouted: 'Tell my people never to trust a Turk!' "

During this conversation, we were sitting in the arbor-like pavilion, built from stones of the ruined castle. Sultan Pasha had again faded modestly away and left us with his two brothers.

After the pause which followed the tale of old Thoukan's dying words, Mustapha turned to me earnestly and said: "*Wellah*, the *Francewi* [French] are worse!"

I thought he meant the dynamiting of their home—though as a matter of fact he had wholly different grievances in mind—and I asked if he would tell me the circumstances that had led up to it.

"Fouad here, perhaps, will relate it," Mustapha replied. "He also rode with Sultan Pasha."

I guessed that it was Atrash family modesty—or pride—that stopped his own lips, as Fouad, son of Ali bey Obeyid, began the recital. At the very moment of his beginning, Daoud Izzedin came to my side and whispered: "This, you know, is the story of Sultan Pasha's greatest deed—of his attack on the French tank."

"In 1922," Fouad meanwhile was saying, "as the French High Commissioner, General Gouraud, was motoring from Beirut to Damascus, he was fired on by a party of Arabs, who may have been bandits or perhaps patriots. A secretary was killed and an Arab military aide badly wounded.

"A certain Adhan Hanjar, a Damascus Arab, was suspected by the French of complicity in plots that preceded the shooting and perhaps led up to it. They sent out an order for his arrest, and he fled to the Mountain of the Druses. After he had entered our territory, he was arrested on the road, in the presence of a number of passing Druses. As the French soldiers took him, he shouted: 'I am the guest of Sultan Pasha Atrash. I was on my way to his house.'

"You must know that in the Djebel a guest is something sacred.

"The Druses who had heard him hurried here to the Atrash castle. It was a time of peace, and Sultan Pasha was riding with his falcons and hounds. In his absence they told their story to his mother.

"When he returned, she met him at the door of the castle and cried: 'You, my son, the earthen floor of whose banquet-hall is black with grease from many sheep slain to entertain guests, must now give protection.'

" 'When have I ever failed?' he replied.

" 'Adhan Hanjar,' she said, 'came into the Mountain and on the way to your house he was taken and thrown into prison at Souieda.'

"Sultan Pasha burst into tears and sang the Druse war-song:

We are the Children of Maruf!
Among our rocks is sanctuary.
When our spears grow rusty,
We make them bright
With the blood of our enemies.

"When he had finished singing, he prayed, and sent a letter to the French garrison at Souieda, saying: 'This man, though he had not set foot in my house, was coming as my guest, and I beg you by our sacred laws of hospitality to free him on my word until his cause may be heard.'

"The French sent no answer.

"That night Sultan Pasha, with his two brothers here, Ali and Mustapha, and five other men, went to storm the little jail. They found it empty. The French officials had taken Adhan into the citadel.

"Sultan Pasha rode home again and before dawn sent messengers of war throughout the Mountain. Meantime the French had sent three tanks to take the prisoner to Damascus. They were small tanks, manned with two officers each.

"We of Souieda had heard the news. A few of us rode to Kurieh to meet Sultan Pasha here, and others prepared to join him later. When I arrived at Kurieh, he had already four or five hundred warriors assembled, and with this force we rode on toward Souieda to begin the attack. When we reached a hilltop looking down westward on the plain, we saw the three tanks from Damascus crawling like bugs. As we continued to ride toward them, Sultan Pasha's power surged suddenly within him. With a great shout he urged his white mare into a gallop, and then into a run. When he reached the plain, he was riding on, nearly a quarter of a mile ahead, full tilt, against the first tank.

"He was fired on, but escaped untouched, though four bullets went through the folds of his *abba*. The top lid of the tank had been left open because of the heat. Throwing away his gun, Sultan Pasha rode his horse at full speed against the tank, leaped from the saddle on top of it and with his sword slew the captain and lieutenant who were inside. In his battle fury he was not content to kill with a single downward stroke. Twenty sword-thrusts were found in the captain's body afterward. We had come up meanwhile, and, though twelve among us were killed, we disabled the other two tanks.

"We knew that after this the French would come to attack Sultan Pasha's castle and his village. Sultan led us by night, several hundred horsemen, to a mass of ancient ruins yonder, overlooking the village, from which all the inhabitants had gone. We hid ourselves and our horses so well that the French who came over in airplanes to reconnoiter saw nothing. Then a force of cavalrymen and foot soldiers, mixed French troops, Arabs and negroes, entered the village and prepared to carry away all the wheat and grain before they began dynamiting. Sultan knew that he could not prevent it, but he hoped to harass them. He said to us: 'Do not shoot until they have entered on the threshing-floors and have laid down their guns.'

"But one of our men got excited and fired too soon. We had a little battle. The next day the French sent more troops, carried away all the grain, and smashed Sultan's castle with dynamite and bombs.

"When a peace was made later, Sultan Pasha came

into Souieda and was carried on the uplifted hands of his soldiers as they rode horseback through the streets. Our people and even the French troops scrambled over one another in the crowds in order to catch a glimpse of him. The French themselves offered to rebuild his castle, but he refused them courteously, saying, 'A house that cannot protect its guest is unworthy to stand, and you did right to destroy it.' And thus it lies as you see to this day."

In one of the five intact chambers of the castle, Katie and I slept that night, again Oriental-wise on pallets. Daoud and Fouad Obeyid slept in an adjoining chamber.

Two days later we were pushing farther back into the Djebel, to visit another great Druse war-chief of the same family, Hussein Pasha Atrash, lord of Anz. We had to abandon the Cadillac and take to camels.

Anz, which we reached just before twilight, was a huge rambling castle-fortress on a hillside, with some hundreds of flat-roofed, thick-walled stone houses massed close beneath it, on the slope.

Servants met us at a gateway in the castle wall, and followed us, leading our camels, into the courtyard with its stables and granaries.

A steep, straight, narrow flight of steps led upward for more than a hundred feet to a colonnaded terrace, which overlooked the valley. From the terrace, we entered the main reception hall, high-ceilinged, richly rugged and tapestried in Oriental style, but with velvet-upholstered, gilded furniture of European design brought on the backs of camels from Damascus. In one corner of the room stood an enormous European bed of state, high-posted, and with an elaborate canopy. It was the only bedstead we ever saw in the Djebel Druse, but it was a most noble one, and we slept on it that night.

A moment after our arrival in the reception hall, Hussein Pasha entered. He bowed profoundly, repeating to each of us: "Welcome, my house is honored." He was a thick-set man of middle age, with a face of great strength. He wore the head-dress of an Arab prince, white silk *kafieh* held in place by a double gold band, and a black *abba* embroidered with gold and silver. It turned out, however, that he had donned this splendor simply to do us honor, for next day and on succeeding days he wore the ordinary Arab dress. More permanently gorgeous was the young black slave who stood at his elbow.

We went out and sat on the cooler terrace, in the twilight, while lanterns and lamps were hung, and presently Hussein's children appeared, shyly, to meet the strange guests. The elder son, perhaps seventeen, had braided hair and the same sort of costume as his father. A twelve-year-old boy, whose hair hung loose over his shoulders like that of a medieval page, wore red velvet, and a little five-year-old was dressed in a miniature British military uniform, which had been made to order in Jerusalem. A two-year-old baby daughter, who was brought out to sit on Hussein Pasha's knee before dinner, was like a little doll or a princess from some fairy-tale. Her eyelids were blackened with kohl; her face was painted, delicately and with art; her hair was twined with bright coins and jewels; her finger-tips were stained pink with henna like the rosy dawn. And with them she tugged at the mustaches of the fierce papa whom she adored.

Hussein Pasha had been described to me by a certain French officer in Beirut as a bandit—"a savage bandit."

The British held him in quite different esteem, for in the latter part of the World War he had helped to raise three regiments of Arab cavalry to aid Allenby and the Allies against the Turks, had given several hundred camel-loads of grain from his own stores to feed the troops; he became a colonel of native forces in the British army, and was cited for personal bravery in the official British dispatches.

As for us, we found the "savage bandit" a delightful host and a charming man.

Dinner was served on the terrace by two black slaves who might have stepped from the pages of *The Thousand and One Nights*, with their flowing robes and jeweled daggers. But if they furnished a Haroun el Reshid background, the meal itself was "modern" to the last touch. There was a long table with spotless napery, a profusion of silver, tall-stemmed glasses, and Sèvres porcelain. The champagne was Cordon Rouge 1912.

Under its mellowing influence, Hussein Pasha, employing a polyglot French-English, became absorbed in repeating for Katie's benefit an edifying tale which he had just told in Arabic concerning a certain Jew and twelve watermelon seeds. The tale was temporarily interrupted by a dish of partridges, and Hussein Pasha, now feeling quite at home in his own castle, absent-mindedly seized one of the birds in his great warrior's fist, and bit therefrom a kingly chunk, flesh, bone, gristle, and all.

And it was then that I began to love him, for out of the embarrassment that flitted across his face as his jaws crunched the mighty morsel, there gradually appeared an apologetic grin, and turning to Katie, he said: "Please do not blame me, madam; it is my old association with those English; among them it is fashionable to eat birds with the fingers!"

The days we spent at Anz are among our best memories of Arabia. They gave us an opportunity, too, of further contact with the unchanged life in the remoter villages of the Djebel.

One afternoon Hussein Pasha took me to Liheh to attend a village court where the old Druse justice was being administered. It was in the *mukhaad* of the chief elder, who was to act as judge. Other of the sheiks and elders sat with him. The complainant, a Christian farmer from the Hauran, stood before them, bewailing the fact that he had been robbed of four camel-loads of grain in this same village the night before. He was permitted to introduce Druse witnesses to support his statements. After a conference, the chief elder rendered judgment: "Even though it may not have been a Druse who robbed you; even though a Bedouin or other stranger may have been the guilty one, the shame and responsibility are upon us, since in the village you were our guest. From the village common stores an equal amount of grain will be immediately returned to you, and we ask you now formally to accept our apologies."

Afterward, apparently as a minor detail, the elders set about trying to find the thief.

I asked Hussein Pasha what punishments were ultimately inflicted on offenders. He said: "In Souieda there are jails under the French law, but we have no jails or prisons here. If the offender is a stranger, he is fined and never permitted to come into the Djebel Druse again. If he is a Druse, he is likewise fined. If his fault is forgivable, he is forgiven. If it involves dishonor, then permanent disgrace and shame are his greatest punishment."

I said to him: "But surely there are crimes for which no disgrace is sufficient punishment?"

He replied: "For that, of course, there is death." And on the way home he told me this story:

"We Druses are no good at trades," he said. "Most of us know only how to fight. We usually get masons from the Lebanon to build our houses.

"A few years ago, a Christian stone-mason from Showair came to the village of Sheik Amir to build a new house for one of the rich men. He brought with him his pretty young wife, a Christian woman, who went, in the Christian way, unveiled. When the house was half finished, the youngest brother of Sheik Amir went one day to the mason's house and took his wife by force.

"She immediately told her husband, and he, in fear, gathered all his belongings together, put them on a couple of donkeys, and went away with his wife in the night. The next morning the man whose house he was building followed him on horseback and asked him angrily why he had left the contract unfinished. The Christian replied: 'My honor is already gone, and if I tell you why, my life will be gone, too. The man who wronged me is a Druse whom even the Druses fear. What could I, a Christian, do against him?' The employer then forced the Christian to tell him what had happened and to go back with him to the village.

"He went straight to Sheik Amir and said: 'You and I and our village have lost our honor, and it can only be regained by the shedding of blood.' There followed a great gathering of the elders and warriors. The guilty

brother himself came, fully armed like the others.   While
the warriors stood in a great circle with their horses, the
forty or more sheiks and elders sat in a smaller circle and
were served with coffee by the servants of Sheik Amir,
who was the host, because the conference was on the outskirts of his village.

"Then the rich Druse whose half-built house had been
abandoned arose and said: 'O Sheik Amir! suppose that
you were a poor man, and, with your wife, went to work
in a town among strangers; and suppose that, while you
were working, a man of the town entered your dwelling
place and took your wife by force!'

"Sheik Amir leaped to his feet and drew his sword to
kill the speaker—not because he dreamed that the affair
concerned his own brother, but because he was outraged
by the reference to his wife in a connection so horrible.
The other sheiks, however, leaped upon him and held him,
perceiving some secret meaning in the words.

" 'O Sheik Amir!' he continued, 'kill me later if you
wish, but now answer me this question: If such a tragedy
occurred, what punishment should the guilty man receive?'

"Sheik Amir replied, 'He should surely die.'

" 'Suppose a Druse had done a thing like that?'

" 'If he were my own son, he should die.'

" 'Do you stand by that judgment?'

" 'I repeat, if the man were my own flesh and blood,
still he should die.'

" 'Is that the judgment of all?' shouted the speaker.

" 'It is our judgment,' replied the sheiks.

"The Christian was brought in, too much frightened to
speak. His employer, after telling the story for him,

said: 'I command you to point out the man.' Tremblingly he did so. The truth was plain. According to custom, if a Druse does something that merits death, his own family exacts the penalty. So Sheik Amir slew his own brother there, and thus the justice was accomplished."

An hour later the man who had told me this bloody tale of savage justice was seated in his orchard-garden with children on his knees and tugging at his *abba*. One of the slaves had climbed a mulberry tree to fill a silver bowl with fruit, and now Hussein Pasha was popping the mulberries into the mouths of the babies. On one knee was his infant daughter. On the other was a coal-black pickaninny, child of the slave. He stuffed their eager mouths indiscriminately and wiped their smeared faces with the fold of his robe.

When we walked back from the orchard at twilight, the little daughter was carried asleep in Katie's arms, and the black baby was perched on Hussein Pasha's shoulder.

Chapter IX

THE GOLDEN CALF

THOUGH French officials back in Damascus had tried to dissuade us from visiting the Mountain of the Druses, it was a missionary who had given us the really exciting warnings.

We had listened with scandalized faces as we drank his tea—hoping meanwhile in our unregenerate hearts that the half of what he told us might be true.

"They hold secret and abominable rites in the worship of a golden calf," he said.

"They believe in black magic. They practice awful cruelties on women. They bury corpses in the walls of their houses."

As confirmatory evidence, he had unshelved a copy of old Silvestre de Sacy's book and read: "It is a secret cult, rendered to the head of a bull or a calf, rudely made, of gold, silver, or bronze, which they keep in a box hidden from all eyes, and open for the veneration of the initiates."

Then there was a curious story, which he had got at first hand, of how a Maronite shepherd, hearing cries and groans from a Druse farmhouse, had peeped through a chink in the wall and had seen a woman lying on the stone floor, with her neck encircled by a heavy iron collar "that seemed fastened directly or with one link only to the paving-stones, so that she could not lift or turn her head."

I was particularly interested in that story because it

seemed somehow not like a product of the unaided imagination. As a matter of fact, there was turning out to be more than a grain of truth, though swollen in some cases, distorted in others, in everything he had told us.

In Souieda, the Druse capital, and in the castles of the Atrash family, we had found a rich feudal aristocracy,

A SACRED BULL ON THE ISHTAR GATE AT BABYLON

holding fast to Druse customs and traditions, yet partially sophisticated through contact with Damascus, Beirut, and the coast. I was beginning to know my hosts so well and trust them so much that I had no hesitancy in talking to them of the tales I had heard in Damascus. At some they were amused; at others angry. In most cases they were candid and even anxious for us to learn the truth. Northeast of Souieda and behind the terrific basalt and lava walls and gorges of the Lejah, whither we were taken on horseback by Hussein Pasha Atrash to little villages and clusters of stone houses unmarked on any map, there are Druse peasants as far removed from civilization as if they lived in the mountains of the moon.

Some of the old-fashioned, superstitious Druses, Hussein Pasha said, believed in demoniac possession. They chained down a man or woman troubled by an evil spirit in just such an iron collar as had been described to us. They did it not from cruelty but with the idea of driving out the devil, who would tire of a cramped body and go in search of a more comfortable habitation. An instance of the fear of evil spirits I saw with my own eyes in a house where we stopped for water. A Druse mother fell into a rage because her husband, hurrying eagerly across the room with a jug to serve us, had brushed her baby's empty cradle with the skirt of his *abba* and made it rock. While she berated him, Hussein grinned and whispered that spirits like to rock or swing, and therefore sometimes jump into empty cradles for a "free ride." Then, after the baby is put back in the cradle, the spirit finds itself crowded and pinches and plagues the child.

One of the objects of our trip into the Lejah was to find a certain sorcerer, reputed to work wonders. He turned out to be a tall, powerfully built old man, white-bearded but muscular, apparently the most important person in his village, since his house was the largest. He was flattered by our visit and bowed low before Hussein Pasha, but did not kiss his hand as most of the peasants did. He insisted on making coffee and wanted us to stay the night. After the coffee drinking, he displayed his powers—magical, possibly, though not necessarily black.

First, he suspended a Bible from the ceiling by a cord.

Next he read the passage from the Koran that denies the divinity of Christ. As he read, the Bible began to jerk and gyrate violently, finally breaking the cord and falling to the floor. By reading other passages from the Koran he seemed to make an egg in boiling water jump out of the pot and break on the floor and seemed to transfer the water from a full jug to an empty jug ten feet distant. I say "seemed," because I believe there must always be some physical explanation for physical phenomena.

The idea that Druses who die are interred in the walls of their houses was based, I found, on the fact that until a generation ago the elders, or *akils*, were thus buried, and still are, in the remoter districts. We saw no Druse funeral in the Lejah, but I had the good luck, on another occasion, to attend one in the mountains of the Lebanon. I had arrived at Ibadyah to spend the night as guest of the uncle of Daoud Izzedin. Ibadyah was a village peopled by Christians, Mohametans, and Druses in about equal numbers.[1]

About nine o'clock, after we had dined, a man stood below in the street, shouting, "Hear, oh, hear!" We went to the windows, and he cried out: "Said Najar is dead." This was equivalent to a funeral announcement as well as a death notice, since the Druses did not practice embalming and always held the funeral on the morning following the death. Daoud's uncle told us that Said Najar was a Druse farmer who had been noted for his physical strength and his courage in war. "Once," said the uncle, "I saw

[1] The Djebel Druse is populated solely by Druses, but they are also found in the mixed populations throughout all the mountains of Syria. They frequently adopt many of the outward forms and symbols of Islam and perhaps partially believe in them, though holding fast at the same time to the secret tenets of their own mysterious faith.

him lift a *jurn* [granite mortar] above his head with one hand and carry it for fifty paces."

Early in the morning, when we set out on foot toward the house of the dead man, we met a procession headed by the bearer of the banner of Islam, green silk embroidered in gold with Arabic characters, *Bismillah al-rahman al-rahim*—"in the name of Allah, the Merciful, the Compassionate." Then, carried high above their heads by six men who let it rest on the very tips of their outstretched fingers, came an empty pine coffin covered with shining tin or nickel, bright as silver, and resembling a sarcophagus with a lid shaped like the body of a man. Wildflowers, yellow and red, were stuck through the handles of the coffin. Among the marchers who followed were Maronite Christians, Druses, and Moslems, distinguished by their different costumes and headdresses. Men of all three sects, including Christian priests in the robes of the Greek and Maronite churches, took turns at carrying the coffin and also the banner of Islam, replacing each other every hundred yards or so as the procession wound through the village street.

I said to Daoud: "I think this is the strangest sight I have ever seen in your fantastic Arabia—a Christian priest with his vestments and crucifix, holding high with both hands the 'infidel' flag of Mahound!"

"Bah!" said he. "It's nothing at all. Or anyway, it's fifty-fifty. If you come here when a Christian dies, you will find both Druses and Mohametans helping to carry the crucifix with Christian banners at the head of the procession."

After the coffin came first the young men, warriors and farmers. They sang as they marched. They were followed by the Druse elders, venerable in white turbans and long black cloaks. Since the law of the Druses is that the elders must always maintain their dignity and never show emotion, they neither sang nor participated in the ceremonies. The singing was all to the same tune, a sort of melodious couplet in four-four time, with the last note of each line elided. The words were verse, either written or extemporized on the spot, in honor of the dead man. A chorus of four men only, walking immediately behind the coffin, tried over a new couplet, and after they had practised it a half-dozen times, they gave the sign and the procession began to sing it like a Greek chorus.

The songs were neither in praise of God nor in supplication to God. They were merely expressions of praise for the dead man and sorrow for his family. Daoud told me that they must stick close to facts. In this case, the only traits that could be praised were the dead man's physical strength, his courage in war, and his generosity; 't seems that he had not been pious or prosperous or particularly intelligent.

The first couplet they sang was:

> Whom is Allah taking today?
> Perhaps it is Antar, that great warrior.

Since Antar was one of the great Arab warriors and heroes before the time of Mohamet, to suggest that the soul of Said Najar was the soul of Antar was a tribute to his strength in battle.

Other couplets ran in this wise:

> A lion is dead
> And the forest is in darkness.

When such a lion dies,
All spears should be lowered.

There are plenty of stars in the sky—
Only the moon has been eclipsed.

Patience is better;
For death is the lot of all.

The procession had now reached a sort of square or courtyard outside the stone house of the dead man. The elders seated themselves on the ground in the courtyard, leaving the central space clear, and there the procession, still with the banner and the empty coffin held high, marched slowly round and round. From time to time people composed new couplets, wrote them on scraps of paper, and handed them to the singers.

Meanwhile the body had been washed and dressed and was lying on a mattress in a big tent on the hillside, just below the dead man's house. The tent had been put up because the house was too small to contain the women who had come to mourn with the wife and sisters. All these women, dressed in white and veiled, were crowded into the tent, watching over the body, while the men marched in procession outside. The women did not sing, but whispered among themselves and raised their voices from time to time in cries of lamentation.

Presently there was a sound of singing from a distance, and down one of the winding streets, between stone walls, came a delegation from a neighboring village, led by Druse elders, Greek priests, and Mohametan *imams*. The local singers fell aside to allow the visitors to march behind the coffin and intone their couplets. Similar processions came from other villages until there were finally perhaps six or eight hundred men marching behind the coffin and singing. Meanwhile water was passed freely in stone jars, but no food and no other drink of any sort was offered, since it is a point of honor that visiting guests at a funeral must take no refreshments at the home of the mourners.

Toward noon the marching and singing stopped. Quickly and without ceremony six men went into the tent with the coffin, thrust the body into it unceremoniously, and, hurrying out with it on their shoulders, took their places again in the procession. The veiled wife and daughters pathetically waved a last farewell.

The procession wound down a steep mule-path, through gardens, among trees and irrigated vineyards, to a tomb on the mountainside. It was a solid vault about ten feet square, built of stone, without door, window, or entrance of any sort above ground. Two feet underground there was a small opening, closed by a rude, flat natural stone. It was necessary to dig a trench, uncover this stone, and lift it away.

As the coffin lay in the trench, ready to be pushed through the hole, a young man with a beautiful tenor voice stood and sang like an angel. It lasted for perhaps ten minutes. It was a series of variations on the two words *Allah Akbar*, meaning "God is great." The crowd now cried out: "May Allah accept his soul in paradise!" There was a pause, during which every one looked toward the elders; another pause and whispering among the elders; then they all repeated quietly: "May Allah receive his soul!" As Daoud explained it, the elders have the right to withhold their prayer, and if the dead man's life has been notoriously evil, they sometimes do withhold it, to the great unhappiness of the family.

What followed was a quick, rough business. Four or five of the strongest men laid hold of the coffin to push it through the hole into the vault. The lid was too big and the coffin jammed. Although the lid had been nailed down, the men pried it off, disclosing the body, and I

THE ARCH OF CTESIPHON IN THE TIGRIS VALLEY

noticed heavy tattoo marks on the hands. The coffin still would not go through. The men pulled it back hastily, and one of them crawled into the hole on his hands and knees. Then, pushing and pulling, they got the coffin in. Afterward the lid was passed through to the man inside. In a moment he came crawling out, perspiring and evidently glad to have finished with a bad job.

After the funeral, while the earth was being shoveled back into the trench, the dead man's will was read. I noticed, as we went away, that two men sat down in

front of the tomb as if they were going to remain in-
definitely.

Daoud said: "Yes, people will take turns at guarding
it for five days and nights."

"How can they fear jackals when the entrance to the
tomb is buried underground?" I asked.

"It is not jackals they fear, but ghouls and *jinn*."

Now that the ceremony had come to an end, the warriors and farmers accepted bread and meat, lemonade
and *halvah*, a sort of candy, offered by the villagers at
small stands. The elders, however, refused to eat or
drink. Many of them trudged home for miles through
the hot sun without having had any food since early
breakfast. The law for them is that they must touch no
food within the boundaries of the village where a funeral
has taken place.

This sharp division between the elders [*akils*] and the
warriors [*jahils*] cuts like a knife through crowds in the
village streets, through groups, through families. Even
without their different modes of dress, the *akils* are set
apart by every word and gesture. Though they are
chiefly the older men, there are many under forty, and any
Druse after the age of twenty-five may become an *akil*
if he leads an honorable life and is willing to assume the
obligations and vows.

Among the families that we visited in Souieda, that of
Suli bey included one son, Ismael, who was an *akil*, and
two sons, Adham and Mustapha, who were *jahils*. At
dinner, Ismael ate slowly, gravely, and sparingly, but his
two brothers, who had been riding hard that morning,
wolfed their food with appetite and pleasure. Mustapha
and Adham smoked their own cigarettes and mine, and

Adham produced a small bottle of *arak*, distilled from grapeskins, a spirit as clear and strong as corn whiskey, which he drank with us. Ismael, being an *akil*, could neither smoke nor drink.

In matters of sex, also, Ismael had to follow much stricter laws than those laid down for his two brothers. He could and did have one wife, but outside the monogamous marriage relation, he was vowed to absolute chastity. His brothers might dally with the pretty gypsy Bedouin dancing-girls who often passed through the Djebel with their tambourines and donkeys. The worst punishment the young warriors could suffer would be the same kind of lenient "bawling out" that the Yale freshman gets when Papa learns of his entanglement with chorus girls. But for Ismael it would mean bitter shame and public disgrace.

As an elder, Ismael was pledged, at the request of any Druse, to give advice and even material help in time of need. Further, according to his vows, he must never lose his temper, never show excitement, never run, never elevate his voice, never express hunger or thirst, and never boast. He was not permitted to fight in raids, tribal quarrels, or personal feuds, but could take up arms only in defense of the nation.

All Druses profess the same religion, are familiar with the Druse scriptures, the *Kitab el-Hikmet*, or "Book of Wisdom," and are permitted to take part in services in the temple. But only the elders compose the inner circle of initiates. To them has been revealed a set of mysteries never divulged, so far as I know, to general knowledge or to the remainder of the Druses themselves. I believe that these mysteries are symbolic rituals with secret

words and litanies. A Syrian told me that the Druse initiates would say to a man, to test him: "Do you plant
cardamon-seed in your fields?" If the man was not an
initiate, he would answer "Yes" or "No" as the case
might be. If he was an initiate, he would reply: "The
seeds are planted in our hearts." I don't believe this is
the true "word." If I did, I wouldn't repeat it; but I do
believe the Druses, like Freemasons and Rosicrucians,
have secret formulas and passwords.

When on a second visit I told my principal host, Ali
bey Obeyid, in Souieda, of my desire to see and learn all
that could properly be disclosed to me of his religion, he
suggested that we should call on a friend of his, the old
Sheik Faris Turkan, a learned *akil* who had lived in
Damascus and who could speak excellent French. Ali
bey's only tongue was Arabic, and my incomplete knowledge of that language was scarcely equal to complicated
theological discussion.

I was not prepared for the cordiality and frankness—
up to a certain point—of the Sheik Faris. He seemed
happy and pleased to help me. He said: "You have
doubtless heard from Moslems and Christians alike that
we worship a golden calf's head and that we have ceremonies in which naked women dance and voluntarily
undergo strange tortures. I suppose you have heard also
that we practice magic. At any rate, you have been told
that at the core of our faith lie hidden dreadful secrets.
Fortunately today is Friday. Suppose you come with
me tonight to our temple and see for yourself what our
religious practices really are."

That night at nine o'clock we went to the temple, a
big, square, one-story stone structure, with walls three

feet thick, like a fortress or powder-magazine, without dome or minaret. It was set on a little hill, more than a hundred yards from any other building, on the out-skirts of Souieda. The interior was a bare room, about fifty feet square, with a vaulted roof supported by pillars and arches of masonry. Through the center hung a heavy black curtain. I imagined that it shut off some of the mysteries, but I was wrong. It was simply like the screen in a Mohametan mosque, and behind it were the Druse women. A non-Druse told me later that beneath this temple at Souieda, as beneath every Druse temple, was a crypt where the mysteries were celebrated, but on that point I have no personal knowledge.

The only furnishings of the big room were rugs spread on the floor and a half-dozen basket-stands, or taborets, of plaited colored straw, shaped like mushrooms. From the ceiling hung chandeliers with lighted kerosene lamps.

Some thirty or forty Druses, all elders, were gathered in little groups on the floor, not cross-legged like Turks, but squatting on their heels. All arose when we entered, and touched their hands to their foreheads. Those whom I had previously met came and shook hands with me.

Manuscript copies of the "Book of Wisdom" or rather, I think, of the parts of it that all Druses were permitted to hear were laid on top of the basket-stands. I was told that these scriptures were in part dictated by God to Hakim, founder of the Druse religion in the eleventh cen-tury, and in part written by Hamza, the Persian mystic, who developed the new faith. There was no leader or preacher, but various elders sitting beside the baskets took turns in reading passages. Of these I could understand only a few words because they were in classic Arabic.

But the Sheik Faris willingly translated them to me in whispered French. They were chiefly conventional precepts of morality and conduct, drawn in some cases from the Bible or Koran. One was almost identical with the verse from Deuteronomy: "When thou beatest thine olive tree, thou shalt not go over the boughs again; it shall be for the stranger, for the fatherless, and for the widow."

After three-quarters of an hour of reading, the worshipers repeated sentences in unison. These sentences, they said, were prayers, but to me they seemed more like affirmation or recital of a creed, except for one, which was: "To thee, O God! we come determined to do what is right in thy sight. Let our eyes, O God! sleep in thine obedience." The statement sometimes made that the Druses do not pray is absurd. Besides having heard the prayer just quoted, I saw Sultan Pasha Atrash and dozens of others praying at various times. All Islamic Orientals, including the orthodox Moslems, consider begging for specific things in prayer to be an "impertinent interference with the Creator." He is all-just, and everything is settled by fate, *kismet*, which is in his hands. Therefore it is silly to ask for rain or for the life of a sick child. All Moslem prayer and all Druse prayer—if thoroughly orthodox—is pure praise of God, recital of his attributes, and concurrence in his will. When Druses are under emotional stress, however, they make requests of God, as Sultan Pasha, for instance, prayed for peace. But they ask by circumlocution—not by direct imploring.

The religious ceremony in the temple ended as casually as it had begun. I could hear the women on the other side of the curtain gossiping as they went away.

The elders again gathered into little groups and began talking busily about crops, commercial affairs, politics, and their latest quarrel with the French. The old Sheik Faris took me off into a corner to enlighten me further on those parts of the Druse doctrine that did not touch the forbidden mysteries.

"You see," he said, "that we are pure unitarians. We have a story, not in our scriptures, that, after God had created heaven and earth, men sinned. God began sending prophets to lead them back into the right path. He sent Noah, but only his own family followed him. He sent Abraham, and his own tribe followed. He sent Moses, and all the tribes of Israel followed. He sent Jesus, and the Gentiles followed. He sent Mohamet and the entire world followed—except the Druses. Then God sent the Angel Gabriel and spoke through him to the Druses, saying, 'I have sent many true prophets, and all the world has accepted one or another, but you have followed none.' The Druses sent back word by the Angel Gabriel: 'God is enough for us.' Of course this is not accurate as either history or theology, but it is interesting for its emphasis on Druse adherence to one God and to God alone. As a matter of fact, we were Moslems in the eleventh century when Hakim, who was the Sixth Fatimite Caliph, became convinced that he had a new revelation direct from God, and we were the converts to his new religion. We believe that the teachings of Jesus, Mohamet, and the other prophets are true, but partial and incomplete."

I could not discuss with Sheik Faris the question of the mysteries. It would have been neither discreet nor courteous. But I did risk mentioning to him the fact that universally the Druses are said to worship a golden calf. He replied: "We worship only the one pure God, but God is in all things, the sky, the earth, fire, water, men, animals, and vegetables. Consequently among all peoples He has been adored by many of His symbols."

This point of view may be partly responsible for the readiness of the Druses to observe outward forms of Christianity and Islam. As a matter of fact, they will sometimes make the sign of the cross and dip their fingers in holy water, and will repeat Moslem prayers. I was told by one Druse elder, in all seriousness, that to do these things was "polite and harmless."

But the persistent story of the secret worship of a golden calf was what interested me most deeply in connection with the faith of the Druses. I was beset with obvious difficulties in my efforts to get at the truth about it, and I am not sure that I ever did. The worst handicap was my genuine admiration of the Druses, their extraordinary kindness to me, and an unwillingness on my part, then or ever, to betray their friendship.[1]

Among the many Druses whom I ventured to question in regard to the golden calf was Suleiman bey Izzedin, the great Druse historian. Though at the time a semi-invalid, he consented to talk with me because of my friendship with his son, Daoud. The house of the Izzedin family was Europeanized in furnishings, but a veiled girl servant, shuffling barefoot on wooden clogs, conducted me to Suleiman bey's bedchamber. It was a lofty room, white-plastered—elegant, but austere. The

[1] The substance of this chapter, published in *Asia,* was translated into Arabic and widely circulated in Syria with the benevolent approval of leading Druse *akils,* who refrained, however, from confirming or denying its accuracy.

historian, a man of sixty, with thick, close-cropped iron-gray hair and black mustache, was propped up on pillows, in a high bed with posts and a canopy. He wore a heavy white linen night-shirt, buttoned close at the throat and wrists. The bed was littered with books in Arabic, French, and German.

Suleiman bey spoke perfect English and discussed freely matters on which Druses are usually evasive—the cruelty of the Mountain Druses to women suspected of infidelity or frivolity; the Maronite massacres that are the worst blot on Druse history; the curious deification of the Caliph Hakim. But when I finally approached the golden calf of the Druses, he refused to admit that it existed or ever had existed. "It is an absolutely groundless calumny," he said, "invented by the Moslems and Christians. It is like the story that the Jews crucify Christian babies at Easter. We have never worshiped a golden calf. We have never worshiped any idol. We worship only the one pure God." And he would not return to the subject.

Even Amir Amin Arslan failed me here, though I am indebted to him for accurate, unbiased information on all other subjects relating to Arabia. He said: "The Druses are the sole people on the edge of the desert who keep cows. The Bedouins have only goats and sheep. Wherever the Bedouins came on Druse villages, they found cows, well kept, carefully tended. From that fact grew up, perhaps, this superstition." It was a feeble theory. From a man of Amir Amin Arslan's great intelligence and sophistication, it was the more unconvincing.

At last, however, I got something more definite. I have promised that the man who gave it to me shall be nameless. He was a Druse, but a Druse who had apparently read everything in comparative religion from Frazer's *The Golden Bough* to Reinach's *Orpheus*. I spent an evening with him alone.

I said to him: "Look here. I am going to write about this golden calf or calf's head when I get back to America. I admire and love the Druses for their courage and hospitality. I am under obligation to them. I hope to have them as friends all my life and some day to return to the Mountain. But I'm not going to ignore what seems, rightly or wrongly, to have been universally believed about them for centuries. I don't want to go back and write a lot of spectacular drivel based on stories told me by native Christian priests, by Maronites, or by well-meaning but credulous missionaries. I'm not inviting you to break any oaths you may have made or to reveal any of the 'inner mysteries' but I do want whatever help you can give me without overstepping those bounds."

He stroked his beard thoughtfully and replied: "Suppose I were an observant and intelligent Chinese. Suppose I went for the first time into one of your churches and studied its paintings, its sculpture, its visible symbols. Should I or should I not be justified in believing that you worshiped God in the form of a lamb? We need not consider whether I should not be justified also in thinking that you had a place for torture in your religion and that you ate your god. Nor need we consider what you could reply if I asked whether these things were true. You might say: 'They are true.' You might say: 'They are untrue.' Yet neither answer would be the exact truth. Let us stick rather to the animal symbolism. If I had

read your scriptures and in a hundred places found the
word 'lamb' recurring as one of the names of God, should
I not feel sure that you adored a lamb? If I asked a devout nun: 'Do you adore the lamb?' she would reply,
'With my whole soul I do adore the lamb.' Yet if I
wrote 'The Christians are a strange sect of idolaters who
worship a lamb,' it would be a calumny."

I thought that I was getting somewhere at last.

"Are there, then," I asked, "in your scriptures, in your
Kitab el-Hikmet, passages that refer to the calf?"

He replied: "I violate no secrets by answering that;
for a certain Syrian Christian doctor, the Sheik Nusralla
ibn Gilda, stole a copy of the *Kitab el-Hikmet* from an
akil at Bakhlin, the village of the Jumblatts, and presented it to King Louis XIV. It is still in the old Biblio-
thèque Royale, and there is a copy in French in the Vati-
can. Therefore I am about to reveal nothing that you
could not get, with time and money, from one of those
sources.

"It is not permitted me to show you a copy of the
book, but I can quote you certain passages:

" 'Hakim [the Druse Messiah] showed us a silver box,
in which was a golden head, which was to be the symbol
and emblem of his physical incarnation after his disap-
pearance, and we prostrated ourselves before it.'

"And later this: 'Take care of the mysteries hidden
behind walls. It is not permitted for the book to be
taken out or copied, nor the box in which is the figure of
the physical incarnation of Hakim. It is not permitted
that the figure be aught but gold or silver. If this book
or figure be found in the hands of an infidel, he is to be
taken and cut into small pieces.'

"Very much later, one of our prophets wrote: 'You have misunderstood the divinity. You have confounded him with the calf, and with Iblis [Satan].'

"Again: 'The calf has become the rival and adversary of him who put into execution the divine laws.' "

After a long pause, which I did not break, the Druse continued: "My friend, I tell you so much as this because with long research you could have discovered it elsewhere. The final, concrete answer to your question I cannot give, but I have supplied you with certain data. You will draw your conclusions according to your own bent."

I presented them to him then and there, hoping that he might make a tacit denial or affirmation. They are, by the way, the opinions that, rightly or wrongly, I still hold. I said: "You will permit me to go much farther back than Hakim. A golden calf was the first symbol of God that the Israelites set up and worshiped after their flight from Egypt. Before that, the bull, the cow, and the calf, both here and in Assyria, Babylon, and Egypt, were symbols of divinity. I will suggest that your Hakim adopted, incorporated into his new religion, this symbol, already, perhaps, adored by many of his converts. I will suggest that the Druses first looked upon it as an emblem; that later they worshiped it idolatrously and were denounced by their prophets; and that they have retained it secretly to this day, not as an object of idolatry, but as the image or symbol originally intended. I might even risk going so far as to suggest that among the Druses, as among all peoples, there may be groups who confound the material emblem with the spirit behind it."

He smiled and said: "Well, it's an ingenious theory." And that was all.

Though I make no claim to have penetrated the arcana of the Druse religion, I learned from another Druse some details of the preliminary ordeal that a candidate is said to undergo before he becomes an *akil*-elect, entitled to be instructed in the mysteries. Though the form of initiation is the same for rich and poor, I imagine it is sometimes carried out among the latter in less sumptuous detail.

First, the candidate fasts for three days and two nights, and on the beginning of the third night, still fasting, he attends an elaborate feast of the *akils*, where the daintiest and most delicious meats of savory odor are spread before him. He must take up these meats and toy with them while the others eat, but he must taste nothing. At the end of the feast, all of the others file out, leaving him alone, with some of the best dishes untouched, still before him. He stays there for the remainder of the night, still fasting. There is none to spy upon him. But, if he succumbs to desire and eats, he must confess of his own free will on the morrow, saying simply, "I am not suited to become an *akil*." He can do this without shame or loss of honor, and the *akils* reply: "It is no mean thing to be a lion among the warriors."

If he has withstood the test, then, after he has broken his fast and regained his strength, the second phase of the initiation occurs. He goes voluntarily for three days without water, riding hard beneath the desert sun, and on the third night, with his throat parched, his lips cracked, and his tongue so swollen that he can scarcely speak, he sits with the *akils* while they refresh themselves with cool sherbets and water perfumed with attar of roses, on which rose-petals float. He takes a goblet in his hand with the rest, but does not touch it to his lips. He remains alone all night, with the cooling water within reach.

If he withstands this temptation also, he is subjected, a week later, to a third. This time, in the banquet-hall he is plied freely with delicious wines and highly-spiced

A MODERN HIGH PRIESTESS
OF THE ART OF LOVE

meats. He is not to become drunk, but neither is he to refuse the winecup. After the banquet he walks through a door, which is locked behind him.

In the room where he finds himself, amid cushions, rich rugs and hangings, with a taboret on which are set out fruits and sweetmeats and more wine, there lies on a divan a beautiful naked girl. She is probably a Bedouin dancer or a Circassian—in any event not a Druse—chosen for her beauty and her expert training in the physical art of love, which Orientals respect as akin to poetry and music

—an art whose high priestesses are sometimes held in high public honor. She has been well paid and knows her duty, and she has absolute license in the matter of methods. She is at liberty to dance before the Druse novitiate, to flee from him, to caress him or leap on him like a tigress, to wrestle with him, to bite, curse, insult him, or to writhe appealingly at his feet. She may even make him drunk with wine, if she can. And he, on his part, may wrestle with her and throw her from him and repulse her or insult her if he likes, but he is forbidden to bind her, to strike her, or to do her bodily hurt. His duty is to preserve himself against her wiles and her allures. If he fails, he is without dishonor, and she is entitled to an additional gift. In the morning, when he says: "I am not suited to become an *akil*," the *akils* reply with indulgence: "It is no mean thing to be a lion among the warriors."

But if he has withstood the temptation of the flesh, as well as the temptation of hunger and the temptation of thirst, he is presently made an *akil* among the *akils*, and only then are the "inner mysteries" revealed to him.

Of these inner mysteries, as I have said before, I know absolutely nothing.

The reticence of the Druses about their mysteries does not, however, include their curious doctrine of reincarnation. They take great pride in it, discuss it freely, and cite endless corroborative cases. The belief is not indigenous and is not shared by any other sect in Arabia. The Druses undoubtedly got it from India, but have developed it into something quite different from the Indian doctrine of the progress of the soul through rebirths until it is finally "reabsorbed in the deity."

According to Amir Amin Arslan, the Druses hold that a Druse soul flies at the moment of death into the body of a new-born Druse baby—an abode which may be better or worse than the one it has just left, though not so by reason of any such law as *karma*. The soul of an old hero may be today in the body of a coward or thief. On this point the Druses have a unique theory of divine justice. They look forward to a trial of souls when this world is brought to an end. Each soul is to be judged by the same rules. But every soul has previously passed through many human incarnations. It is born sometimes into a bandit's family, sometimes into a drunkard's family, sometimes into a scholar's family, sometimes into a hero's family, sometimes into a holy man's family, sometimes into a thief's family. In the end all souls will have had an equal chance and may justly be tried on the day of judgment by their general "batting average." Then they stay in a heaven or go to a hell and cannot complain that God has given them an unfair deal.

One queer detail of the reincarnation theory I got from Sultan Pasha Atrash's brother Ali during my visit to the castle at Kurieh a few weeks before Ali himself was killed in battle with the French. When war is on, he told me, and Druses are being killed faster than Druse babies are born, the left-over souls fly off to a mountain region in western China. There they are born into Chinese-Druse babies and thus recruit a race that, though no one has yet seen any members of it, some day will come to help the Druses conquer Arabia and the world. Neither Ali nor the elders whom I questioned could tell me the origin of this belief, which is universal among the Mountain Druses.

The most interesting of the reincarnation cases I heard was the story of a certain Mansour Atrash. It is vouched for by dozens of persons in the Djebel. This Mansour Atrash married a beautiful girl of twelve, by the name of Ummrumman—Mother of the Pomegranate. Shortly afterward, he was killed in a raid. Those events occurred about thirty years ago. At the exact hour of his death, a fact afterward verified, there was born to a family of Druses hundreds of miles away, in the mountains of the Lebanon, a boy, whom they named Najib Abu Faray. He grew to be twenty years of age without ever leaving his native mountains and then by accident was taken to the Djebel Druse, the old home of Mansour Atrash. As soon as he reached the Mountain, he said: "I must be in a dream. I have seen all these places before; they are more familiar than my own mountains." When he came to the village in which Mansour Atrash had lived, he said: "This is my village, and my house is up a certain street and on a certain corner." He walked through the twisting streets, straight to the house of Mansour Atrash, went to a walled-up recess, had the bricks torn down, and discovered a small bag of money that he remembered having put there in his former life. Later he was taken to some vineyards belonging to the Atrash family, where there were disputed boundaries. He pointed out the boundaries that he said he had laid down when he was Mansour Atrash, and a Druse court of law accepted them. He had now given so many proofs of his identity that he was recognized by the children of Mansour Atrash as their reincarnated father and received ten camel-loads of grain as a present from the Atrash family.

Here is a yet weirder story they told me:

A man in the Djebel Druse was murdered. When he was reborn and grew up again, he remembered the murder and declared: "I am going to seek vengeance." He followed the guilty man to America and actually did kill him, saying: "I am killing the man who murdered me."

I was told, however, that survival of personal memory was rare, and that not one Druse in ten thousand recalled anything of his former state.

Obviously the Druses are a "closed corporation." According to their doctrine the number of Druse souls is fixed. Moreover, there are no converts and no renegades. During the months while I was in that part of Arabia, I annoyed Christians, Moslems, and Druses alike by asking at every opportunity whether, so far as they knew, a Druse had ever adopted an alien creed or a Druse woman had ever married a non-Druse. Except for one Druse sheik in the Lebanon, who turned Moslem for political reasons under Turkish rule in 1865, I could learn of no change in religion. And in each of four cases reported to me of a Druse girl's marrying outside her race, the girl was slain by her relatives. The Druses number two or three hundred thousand, so that, though their men only occasionally take wives from Moslem families, inbreeding has not hurt them. They seem to me as they have been from the time of the Crusades—unconquered still— the proudest and most hospitable and at the same time the fiercest and most warlike little feudal aristocracy on the face of the earth.

Chapter X

THE VEILED LADY OF MUKHTARA

THE most powerful woman among the Druses today—and probably in all western Arabia—is the Sitt Nazira el Jumblatt, the famous "Veiled Lady of Mukhtara." She rules like a queen of ancient times in a wild mountain district of the Lebanon, between the Djebel and the coast. She is the present head of her branch of the Jumblatt family, who were princes of Aleppo in the sixteenth century and claim descent from Saladin.

We had heard, even so far away as Constantinople, many tales of her beauty, her power, the splendor of her palace in the mountains.

When Daoud Izzedin, who was her remote cousin, told us that after our motor car had traversed the next gorge and turned the corner of the cliff, we would see Mukhtara, I was prepared for disillusion. But there it towered against the sky, hundreds of yards above us, like something in a dream. As we drew nearer, we saw that the lower part was a great mass of feudal dungeon architecture covering more than an acre. It was surmounted by two superstructures, which faced each other across an open courtyard. One was of the pure Arab type, with slender, twisted columns, high, trefoil-arched windows, and lacy balconies; the other was Roman Renaissance, with a curved, winding flight of marble steps, leading to a semicircular domed portico with Corinthian columns.

Below it were the hundred or more stone houses of the village of Bakhlin, and, rambling behind it, were walled gardens, with fountains, trees, and a domed tomb.

When we arrived, about noon, the place was buzzing with groups of Druses, Maronites, and Moslems from surrounding villages, waiting in the courtyard for later audience. Our appearance aroused no keen interest. It was only when Daoud got out, approached one of the groups, and made his identity known, as a relative of the family, that they shouted for a servant. An old man with a scraggly beard came trotting, knelt, and kissed Daoud's hand, bowed low, touched his forehead, then led us through a dark stone corridor, up an old flight of steps, and into the more modern part of the palace.

In a sort of antechamber, large and bare, Bakhir bey, a brother of the Sitt Nazira, was seated in a chair, being shaved by the family barber. Bakhir bey wore European clothes and was in his shirt-sleeves. His shoes, which needed polishing, were of patent leather with yellow kid uppers and colored glass buttons; blue sleeve-elastics encircled his elbows. Close to him stood several men, all trying to talk at once. His back was turned to us, and Daoud judged it no time for introductions. We passed on to a marvelous colonnaded inner court, with many flowers in big green wooden boxes and some children's toys, including a little wagon and a velocipede. One side of the court was wide open and overlooked the valley. From a door on the right came hurrying a middle-aged gentleman—tall, thin, and dyspeptic, but amiable—wearing a pepper-and-salt suit and a fez. He proved to be Said bey, first cousin of the Sitt Nazira, and welcomed us with elaborate courtesy and apologies. It seemed that the

Lady was so terribly busy that they had not dared yet to inform her of our arrival.

He ushered us into an enormous parlor, of beautiful Damascan architecture, with tiled floor, gorgeous rugs, and a marble fountain basin in the center. Also there were several pieces of comfortable and expensive but hideous Victorian furniture, a big German phonograph with a green horn, a French barometer in a glass case, and on the wall a number of family portraits. Some of them were good oil-paintings by Arab artists, and one was an extraordinary life-size chromo of the Lady's late husband—made from a photograph, as I was later told, by a mail-order house in Chicago. During the next half-hour, a succession of servants came trailing in with cooling drinks made from lime-juice, orange-blossoms, and attar of roses; gold-tipped cigarettes, stamped with the crest of the Jumblatts; sweetmeats and candies; finally, tiny cups of coffee.

Daoud, privileged as a relative of the family though a distant one, had gone out and had been rambling around the palace. He came back grinning and presently whispered to us that the Lady was receiving a delegation of important political personages, lying late in bed, like a queen, but with a heavy curtain stretched between them and herself. Later, it seems, she was dressed by her maids, behind the curtain, without any interruption of the conference.

Finally, after an hour, the Veiled Lady of Mukhtara, preceded by two servants who announced her solemnly, came into the parlor. She was a large woman with regal carriage, a figure voluptuous and magnificent, though a bit heavy for the present western standards of feminine beauty. She was veiled with black so that no part of her features showed, but her soft black dress and draperies had been cut by a dressmaker who knew something of Paris fashions.

It was now our turn for hand-kissing. She sat down in a rocking-chair, and then invited us to be seated. She talked for perhaps ten minutes, in a voice contralto and musical. She was keen to know exactly who we were and was embarrassingly direct in her questions to Daoud. When she learned that we were his close friends and that we had been with him in the Djebel, she grew more intimate and friendly. She asked Katie about the life of women in America, about feminism and votes for women, and then she inquired, point-blank: "How many children have you, madam?" And when Katie replied "None," she leaned forward, took her hand, patted it, and said: "Oh, I am so terribly sorry! I shall pray for you."

After a moment or two, she suddenly shouted in her deep contralto for one of the servants. It takes generations of aristocratic breeding to produce such an imperious yell. It isn't taught in the books of etiquette, either Oriental or American. The servant came running as fast as his legs could carry him. She whispered instructions, and ten minutes later he returned with her little seven-year-old son, Fouad, a pale, delicate child with black hair and deep black eyes, in a Little Lord Fauntleroy suit of velvet. He will some day be the head of the family— "The Jumblatt," a sort of uncrowned king. It was curious to see my friend Daoud, with whom I have strolled on Fifth Avenue and lunched at the Harvard Club in New York, bend and kiss this child's hand. Daoud told me afterward that General Weygand, former French High

Commissioner of Syria, had knelt before this boy.   It
seemed difficult to believe.   Yet it turned out to be true.
After the boy's father was assassinated, in 1922, General
Weygand pinned on little Fouad's breast the Cross of
the Legion of Honor.   He had indeed knelt—I saw a
snapshot of the ceremony—but I think he was merely
bending down in a natural way to the level of the child's
breast, rather than intending to do formal homage.

The Sitt Nazira was proud of the fact that little Fouad
had a French tutor, and at her request the child recited
for us a poem by Lamartine.

Daoud had told me—and he still sticks to the statement—that no man in Syria outside the circle of her immediate relatives has ever seen Sitt Nazira's face.   Be
that as it may, becoming animated in the course of her
conversation with us, she unfastened her veil and let it
partially drop, held in her left hand, so that her eyes
and the top of her nose were visible.   Glamour and mystery aside, it seemed to me that she was authentically
beautiful.   Her eyes were enormous, liquid black and
wide-set beneath a noble forehead, softened by the wavy
hair that partially showed beneath the upper part of the
veil.   Once, when, in her interest, the veil was dropped
for a moment still farther, I had a glimpse of her entire
face.   Her nose was aquiline, finely chiseled, her mouth
large, perfectly formed, with full red lips and flashing
teeth.   If there was any flaw, it was the heavy, dominant
chin, the chin of a race of rulers; but though it detracted
slightly from the feminine beauty of the face, it added
to its strength.

When luncheon was announced, the Lady excused herself.   She ate alone in her bedroom behind a curtain

while she engaged in another conference. Daoud, Katie and I lunched with Said bey in a high-ceilinged dining-room at a long table that would have seated thirty. There were two servants to wait on each of us, making

A CORNER OF THE JUMBLATT PALACE AT
MUKHTARA

six servants in all, and an endless succession of dishes, both European and Arabian.

I had heard differing versions of a certain hair-raising story of how Fouad Jumblatt, husband of the Sitt Nazira, had been assassinated in "a trap baited with a human being." At luncheon, Daoud persuaded Said bey to give me the real facts.

"Sitt Nazira is a Jumblatt by both birth and marriage,"

he said. "In marrying Fouad bey, she married her sixth cousin. When the French came into Syria under the mandate, they made Fouad bey (who was already the actual governor of the Lebanon Druses) their representative and gave him the title officially. Many Druses resented his acceptance of the French post. They wanted absolute independence in the mountains. They felt that he had sold himself and the family name to the French, so that a French tyranny could be inflicted on them through the power of the Jumblatts. Certain bands of Druse guerrillists—this was as late as 1921—began raiding, fighting, killing French troops that came into the mountains, and even shooting the Druse agents of Fouad Jumblatt. Finally they blew up a couple of bridges with dynamite.

"The guilt was traced to a certain village. Fouad bey sent a big body of mixed troops there and, in his temper, did a crazy thing which no Druse in his right senses would ever do. He arrested the Druse women along with the men and had them all put in a common jail. Among the women was the wife of a certain famous guerrilla warrior by the name of Shekib Wahhab. When Shekib Wahhab learned that his wife had been dragged to jail with a lot of men, he swore vengeance and organized a personal feud against Fouad Jumblatt.

"For weeks Fouad never ventured out of this palace except surrounded by troops in such force that Shekib and his men could not attack. They finally got him by a ruse. Fouad had a favorite manservant who was also hated because he was a sort of jackal and spy. One night, as this servant started down the road to the village, the same road you came up, just beneath the palace walls, he

was carefully shot through the bowels, so that he did not
die at once but lay screaming horribly. Fouad, who was
no coward, rushed out, followed by some of his men. As
he went over to lift up his wounded servant, he was
pierced by more than fifty bullets from the rifles of the
men in ambush behind rocks and trees.

"The French offered a thousand gold pounds for
Shekib Wahhab's capture, but he fled that night back
through the mountains and received protection from the
Atrash family. The Atrashes were later offered even
more money—not to deliver him up, but simply to with-
draw their protection. They refused. But Shekib, himself, rather than force a war on Sultan Pasha Atrash, fled
south to Mecca and became a leader of King Ali's forces
against the Wahabi tribes. A violent character, he presently quarreled with the King, and went away. The
King sent messengers and persuaded him to come back.
He returned, led a raid against the Wahabi, killed seven
of them in personal combat, including Faisal Duwish, a
Wahabi chief, and brought back, as a gift to King Ali,
Faisal's jeweled scimitar and Faisal's head in a leather
bag. Ali kept the head, but gave the sword to Shekib.

"Sitt Nazira has been wiser than her husband. She
has the full confidence of the Druses, and, although she
has never accepted favors from the French, they regard
her with respect and seek her advice on matters of local
policy."

After the luncheon Said bey, with a servant carrying a
great iron ring on which were strung two hundred heavy
keys, showed us other parts of the palace—drawing-
rooms and bedrooms fitted with European furniture;
stables in the old substructure, pillared and stone-arched

like the crypt of a Gothic cathedral. There were stalls and mangers for three hundred and fifty horses; there were dungeons and prison cells, with iron chains and manacles still riveted into the walls. A sort of oubliette, protected by an iron grating, gave a glimpse of the little subterranean river that roared under the palace, spouting up into fountains in the various rooms and gushing out through a lower wall down the mountainside.

The next morning, after taking leave, we detoured to see the palace of Bteddin on another height across the valley. Its big quadrangles, marble courts and fountains, luxurious domed baths and rich mosaic, seemed to me like a million-dollar stage-set for the movies. There was, however, a striking portrait of the late Amir Beshir Shihab, a fierce old eagle with an enormous beard and a little black skull-cap instead of a turban. He had been a great magician in his time and was believed to hold direct intercourse with Satan. When the Amir Beshir's wife died, the old man sent to Constantinople for three Circassian girls and, when they arrived, selected the prettiest one to be his wife. She was Christian and refused to change her religion. She said: "You may torture me or kill me, but I will not renounce my faith." The old man grinned and said: "Not at all. I'll find another wife. You may go to the kitchen and work." A week of scouring pots and pans accomplished what racks and thumbscrews might have been twisted for in vain. She preferred being a Moslem in the parlor to a Christian in the scullery, and made him a good wife.

As we drove on down the mountain, I said I thought the Circassian wench had shown uncommonly good sense. Daoud replied: "Maybe so, for a Christian, but a Druse girl couldn't do it. No Druse girl has ever married any-body but a Druse. Her father or brothers would track her down and slit her gizzard, even if she were asleep in the Sultan's arms."

Although Druse women often wield powerful influ-ence in family and political affairs, I doubt if there is any other country, in the Orient or in the world, where woman is so absolutely a slave in all matters that involve marriage, sex, and "the honor of the home." Father, brother, even sons when they are grown, exercise, ruth-lessly if need be, absolute rights of life and death over all the women of the household. And this is the law among both rich and poor in the Mountain of the Druses.

On her marriage every Druse bride presents her hus-band with a dagger, over which she has knitted with her own hands a red woolen cover, enclosing it completely like a sewed-up purse. This dagger is the symbol of the death penalty she will pay if she is unfaithful. The knitted, sewed-up cover is the symbol of the law by which her husband himself cannot unsheathe the knife unless all her own male relatives are dead, but must return the dagger and the girl to her father or brothers, who pro-nounce and execute the sentence.

"It is not for personal vengeance," said the young Sheik Fouad Obeyid to me at Souieda. "It is not for anything personal at all. It is for the purity of our race. It is for the good of unborn Druses. Woman is the sacred cup in which our strength and life and honor are handed from generation to generation. If the cup is polluted, it must be broken and thrown away."

They are equally ruthless in enforcing the law that no Druse woman can marry outside her own race.

Here, briefly, is one recent tragedy that I authenticated from various sources. I recount it not to criticize the Druses, but to illustrate the extremes to which they go to protect their racial purity in a country where mixed breeding is the rule. The pretty daughter of a comparatively poor Druse family in the Mountain obtained her father's permission to go to work as a servant in a Druse household in Beirut. A few months later he learned that the girl, dazzled perhaps by the life of Beirut, which is like a little Paris, had left her Druse employers, had gone to work as nursemaid with a Jewish family, had taken off her veil, and was dressing in European style—short skirts, high-heeled shoes, and silk stockings. One of her brothers was a member of the rural constabulary. He went one night in uniform to the Jewish household, arrested his own sister without a warrant, and took her back to the Mountain. She was locked in the dark cellar of her father's house for a week and was daily "persuaded" to repent. Finally, when she had agreed and sworn to retain her veil and work only for a Druse family, they let her go back to Beirut. Six months later it was learned that she had met a French sergeant and was planning to marry him and go with him to Marseilles. There was no marriage, no seduction—merely the engagement. The brother went again and "arrested" his sister. She was taken back to her home in the Mountain, where a family conference was held, and she was condemned to death. On the following night, they took her on mule-back down into a gorge, strangled her, and buried the body among the rocks.

In Shuweifat in the summer of 1923 a similar episode occurred. A Druse there married a Druse girl who had

lived in Damascus. Later he discovered that a year before she had been involved in an affair with a Damascene
merchant, a Moslem. He uttered no reproaches, but took
her to her parents' home. When he arrived there at dawn,
the girl's own mother forced a confession from her, and
her father took her into the cellar and cut her throat,
"without waiting for breakfast."

COLONNADE OF THE SULTAN SELIM COURTYARD
AT DAMASCUS

Another Druse girl—these really are rare cases, num-
bering fewer, I think, than a half-dozen among all the
Druses of this generation—married her first cousin. She
was unfaithful, and he told her brothers, who, of course,
were also his first cousins. Because of their interrelation-
ship it was a double family disgrace. Rather than face
the gossip that would follow if the girl were put to death
in the usual way, they forced her to leap from a cliff under
circumstances that might seem accidental.

I want to repeat and put all the emphasis I can on the

fact that such occurrences are extremely rare. I want to add, in justice, that it seemed to me Druse women generally were free and happy—within the law.

And, furthermore, there is no dearth of true-love romance in the Mountain of the Druses. One recent courtship and marriage, of which I had direct knowledge, was as lyric as the Book of Ruth. A girl named Mara, daughter of the rich Sheik Shibli, fell in love with a poor young laborer on one of her father's farms. He was of the peasant class, but handsome, and brave in battle. The girl went to her father and said: "I love this man."

"Have you told him?"

"Never, Father."

"Does he know it?"

"He would not dare to know it."

"Has he looked upon your face?"

"Once, at the well, for an instant, he saw my eyes above the veil, but he has never looked upon my face."

Old Shibli replied: "Do you not know that this is a common man and that if the father of your children is not a great man, your children will not be great?"

She answered: "He is brave, and, if my children are brave, I shall be content."

A month later, old Shibli gave the laborer extensive lands, and a happy marriage followed.

Marriage among the Druses, as among the Moslems, is a civil contract. It is not accompanied by religious ceremonies. The procession in which the bride is fetched from her parental home to the house of the bridegroom is noisy and full of color. One afternoon—I think it was when we were returning from Anz to Souieda—we chanced upon a village wedding. First we heard the firing of rifles and pistols, accompanied by a deep, rhythmic chant. We left our car and entered the village afoot.

At the head of the procession marched the bridegroom, a lean, thin-faced youth with plaited hair. He wore a long embroidered tunic with a short bright-blue coat, wide-sleeved and heavily braided. On his head was the flowing white *kafiyeh*. Next came the bride on horseback, side-saddle, swathed in white draperies from head to foot. Behind her marched the warriors, thirty or more, firing guns and pistols in the air, waving curved swords and daggers, all singing or rather shouting their deep-throated chant, endlessly repeating the four syllables, accented and of equal length, like drum-beats:

"Beni Maruf!"
"Beni Maruf!"
"Beni Maruf!"

Each line was "boom, boom, boom, boom" in perfect time to the marching. It means "We are the children of Maruf," a legendary Druse hero of the thirteenth century. Behind them marched the village elders, grave and silent. A scattering of women and children brought up the rear. Some of the men invited us to the bridegroom's house. Unfortunately, we had to get on to Souieda.

Of the women I actually met in the Djebel Druse, the one whom I shall always remember most vividly is the Sitt Zainab Umm Yahyah el Atrash—"great-grandmother of the warriors." She sat hunched in her black robes, like a gaunt old eagle, hawk-nosed and pale-blue-eyed, on the grass mats of an elevated stone divan in the banquet-hall of the castle at Orah. I saw generations of fighting men who had sprung from her womb—grizzled Atrash sheiks with their sons and grandsons, clanking with cartridge-belts, pistols, daggers, and jeweled swords, who knelt upon the grease-blackened, earthen floor and kissed her withered hands.

Among them was Sultan Pasha Atrash—this was in the late summer of 1925, only a few days before the actual war began—who had come for solemn counsel to his great-aunt, a woman almost ninety. What she told him I do not know, for they spoke in whispers. But I do know that within a week the Druse war-song was ringing from the Hauran plains to the crags of the Lejah.

Among the Dervishes

Chapter XI

IN THE PALACE OF THE MELEWI [1]

"ON reaching the palace gateway," said Ahmed, "your breast will meet a great iron chain stretched across. You will please to bow beneath it and walk under, for this is a *devoir* required of all.

"On entering the presence of the Sheik el Melewi, you will please to bow again, more low, with touching of hand against forehead, for he is a most holy man."

Ahmed was a pompous, pudgy-faced little Arab in store clothes and patent-leather shoes, with a fountain-pen clipped in his waistcoat pocket—a kind of interpreter and upper servant, who had been sent to meet us in the market-place of Syrian Tripoli and guide us afoot to the Dervish palace monastery in the hills behind the city.

As we zigzagged through a labyrinth of narrow streets, Ahmed stepped ahead, and my friend, Dr. Arthur Dray, whispered: "It is true about the chain, but as for the rest of it, I have known the Melewi for years, and I am inclined to think our welcome will be less formal."

Presently we emerged from the town, up a flight of stone steps, which led to a footpath above the gorge of a little river. On our right towered the Crusader's castle which legend says was Melisande's. Another turn brought

[1] The original Turkish word is Mevlevi, and the "v" has been generally retained by English writers. In current Arabic, however, the "v" sound has been elided in the first syllable and changed to "w" in the second. The accent is on the first syllable.

the Melewi palace into view, its white dome half-hidden by the trees, its walls and terraces rising sheer from a cliff above the river, with a water-mill, granary, and storehouses in the gorge below.

We came to the gate, an open arch, barred only by the chain Ahmed had described, and which led into a tunnel passage at the base of a high wall. The place was silent and seemed deserted. We bowed perforce to pass beneath the chain and stood out of the sun while Ahmed went in to announce our arrival.

A few moments later, the monastic silence inside the palace was shattered by a series of prolonged and mighty roars. They came from a human throat, for words were distinguishable. But it was as if the bull of Bashan were bellowing in Arabic: *"Ya Mustafa! Ya Nur! Ya Hamid! Aiee, Kanja!"*

Dr. Dray grinned cheerfully. "I seem to recognize the voice," he said. "That will be the holy man himself. He is calling the servants."

The roaring ceased as suddenly as it had begun, and down the passage came hurrying the owner of that mighty basso, the Most Reverend and Holy Sheik Shefieh el Melewi, Hereditary Governor-General of the Tripolitan Whirling Dervish See, and lineal descendant of the Blessed Prophet.

He was bareheaded, with baggy white trousers, a short white blouse of finest texture buttoning in front like a vest, loose slippers of red Damascus leather on his otherwise bare feet.

He shouted welcome in French and Arabic as he came, embraced Dr. Dray like a grizzly bear, shook hands with me, deplored the hot weather, and led us to a terrace where he hoped there would be a little breeze.

The Sheik el Melewi was past sixty, but solid as an oak tree in its prime. Here was no vague, anemic saint, but a Lion of Islam. His hair, clipped close, was grizzled, and his short, thick beard was white; his skin was healthy and ruddy; his frame compact, heavy, muscular. He fairly radiated physical strength, and the wide-set brown eyes, now twinkling with pleasure, beneath a broad, high forehead, suggested an intelligence equally active and powerful.

The enthusiastic welcome, I learned later, came from the fact that he and Dr. Dray—for long years resident in Arabia—had literally gone through fire and blood together, working to balk the cruelty of Jemel Pasha when that arch-devil had been in the Syrian saddle during the World War, and had formed a lasting bond of friendship, though they hadn't seen each other for a couple of years.

The terrace on which we had emerged was parapeted on the left, overlooking the gorge and little river, which cascaded among the rocks, fifty feet below. A stone staircase led downward, from a break in the parapet, to the roof of the mill, and thence to a lower garden.

On our right, hung the high dome, and beneath it, like a stage in a theater, opening toward us, was the *tekkeh* or dance-floor—an elevated wooden platform some forty feet square, with a light wooden railing. Ten feet above the dance-floor, on the three walls which supported the dome and formed the back and sides of the structure, were narrow, overhanging balconies. The middle balcony was for the musicians; the southern balcony for special guests; the northern balcony, protected by a lattice screen, was for the ladies of the *hareem*, who could watch the dances while remaining themselves more or less invisible.

At the lower end of the terrace was the wing under which we had entered by the tunnel passage. At the farther end, a short staircase led up to the main doorway of the palace proper, with a big reception hall furnished in European style, where the Melewi permitted me later to take some photographs, and a corridor leading to the *hareem* and private apartments of the palace, which we, of course, never entered. The monastery quarters, with cells for the eighteen resident dervishes, lay on the hillside, behind the dome.

Almond trees were planted on the terrace; there were potted plants and flowers, and a circular fountain with bright-colored fish and a jet of water spouting upward from its center; a brook from the hillside had been led under the palace walls, emerging to flow through a mossy, stone channel and disappear rumbling again into the darkness below. From a row of tubes set in the wall, fourteen jets of water spurted into this little watercourse.

When servants came with soap and towels, we washed our hands and faces at these spouts. Meanwhile European chairs were brought and a table was set, *farengi*-fashion, under a tree, in preparation for luncheon, with white damask cloth and a profusion of silver tableware.

Asceticism obviously had no part in Dervish hospitality, for presently we found ourselves smoking exquisite gold-tipped cigarettes from Cairo and sipping a delicious pale-green liquid, mixed from freshly crushed white grapes and lime-juice. The Sheik el Melewi smoked and

A GATEWAY OF SYRIAN TRIPOLI

On the Street Leading to the Whirling Dervish Palace

drank with us, chatting with Dr. Dray, shouting an occasional order to the servants about luncheon.

A terrorized squawking of hens being done to death down by the river indicated that the wait might be long, and it was more than an hour later, almost mid-afternoon, when luncheon was finally announced.

A fourth at the table was the sheik's brother, a tall, gray-haired, clean-shaven man of fifty, charming, but quiet and restrained.

The luncheon was an Arabian Nights feast of more than twenty courses and lasted for two hours. Whole roasted chickens, and chicken pilaff with rice, almonds, and raisins; lamb on skewers; lamb wrapped in grape-leaves and cooked in olive oil, lamb stewed with egg-plant; lamb cooked with peppercorns; delicious salads; cucumbers peeled at the table and eaten as we eat fruit; no less than six desserts, beginning with a great pan of custard, running the gamut of pastries with ground-up nuts and honey, to end at last with watermelons cooled in the fountain.

The most holy sheik had an appetite that would have been the envy of any sinner—but through all the exuberance of his welcome, through the elaborate material luxury of our entertainment and his obvious whole-hearted enjoyment of the delicious food, I sensed continually that there was another side to this man and felt that his abundant physical vitality was not incompatible, perhaps, with powers which might be equally unusual in other directions. I had been told that he was a great mystic, and I was not prepared to doubt it on the superficial evidence.

Nevertheless, my mind was still floundering with its own preconceived notion of dervish sainthood. I had expected, candidly, to meet a pale ascetic—not actually lying in rags on a bed of spikes, but at least so absorbed with the inner vision that he would be wholly indifferent to worldly and material things. I found this mental picture difficult to reconcile with the reality before me as I watched the Sheik Shefieh inhaling the smoke luxuriously from a gold-tipped cigarette and savoring his coffee like a connoisseur.

In fact, it bothered me so much that I ventured to tell him what was going on in my head, almost as plainly as I have set it down here. He was neither amused nor offended. And he was quite willing to discuss the point.

"Do you know anything about mysticism?" he asked me, and I replied: "A little; but I am sadly ignorant, as you see, about the Dervishes."

"There are many Dervishes of other sects," he answered, "who would match perfectly the ascetic type you had in mind—and who shall say whether they are more or less holy?—but ascetics are not found generally among the Melewi.

" The term 'Dervish' is applied to more than thirty different sects of Islam, whose monasteries are scattered throughout the entire Moslem world, from the Bosphorus to China.

"These sects are alike in that all are mystics, and alike in the sense that all are religious fraternities which have sprung from the Sufi philosophy. But here the similarity ceases. All go by the name of Dervishes, as all members of Christian religious fraternities go by the name of monks. But they differ—even more widely than Christian monastic societies—in rules of living, dress, theology, and ritual.

"The object of all mysticism is the apprehension, through contemplation and ecstasy, of truths more profound than any which can be arrived at by logic or cold reason. The ultimate goal of the mystic is oneness with God, but the paths toward this goal are divergent. One school seeks to attain this higher state through pain and fasting, through destruction of all sensuous pleasures and desires. To this school belong all ascetics of whatever creed who practice chastity, poverty, penance, and self-torture. To it, among Dervish sects, belong the Bektashi, who are beggars vowed to poverty; the Rufai, or Howling Dervishes, who slash their bodies with knives and burn themselves with red-hot irons; the Sadee or Fire-Eaters, who practice a magic of their own, seem to devour red coals, and bite the heads from poisonous serpents.

"But we others, we Melewi, believe that soul and body are alike divine—that the soul grows, like a flower, on the body's stem. We accept all material and sensuous beauty as the true mirror of divine beauty. And we seek this divine beauty, this ineffable harmony in which all things become as one, through the most perfect and most spiritual of material beauty-forms—the rhythm of music and the dance.

"One of our legends is that the Prophet, after experiencing a transcendent illumination, imparted to Ali certain inner mysteries, enjoining him to keep them secret, since they were not for the common mind. The secret swelled in Ali's breast, and he fled to the desert for fear it would burst out. He came to a little oasis and, seeking to drink at a spring, opened his mouth, and the secret spilled out into the water. Months later, a wandering shepherd found a reed growing in the edge of this spring, which he cut and fashioned into a flute. When he played upon it, melodies of such ravishing beauty were born that his flocks forgot to graze, and when other nomads heard him playing, their hearts were melted and they wept for joy. Finally, it chanced, the shepherd's piping was heard by Mohamet, who swooned, and then said: 'Ali has betrayed the secret, for this flute sings of the holy mystery.' "

As the Melewi paused, I thought of how this vision had come in similar form to many men in other lands and times. I thought of the Pipes of Pan which sang "of the dancing stars, of earth and heaven, and love and death, and birth"—of William Blake, Thompson, and the other Christian mystics who had found God through beauty—and of Keats' ecstatic ode.

I tried to quote its last few lines and translate them as best I could into Arabic. The venerable sheik was deeply interested.

"Our own Pir," he said, "was such a poet—one of the greatest in all Islam, and he, too, wrote concerning the ultimate identity of beauty, truth, and God. His name, which you may know, was Jelal-ed-Din, a Persian Sufi who came to Konia in the sixth century (the thirteenth century by Christian reckoning) when the Turkish sultanate was established there. He taught philosophy in the royal college and founded the Melewi order. Konia still remains our center, and there in his great palace dwells our sheik of sheiks, Mohamet Bakhir Chelebi, one of the holiest, and also one of the richest, lords of the Islamic world."

I asked our host about the present extent and power of the order. He told us that it numbered upward of a thousand monasteries, some rich and some poor, distributed chiefly throughout Turkey, Arabia, North Africa, and part of Persia. The most important, he said, were in Konia, Constantinople, Aleppo, here in Syrian Tripoli, Damascus, Jerusalem, and Cairo.

The Melewi monks permanently resident in the monasteries would number, he thought, less than thirty thousand, but lay members of the order would increase the total to a hundred and fifty thousand—perhaps even more. The lay members, he told us, had included several ruling sultans, and now numbered many native princes and men of political importance. In Tripoli alone, he said, the lay membership included an ex-mayor of the city, a former chief of police, and a famous professor of literature. These pursued the normal avocations of life, but came at stated times to the *tekkeh* to participate in the rituals and dances.

The sun was still high and the air was sultry when we finished our talk. The sheik and Dr. Dray retired for a nap. I strolled down the winding stairway into the garden, stretched myself out on the grass beneath a tree beside the little river, and presently fell asleep.

I was awakened in the cool evening, just before twilight, by a voice calling, "*Ya, Howeja Inglese* [oh, English sir]"—a servant, sent to find me. He was followed by a handsome girl, barefooted and unveiled, bringing a bowl of *labne* [milk curds], which, kneeling, she offered me as I lay on the grass. Her short skirt was a bit ragged, but she wore a little bolero jacket bravely embroidered with tarnished silver. A tousled mane of red-brown hair made her almost a beauty.

"*Selim dayetak*," I said ["may your hands be blessed" —a polite common phrase of thanks], and then, since she was very pretty—and obviously not Moslem—I felt that it could do no harm to tell her so. She blushed, and laughed, and tossed her head. I gathered that she was *Tcherkesse Nazrana* [a Circassian Christian] and a sort of dairymaid. She was also "*mebsoud k'tir* [very happy]." Then the conversation languished. She sat on her heels for a moment or two as I ate the *labne* and watched me with her big, green cat-eyes flecked with golden brown. A nightingale was singing, and the little river murmured over the rocks.

I reflected on Mohamet's description of paradise— "there shall be palm trees and pomegranates, fountains and pleasant gardens beneath which rivers flow, and beauteous fair damsels having large eyes."

And I wisely reflected also that it was high time to betake myself elsewhere.

Dr. Dray was on the upper terrace alone, yawning, and soon ready for bed. We saw no more of the Sheik el Melewi that night. The ceremonial dances were set for the next evening—a second Friday of the month. We had a final cigarette and retired. In the high guest-chamber which we both occupied were two brass bedsteads and other European conveniences. A nightingale still sang in the garden beneath our window, and I was a long time dropping off to sleep.

I was anxious next day, before witnessing the dance, to learn more from the Sheik el Melewi himself of its inner purpose and meaning. Dr. Dray was doubtful, but I urged a sincere interest, and he consented to transmit my request.

I think the Melewi sensed that my wish was based on something more than simple academic curiosity. At any rate, he sent for me to come to him alone, and I found him seated Oriental-wise on a little divan in a sort of bare-walled chapel. He was the same man who had made the palace reverberate with his shouting on our arrival— and yet not the same. He now wore the tall Dervish hat, wound at the base with the green silk scarf of office, and was robed in a gray mantle. But the change went deeper than mere outward form. His arms were folded on his breast. His face was grave, and his voice was gentle as he bade me be seated. I touched fingers to my forehead and sat on a grass mat at his feet.

He was silent for what seemed a long period of time, and then he spoke: "I had intended, on arriving at the rosebush, to fill the skirts of my robe with roses to offer the brethren on my return. But when I arrived at the rosebush, its odor so intoxicated my soul that the hem of my robe escaped.

"No words, my son, can impart from one man to another the final secret. For God is the divine harmony in all things—in the circling of the earth and stars, in the measured heart-beats of the human body, in the rhythmic act of procreation; in fire and water, in the rolling thunder and rushing winds; in the flight and songs of birds or tiniest insects; in the breath of life itself as the air is drawn into the lungs and expelled through the nostrils.

"All paths can lead to God, and each must choose the one seeming best for him. But you would have me speak of the path we Melewi have chosen—how, through rhythm, we seek to merge ourselves with the divine harmony.

"We have found that it leads to three stages or conditions.

"The first is simple bliss. The soul is exalted, yet at peace. It seems to lose identity, to become nothing in itself, yet to embrace all creation. We name it negative unity.

"The second is power, and not all men can attain it, for it requires a deliberate use of consciousness and will at a moment when the soul has lost all ordinary desires. In this state are performed the so-called miracles. They include power to understand the thoughts of others, knowledge of far-off events, but never of future events; sometimes the power to influence a material event. These powers are mysterious, but no more so than your western radio or telephone, which by tuning in with a certain vibration can make you materially aware of a far-off event; nor than the string of a great harp, which, tuned and set vibrating at a certain rhythm, can smash a crystal glass at a distance.

"The third state is positive unity, in which the soul is flooded not merely with a sense of emotional beatitude, but creates conscious visions of beauty and glory and is aware of its own high state. In this state and beyond lies the final mystery, which is ineffable, and also dangerous to certain minds, for it frees mighty forces, potent both in good and evil.

"These things which I have told you are hollow and empty, save as you yourself can put meaning into them; yet perhaps they will help you, tonight, toward a partial understanding of our ritual."

It was nine o'clock in the evening when Dr. Dray and I mounted to the southern balcony, beneath the dome. The pavilion was brightly lighted from above by kerosene lamps. The dance-floor was empty save for a sheepskin dyed brilliant red, which was laid in front of the *mihrab*

THE PALACE-MONASTERY OF THE WHIRLING
DERVISHES AT TRIPOLI

[niche] in the southern wall beneath us, indicating the direction of Mecca. The orchestra was already seated, on a level with us, in the balcony at our right—reed-flute, zither, drum, and a singer—in their tall brown hats and robes of the same color.

Directly opposite in the north balcony, but behind a latticed screen, were five women, white-robed and veiled. Except for the briefest glimpses of their eyes as they occasionally drew aside the corner of a veil to look at us, we could see nothing of their features, but I got the impression that one was old, and that three of them, at least, were young and possibly beautiful. They were the wives and a sister of the Melewi and his brother.

In complete silence, twelve Dervishes entered, in solemn procession, single file, with their tall brown hats and long black mantles—barefooted, heads bowed forward, with arms crossed on their breasts, each hand clasped to the opposite shoulder. They disposed themselves in two rows, seated on their heels, right and left, facing each other, heads still bowed.

A thirteenth Dervish entered and seated himself in the middle of the dance-floor, facing south toward the red sheepskin and the niche beneath us. He was the Sema Zan, or elder, who would act as a master of ceremonies. His cloak was brown, like those of the musicians. Black is worn only by the dancers.

Some were short-bearded; others clean-shaven. They ranged in age from past fifty to one or two youths who seemed under twenty. They kept their heads bowed and their eyes almost closed.

When the Sheik el Melewi entered and sat upon the sheepskin, they made no salutation, but remained silent, motionless. His robe was pale gray, of glistening, fine texture. His hat was taller than the rest, wound at the base with a great ceremonial green turban.

The ritual began with a mystic hymn followed by the orthodox *Fatiha* in praise of Allah and with special prayers which named the Chelebi, Jelal-ed-Din, and Mohamet.

The musicians then began a slow march, in retarded four-four tempo. The sheik, who had arisen, stepped forward off the sheepskin, turned, and made two profound bows, one from the right and one from the left, toward the spot he had quitted. This was to invite the spiritual presence of Jelal-ed-Din, founder of the order.

He then returned to stand on the sheepskin, while the Dervishes arose, one at a time, and with a space of some five feet between them, began a slow circling march round the dance-floor. Passing before the sheik, each Dervish bowed to him, and then turned to bow to the Dervish who followed in the procession. They circled the floor three times.

The tempo of the music changed to a weird rhythm I could not follow, while the reed-flute began a soaring melody. The march ceased. The Sema Zan divested the Dervishes, one by one, of their long black cloaks, revealing the voluminous *tesseri* [skirts] which dropped to their bare ankles. These skirts were tight-fitting at the waists and wound tighter still with girdles, above which they wore short-waisted jackets of various dark colors, with long, tight sleeves.

The Dervish whose robe had first been discarded came and stood before the sheik, with his right great toe crossed over his left, and with arms still folded. He made a profound obeisance and kissed the sheik's hand. The sheik then touched his own lips to the Dervish's hat. The music had again changed. The flute still sustained a singing melody, backed by the sweeping harmonies of the many-stringed zither; but the drum began a steady, unaccented tomtom beat, in one-one tempo.

And now the single Dervish began slowly the *zikr*, or turning. He drooped his head on his left shoulder, closed his eyes, and balancing on the left heel as an axis, communicated the rotary motion with his right foot, keeping both feet close together. The whirling was at first very slow, but gradually increased in speed, while his arms seemed to unfold and stretch out automatically, until the right was horizontal from shoulder to elbow, bent vertically upward at the elbow, the hand bent backward, palm up; while the left arm stretched straight horizontally, palm down. As the speed increased, the skirt unfolded, ballooning upward and outward, until it whirled in a great circle almost waist-high above the baggy white drawers.

One after another the twelve men went through this ritual until all were whirling, save the sheik himself and the Sema Zan.

Even when they had attained their full momentum, they did not whirl at equal speeds. The revolutions varied from sixty-four per minute to about thirty. The average was around fifty, almost one complete revolution per second. Their bodies were rigid. They spun like tops which had "gone to sleep." Their faces were calm, expressionless. There was no questioning the fact that they passed actually into a trance—into the state of *hal*, as they name it technically.

At the end of eleven minutes, the Sema Zan arose and stamped vigorously on the floor—evidently a signal to stop. But only two of the dancers heard it, and he had to clap his hands and stamp again loudly, as if to awaken people from a deep sleep, before all heeded him and became stationary. They did not wobble as dizzy men would, but stood motionless as statues, heads bowed forward and arms crossed again on their breasts.

Slowly they marched three times round the *tekkeh*

floor, and as each passed the sheik the third time, he again began whirling. On this second occasion they whirled for nineteen minutes. When the third, final signal came to stop, they sank to the floor and remained seated while the Sema Zan went from one to another, replacing the black mantles on their shoulders. They were still like men in a dream.

The music ceased, and in the silence came the deep voice of the Sheik el Melewi:

"The man of God is exalted without wine.

"The man of God is beyond good and beyond evil.

"The man of God is beyond religion and beyond infidelity.

"The man of God has ridden away to the place where all is One."

And I realized that here, even more than in the words he had spoken to me that afternoon, lay a key to the deep inner secret of the Dervish faith. It was pure pantheism, in its most daring and advanced form. To these exalted souls, God was neither Father, Master, nor Judge. God was life itself. And to each of them, when he made himself one with all life through the ecstatic vision, the secret hundredth name of God was "I."

I went to sleep thinking about this, and the next day when the Melewi asked how the ceremony had impressed me, I told him my thoughts unreservedly.

His face was sterner and more serious than I had ever seen it. He lifted a solemn, warning hand.

"Beware, my son. Deep peril lies here, and destruction for weak minds. The fool, when blinded by an illumination too great for his understanding, cries out 'I am God!' and is destroyed for his blasphemy. Yet man may say without fear: 'God is I.' " And he quoted Jelal-ed-Din, who had written: "When men imagine they are adoring Allah, it is Allah who is adoring himself."

Then, softening in expression, he told me of a mystic vision he had experienced personally and which, he considered, had contained both truth and deadly danger. He had seemed to be climbing a mountain-top in search of God and had come at last to a great white throne, but dared not look upon the face of Him who sat there. "Dare to lift up your eyes!" cried a voice. He lifted up his eyes, and the face which he beheld was—his own.

I began to feel that the things I had heard about the Sheik el Melewi from native Arabs who considered him a holy man were in a very deep sense true. And I reflected that, proud and dangerous as the Melewi doctrine seemed, it was not so very far removed from that of the Christian mystic who proclaims that no man can find God except in his own heart.

Chapter XII

DAIDAN HELMY'S LEAP (AN INTERLUDE)

ONE moonlight night I stood alone beneath the almond trees, on the terrace of the Whirling Dervish palace, in the hills behind Tripoli, and leaned over a parapet to look down on the little river among the rocks below.

Presently I heard the soft, slow padding of slippered feet on the flagstones. It was my friend and host, the venerable Sheik el Melewi. He took my hand, but did not speak. We were both caught in the spell of the Oriental night. The scarcely audible melody of a reed-flute floated from a darkened window beyond the white dome of the *tekkeh*.

We stood for a long time silent beside the parapet, and then the sheik said slowly, like one communing with his own memories: "It was from here that Daidan Helmy leaped, in the darkest hour of his life and mine."

I wondered what tragedy lay behind his words and was eager to hear more, but only in case it was his wish to speak. So I made no reply, until he added: "You have heard, perhaps, of Daidan Helmy?"

"No," I answered. "He was your friend—some one you loved?"

"Scarcely that, but surely not an enemy, though he brought sorrow and death to my household. I supposed that his name might be already known to you because Daidan Helmy was—and still is—the greatest of all

Melewi Dervish musicians, and, therefore, the foremost of all Islam. When he sings, it is like the voice of the archangel Israfel. But let us sit by the fountain, and I will tell you his story. As it unfolds, you will see that

A COURTYARD FOUNTAIN IN THE
WHIRLING DERVISH PALACE

the unwitting evil he wrought here was but one dark thread woven into a tapestry of many colors which made a design of harmonious beauty at the last.

"I would have you see him as I knew him first, in our chapter house at Damascus. He was leader of the orchestra, and a gifted player on the three principal Dervish instruments, the *nei* [reed-flute], the *ne-airat* [zither], and the *aout* [lute]. But most marvelous of all was his voice—a voice of silver and gold. And he had made a vow in childhood to sing only songs in praise of Allah and the divine mysteries.

"On the nights when the Dervishes danced in Damascus, high-born Moslem ladies, and often *farengi* ladies, too, flocked to the *tekkeh* and crowded the galleries, to sit enraptured as he sang.

"He was a young man, handsome, with deep, shining eyes, smooth-skinned and with flowing black hair, wholly absorbed in the beauty of music and in saintly contemplation—indifferent to admiration and worldly fame.

"Yet his fame grew until it came to the ears of the grand master of our order, Mohamet Bakhir Chelebi, on whom be peace, and he was invited to the court of the great Dervish palace at Konia in Turkey, where he sang as he had never sung before. The assembled brethren were exalted, and ladies of the palace, veiled and hidden behind latticed windows, listened entranced as had their sisters in Damascus.

"The lamentable events which then happened secretly at Konia are now known to all the Melewi. Among the ladies of the court was a beautiful young girl, Firdoos by name, daughter of the Dervish Sheik Adham, and niece of the Chelebi himself. As she sat veiled and listening enraptured, in company with the rest, she drew aside the corner of her *tcharchâf*, as any young girl might, peeped through the screen, beheld the singer, and the dart of love pierced her heart.

"The way of a love-driven maiden is ever in all lands the same. One evening then, as Daidan Helmy was walking alone in the palace garden, she appeared at a window above his head and contrived to let her veil fall, so that he beheld her face. His heart, in turn, was smitten by

her glance, and he forgot the solemn vow by which he had
consecrated his golden voice to God alone. He lifted his
voice and sang:

> Your face is like the moon;
> Your eyes are like deep pools
> In which I drown.
> Your mouth is a pomegranate
> From the tree of life.

"And she answered him with another song:

> Your eyes are fire
> That burns into my soul,
> Your voice is honey
> Dripping from the stars.

"Had they considered reasonably, at once confessed
their case, and sought counsel of the maiden's family, no
grievous tragedy would have followed, for marriage is
permitted, as you know, among the Melewi, and all might
happily have been arranged. But they were carried away
by the first sweet madness of their love. They made
secret trysts, where they walked and talked in a cypress
grove near the palace. A woman servant revealed their
meetings to the Sheik Adham, Firdoos' father, who went
in his flaming rage direct to the Chelebi.

"Firdoos was punished and shut up in the *hareem* for
a year and a day. Daidan Helmy was banished from the
court and from Turkey, sent back to do penance in his
own *tekkeh* at Damascus.

"He went away plunged in sorrow, and as the train
bore him over the Taurus Mountains, farther and farther
away from the damsel, he became crazed with grief. I

mean that an actual madness seized him as he sat in the
train compartment. He took his lute and zither from
their cases, smashed them against the walls, then began
tearing off his robes and hurling them from the car window.

"Fortunately, among his fellow travelers were certain
Damascenes who recognized him and said: 'Surely this
saintly one is no common madman.' They restrained him
as gently as might be, sought to quiet him, and had him
conveyed safely to the chapter house in Damascus.

"For many days he was prostrated, and then seemed
partially to recover. He gave no further signs of madness, but brooded unhappily, silent and plunged in misery,
day after day, unable to play or sing or pray.

"The Damascus sheik, who is my friend, and a most
gentle soul, was filled with sympathy, as were all the
brethren. And after a few weeks, when Daidan Helmy
asked for a long leave of absence to travel, with the hope
that it would make him forget his sorrow, the release was
freely granted him, and he departed, followed by their
prayers.

"The tale of his far wandering no man knows—least
of all he—save that he crossed weary deserts and mountains, seeking always forgetfulness. Once, afterward,
when he chanced to see a picture of the great mosque at
Ispahan, it is told of him that he said: 'I was beaten and
driven from this door by the beggars,' and it is also told
that after his return a *haj* plucked him by the sleeve,
looked searchingly into his face, and said: 'Art thou not
such a one, who journeyed on the road to Samarkand?'

"The seasons changed, a whole year passed, and then
one night in spring, as the first *mush-mush* trees were

beginning to flower, Daidan Helmy stood outside the gateway yonder—though we knew him not—and cried: 'I am a brother who asks for sanctuary.'

"My gatekeepers thought he was some wandering Bektashi [a separate sect of begging Dervishes vowed to

A NICHE IN THE YELBOGHA
MOSQUE AT DAMASCUS

poverty], for his hair was long and tangled, his face was haggard and overgrown by a rough black beard, and his garb was not of the Melewi. An old ragged turban was wound round his brow; his cloak was caked with mud and hung in tattered shreds. His legs were dirty and scratched with brambles.

"So he appeared when they brought him before me, and a Bektashi I also thought him to be. But he dropped to his knees and kissed my hand as no Bektashi would have

done, and instead of saluting me with the '*Salaam
aleikum*' of Moslems outside our sect, he pronounced the
ritual Melewi greeting—which is one of the secret names
of Allah.

"I replied with another secret name of the Most High
and said: 'But who art thou, O brother! and how has a
Melewi fallen in this sad case?'

"And he answered: 'I am that Daidan Helmy whom
your own eyes have seen in the Damascus *tekkeh*. I have
suffered, and my heart is dead, but purified, and I would
now return, as is my duty, to my own chapter house to
dwell once more among my brethren.'

"I recognized that it was he indeed. I embraced him
and kissed his forehead, and called for servants who took
him to the baths, and bathed him and rubbed him with
oil, and shaved him and sought to comb out his hair; but
it was matted and they were forced to crop it off close to
his head. And they laid out new proper garments for
him, with the *khirka* [brown robe] and *kulah* [tall hat],
so that he was again a Melewi among us.

"I said to him: 'Will you bide here with us and regain
your strength, or shall I command a motor car from
Tripoli for the morrow, that you may be away across the
mountains to your own *tekkeh?*'

"He replied: 'By your grace and the grace of Allah, I
will bide here for a few days, and then you will supply
me with a little money, and I will take the small boat
from Tripoli to Beirut and go thence by train to Damascus.'

" 'Bide at your ease, few days or many, in the peace of
Allah, and when you are ready to depart it shall be as you
wish,' I replied. And I had a chamber made ready for

him in the *tekkeh*, and ordered that strengthening foods be prepared for him morning and evening. And I bethought me to have a flute laid by the *Mesned* [the sacred poetical book of the Dervish mysteries] on the tabouret in his chamber, so that if his soul felt the need he might solace himself with music.

"On the first day he remained in silent meditation; on the evening of the second day he breathed into the flute, but the melodies were sad and broken. On the third evening—or perhaps it was the fourth—he played again, and the melody rose like an imprisoned bird remounting to the sky, and the brethren gathered in the *tekkeh* to listen, while the servants stopped in the fields below. One said: 'It is an angel singing in paradise.'

"And another said: 'No, it is that one whose heart Allah has healed of its deep wound.'

" '*Inshallah!*' replied the others, and on that instant, as they said it, the melody wavered in its flight, and wailed, and ended.

"But on the next day he played again, and we felt indeed that his wound was healed. So that when the second Friday came, and we made our preparations for the ritual dance, I invited Daidan Helmy to conduct the music, leading our own orchestra, the same which you have heard.

"All went well that night, until the brethren were whirling in their ecstatic *hal*, while the music, led by the notes of his reed-flute, pulsed with rhythms and melodies of heavenly beauty.

"You already know our ritual and have seen how the musicians are disposed on a balcony above our dance-floor, and you have seen how the ceremonial requires that at

certain times I arise from the red sheepskin and stand as
the dancers pass before me. You have observed also that
for this ceremonial I am garbed, as are all *tekkeh* governors, in a robe different from the rest, with a taller hat,
wound with a turban of green silk.

"As I arose upon that night, my eyes were compelled
upward toward the musicians, and when I lifted my face,
Daidan Helmy screamed. As the others ceased playing
in amazement, he hurled his flute downward so that it
struck my breast, and all was confusion. While the
musicians laid hands upon him to restrain him, he
screamed again, and tore one of his arms free.

"Straining toward me, he cried: 'Horror and desecra-
tion! An impostor is here among you! That man is not
our sheik! *Aiee!* The white-bearded demon!'

"My friend, you can guess easily now, as I quickly
understood then, the meaning of that dreadful scene.
This stricken and unhappy soul, carried away by the
familiar beauty of the ritual, entranced by the familiar
music, imagined himself back once more in his own
tekkeh at Damascus so that when I arose, his eyes unconsciously expected to behold the form and features of his
own sheik, a man of smaller stature, darker beard, and
different mien than mine. In the shock of amazement, he
forgot all that had intervened, and his old madness came
upon him.

"Neither I nor any of the brethren could, therefore,
hold him blamable. Rather, we sorrowed for his re-
newed affliction, and sought in all ways we might to calm
him. But the madness persisted, and he would not be
restrained. So we divested him of his hat and robes and
put him in common garments—not for disgrace or shame,

but because it would be unseemly for one whose mind was clouded to wear the consecrated garments of the Order. As he was exhausted from struggling against us, we gave him a sleeping draught and shut him up for the night in his chamber. His hat and garments were sealed in a packet marked with his name and laid away, to be returned to him with all honor when the cloud had lifted.

"These things occurred in the month of Ramadan, so that, contrary to our custom at other seasons, we danced again the following night. The demented man had lain all day exhausted, but quiet, and had suffered willingly the ministrations of our physician.

"But the madness came upon him again that night, and he tore off his garments so that he was naked, and fled from his chamber along a corridor which led to the balcony, and sprang like a goat in his nakedness, crashing through the wooden railing, down upon the floor among us, screaming, 'Woe to the false sheik!'

"We seized him and put heavy chains upon his arms and carried him struggling to a chamber, where he lay upon a pallet like one dead. Yet even so, lest the violence come again, we locked another chain around his waist and fastened it to an iron ring, so that he might not escape to harm himself or others. And we planned that on the morrow we would dispatch a messenger to Damascus, asking that he be transported thither.

"But, alas, on the morrow it was too late. On that same night, the tragedy befell. You are my friend, and I may speak of it. I had a beloved daughter, Yamile, who was still more child than woman, yet at the age when childhood ends and womanhood begins. You know the Moslem customs—how she lived cherished and protected.

But she was not in my thoughts on that ill-fated night of nights. I was distressed and wakeful. I paced here upon the terrace, and finally descended to the terrace below, on the mill-roof by the river.

"One thing you must understand before I continue, else I could not speak at all. The horror which followed was of the soul. The hurt which my Yamile suffered was inflicted upon the spirit alone.

"Yamile, of course, lay sleeping up here—yonder in the *hareem*. I was down there—in the late night—when I heard her sudden cry. And then a dreadful silence.

"My heart stopped in its beating. Then I shouted, and strength returned to me as I climbed upward. Others had already rushed to the terrace. Together we ran to the corridor of the *hareem*, and I tore back the curtain, while they stopped behind me.

"It was not dark. The little night lamps were burning. My daughter lay as if lifeless among the cushions of her divan, and kneeling over her, with his chained hands clasped, was the demented Daidan Helmy. But his face was not mad or evil. It was calm, as if illumined. He did not see me or lift his eyes, but he had heard the rushing of our feet in the corridor, for he said in a gentle whisper: 'Hush! Be still. Walk softly on tiptoe, for my lady sleeps.'

"But then he raised his eyes and saw me, and a rage came upon him, and he leaped to his feet, and sought to strike me dead with his heavy chains. I rushed upon him and held him and called the brethren to my aid, and we overcame him. After breaking the chain which had held him, he had wandered by chance through the corridors, and coming upon the sleeping girl, in the dim light, he must have imagined her to be his own lost Firdoos, at Konia. He had not sought to harm her, but the shock which she had suffered was too great. She sank from day to day into a profound depression that no physician's skill could stay, and died at the end of Ramadan, as the first blossoms were falling from the trees.

COURTYARD AND COLONNADE OF THE AZEM PALACE AT
DAMASCUS

"On that same night, as they were dragging Daidan Helmy away, he tore himself from their grasp at the outer door of the corridor, leaped from the parapet, and broke both his legs on the rocks below. We thought he had slain himself, but fate willed a different ending. He was transported to a hospital in Tripoli. At the end of six months he was made whole of his hurts, and his right mind was restored to him.

"There is no more sadness, but only a blessed conclusion to his strange life's story. He came to us when he was whole again and prostrated himself before me to beg forgiveness for the grief which he had wrought. But there was naught to pardon, for the deeds of one whose mind is clouded are not his own, but utterly in the hands of Allah. So then I placed on his brow the kiss of brotherhood and peace, and we re-invested him with his robes and gave praise for his recovery. 'I would begin my life anew,' he said, 'and rather than return to Damascus, I would beg leave to find refuge in some poor and far-distant *tekkeh*.' So he was transferred far away, to a *tekkeh* below Jerusalem, and was no longer the singer whose voice had been a glory, only one among the humblest of the brethren, and spent his days in prayer and contemplation of the mysteries.

"But when all these matters came to the knowledge of the Chelebi, our grand master at Konia, he pondered them deeply, and sent for Firdoos, the daughter of Sheik Adham, and she came and knelt before him.

"Almost two years had passed, and the girl was now eighteen, an advanced age for a Moslem daughter of good family to be without a husband. She had been sought in marriage, but had refused all suitors, even when urged by her father to choose among them, and it is not the custom among the Melewi to force marriage upon a girl against her will.

"The Chelebi said to her as she knelt before him: 'O daughter! answer me this question. Who will rule here in my stead when I am laid to rest?'

"She replied: 'Why, your son will rule, on whom be peace—he who is now governor and sheik of the great palace monastery at Aleppo.'

" 'Truly answered, my daughter, and he who will one day become the Chelebi has sent to ask your hand in marriage. His beard is silken black. He is in the full glory of youth. When I have passed away your husband shall rule here, and when you and he have passed away, your first-born son shall sit upon the sheepskin throne.'

"This he said to search for what might lie hidden in her heart. She listened in amazement and replied, weeping: 'My lord, the honor is greater than any I ever dreamed, but I am desolate, for my heart died when he who sang was banished and sent away.'

"The Chelebi lifted her from her knees and kissed her on the forehead and bade her go in peace. Straightway he summoned his chamberlain and bade him telegraph the chapter house at Jerusalem to send a swift messenger to the little *tekkeh* where Daidan Helmy sat in exile, and summon him to Konia.

"When Daidan Helmy came, the Chelebi proclaimed a *fetvah* [a sort of religious court or tribunal], and when the brethren were assembled he said: 'It is written that the ways of Allah are past finding out, and it is written that no man can struggle against his fate. If one go mad for the love of a damsel, and then recover his reason, but with his heart still desolate, shall he not be given her hand in marriage, lest the madness come once more upon him, and the answering be heavy upon those who have sought to hold them apart?'

"Then all the brethren, including the father of Firdoos, cried: 'So be it, O most just among Moslems!' A great wedding feast was prepared, and when three days had passed, Daidan went in to the damsel and made her his wife. All of these latter things which happened a

Konia were related to me, my friend, by the Chelebi himself, on whom be peace, and one day if you visit Konia you will hear Daidan Helmy's golden voice, and you will tell him for me that there is no bitterness in my heart. . . ."

The Sheik el Melewi ceased speaking, and a long silence fell again between us, as we sat by the fountain.

Chapter XIII

IN THE RUFAI HALL OF TORTURE

For a holy man and mystic, my friend the Sheik Shefieh was eminently practical.

Master he and catechumen I were journeying as pilgrims on the long, hot road from Damascus northward. But not with the traditional dusty sandals, staff, and scrip. We sat at ease in the wide tonneau of a powerful Renault, luxuriously upholstered by Kellner et ses Fils, who once made carriages for kings and queens. I felt sorry for old Saul of Tarsus, who had gone that road afoot, and wondered if the Lord God had not, perhaps, knocked saintliness into him by means of a sunstroke.

We were whizzing along with the hood of the car laid back to catch the breeze and afford a better view of the landscape. My venerable companion, whose saintliness was already sufficiently established in Islam, had removed his tall Dervish hat and replaced it with a woolen skullcap to prevent superfluous actinic miracles. Except that this cap was black and white instead of scarlet, and his robes pearl-gray, he might have been some stalwart bearded cardinal of the Renaissance. Certainly no cardinal since that robust half-pagan period could have munched with such human relish the green young cucumbers plucked from his own palace garden with which we both refreshed ourselves from time to time.

The objective of our pilgrimage was a monastery of the

AN ANCIENT ARCHWAY

In the Old Roman Street Leading Northward from Damascus

Rufai, or Howling Dervishes—a sect fundamentally different from the Whirling Melewi—in the mountains, between Hama and Aleppo. For the next night, Friday of the Christian week, but the first Moslem Sabbath of the new moon, a ritual Rufai ceremony was scheduled, and the Sheik el Melewi was taking me to see it.

We reached Hama in mid-afternoon Thursday, and I hoped that he would decide to push on so that we could spend the night with the Rufai. But the French gendarmes advised us there was serious danger from bandits after nightfall in the hills; so we put up at a hotel, run European style by an Armenian, where I was sinfully proud to be seen in company with one before whom the proprietor and servants bowed as to a king. We engaged a bedroom with two beds and a private sitting-room, where dinner was served us later. My pious but practical friend, over a delicious melon and Turkish coffee in tiny cups, offered me one of his long, amber-perfumed cigarettes, and intimated that it was just as well. We would see enough—and maybe too much—of the Rufai on the morrow. They were a sincere and consecrated brotherhood, he told me, and had supplied some notable saints to the Moslem calendar, but they were more admirable for godliness than cleanliness, and had a habit of serving even their most distinguished guests with a stew of goat-flesh into which they also dipped their hands. I guessed, and it turned out rightly, that we would find the Rufai chapter house a somewhat striking contrast to his own palace monastery which we had left the day before at Tripoli, with its spacious halls and domes, luxurious terraces, fountains, gardens, and elaborate cuisine.

Friday morning we made a late start from Hama, and

after a minor delay in getting our big car out of a ditch
where it had skidded when the chauffeur tried to run
down and kill a hyena which loped diagonally across the
road, we arrived at our destination. It was a rambling
old flat-roofed stone building, on a barren hillside, with
a wooden wing, weatherbeaten to the color of stone.

The Rufai sheik himself came out to greet us. He
was a man just past middle age, with a Kurdish cast of
countenance, piercing black eyes, sparse-bearded, but with
long, rusty dark hair hanging over his shoulders; barefooted, in a coarse shirt of unbleached hemp or linen,
with a black robe, and a black turban wound round his
low-crowned fez. He made a startling contrast to the
Melewi sheik, whose pearl-gray vestments of finest texture, tall hat, green silk turban, and ivory-handled stick
made him as elegant as a figure from some old illumined
Persian miniature. However, they embraced as brothers.
Both were ruling sheiks. Both were Dervishes. Both
were mystics. But their respective personalities and garb
showed how totally different were the two sects and how
completely at variance were their modes of life.

The Melewi introduced me as a student especially interested in all branches of mysticism—which in a modest
way was true. After offering us water and unsweetened
coffee, in a hall barren of all decoration and furniture
except for a banner of the Prophet and a few grass mats
scattered on the low stone divans built against the walls,
he spoke rapidly to the Melewi for a few moments, and
then turning to me said in slower Arabic that since I was
interested in *turuk* [the paths of knowing], I might
care to look upon one or two of the brethren who on this
holy day were in *melboos* [the mystical state].

He clapped his hands sharply, but no one responded to the summons, and he called out several times: "*Ya Mechmed!*" Finally a Dervish appeared at the doorway, touching hand to forehead.

"What brethren are in *melboos?*"

The man reflected, and replied slowly with four names. Nur-Adesh was one, and I think Fahim, with two other names which I cannot recollect.

The sheik seemed slightly chagrined. He said, with the curious matter-of-factness that so often surprised me among Oriental mystics: "Four. I did not know there were so many. It is regrettable, since there will be four less for the ceremony tonight."

We traversed a bare corridor, mounted a short flight of steps, passed several closed doors in a second corridor, and came to one which the sheik opened.

On the stone floor, in the center of a drab cell, whose only furniture was a worn pallet, a man sat hunched like an Aztec mummy. A broad leather strap, blackened and greasy, was fastened tightly round his body and across his back just beneath the arm-pits, then crossed again over the base of his neck and buckled under his drawn-up knees, so that his head was held down between them. His arms hung free and limp. He was naked to the waist, barefooted, with only a ragged pair of baggy drawers. He was motionless, except for his slow, steady breathing, and seemed unconscious. The Rufai sheik told us that he had fastened himself in this position and would remain so for a day and a night, perhaps even a little longer, when he would return to a normal state of consciousness and probably release himself, but if he were too numb or exhausted he would call out, and one of his brothers

would come and release him. He had already been there
for about ten hours and had long since passed into *melboos*, so that we entered the cell and spoke without the
need of lowering our voices.

In another cell, where we only looked in at the door,
and were cautioned to keep silent, was a Rufai just passing into the "state." He had fastened a rope in a double
loop from the ceiling, had wrapped his left wrist with
rags, inserted it in the loose dangling loop, then twisted
round and round, until the loop tightened on his wrist,
and the rope twisting double became shorter and shorter.
He now hung rigid with his heels some two inches off the
floor, but with the balls of both feet planted firmly, to
support a part of his weight. Even so, most of the weight
of the body seemed to be suspended from his wrist. The
hand was purple, the finger-nails were black, the sinews
of the long, emaciated arm were drawn taut like cords, the
left shoulder was drawn up, while the right shoulder
sagged. His right arm hung limp and free. His head
drooped forward over his sagged right shoulder, like a
man crucified, but by stooping I could see his features.
The eyes were closed, and the face was rigid, but there
was no rictus, no distortion, no twisted grimace sugges-
tive of pain. When he would emerge, many hours later,
from *melboos*, he had only to turn a few times on his feet,
for the twisted rope to unwind of itself and release him.

I felt that I had seen enough, but there was one more
method which the sheik wanted me to see, because, he
said, it was the oldest and most classical among the
Rufai, and the one which was first taught. It was called
chibeh. It turned out to be—or at least it seemed to me
—much less severe than the others. The man sat com-

pactly cross-legged on the floor, with arms folded on his breast, his shoulders balanced a little forward, his chin lifted and his head drawn slightly backward by a cord which was fastened in the braids of his hair and ran upward at an angle to the wall behind him. In this case, the strain was not great. The cord itself was not heavy. A hard tug would have broken it. But it sufficed to hold his head fixed in position. His tilted chin made me think of the iron clamps that I had known as a child in old-fashioned photographers' galleries, and it seemed to me that they might have served the purpose almost as well as the cord.

The Rufai sheik led us back to the reception hall and left us to rest for an hour or two. We dozed on the hard divans, and later dinner was brought to us. It turned out to be the goat stew which the Melewi had predicted with a marked lack of enthusiasm, but we had it all to ourselves and did not fare too badly, since it contained the entire liver, which is always tender and delicious.

When we were conducted that night to the *tekkeh* hall, where the ritual ceremony was commencing, it was like stepping back a thousand years in time and space. The Sheik el Melewi at my side, although in outward garb himself an esoteric figure of the East, suddenly became as familiar and wholesomely commonplace as any friend in New York. It was a great comfort. For there was absolutely nothing else that seemed even remotely connected with the sane, safe twentieth-century world. Even the iron lamps which flared and smoked in their brackets along the wall were flat, bulbous, wrongly shaped. The hall was stone, rectangular, some forty feet long and nearly as wide, low-roofed, murky. A gnarled

and heavy wooden pillar loomed—not in the center of the
hall where a pillar rightly should be—but set near one
of the walls, where it was not needed to support the roof.
I wondered what it was there for. It affected me unpleasantly. There was an overpowering odor of incense,
sandal oil perhaps, but mixed with pungent, unknown
herbs. In a semicircle sat the twenty or more Rufai
Dervishes, on the floor, in low fezes wound with black
turbans, most of them with long, unkempt hair, black
cloaks thrown loosely over their shoulders, naked to the
waist beneath. All were chanting in monotone an endlessly repeated "Al-lah, Al-lah, Al-lah," which continued
uninterrupted by our entrance. In front of them was a
brazier, with a glowing bed of charcoal, from which
emerged the handles of knives, long iron pins, like spits,
with wooden handles, and iron pokers with no handles
at all. Beside this brazier, on a dirty, undyed sheepskin, sat their sheik, garbed like the rest, except that he
wore a shirt beneath his cloak. He arose on our entrance,
came over to us, bowed low, embraced the Melewi, and
then bowed to me. They whispered together. I guessed
from their gestures that he was inviting the Melewi to
come and sit beside him on the sheepskin, but he chose
to remain with me, and we were given seats on a stone
divan covered with matting, aside, against the wall.

For ten minutes more, the monotonous chant continued,
with the two syllables of the "Al-lah" equally timed and
accented, like the rhythmic beating of a drum. Then
one voice suddenly broke into the rhythm, with a loud
"*Ya hoo!*"—literally "Oh, him," but meaning "Oh, He
That is," and signifying that the one who shouted had
felt the Divine Presence. To this first "*Ya hoo,*" the

sheik shouted *"Allah akbar!* [God is great]." Then two
or three others took up the cry, *"Ya hoo,"* while the
underchant in monotone speeded, broke rhythm, until
each in a sort of ecstatic frenzy was calling the name of
Allah in a mad, howling uproar.

Suddenly one of the Dervishes leaped to his feet, threw
off his cloak, leaped again into the air, naked to the waist.
The Rufai sheik leaped up at the same time, seized a
long, red-hot spit by its wooden handle from the brazier,
and began waving it wildly in the air. He must have
waved it for fully a minute. The long, pointed iron pin
was less than a quarter of an inch thick, and the red glow
quickly faded. I imagine it had time to cool consider-
ably. The other Dervish circled, leaping around the
sheik and howling, then backed, with his head pressed
sideways against the wooden pillar, with his mouth gaping
open, and stood rigid, motionless. The sheik inserted the
spit at an angle into his mouth, and with a solid blow of
his fist drove it through the man's cheek and pinned him
to the pillar.

The others had meanwhile leaped to their feet, thrown
off their cloaks, and joined hands, howling and leaping
in a circle around the brazier. Then they broke circle
and precipitated themselves toward the glowing coals,
each one apparently seizing the first hot implement that
came to hand in the confusion. These they waved as they
resumed their mad dancing, and the howling again caught
rhythm from their feet to become a wild, frenzied chant,
savage, exultant, ecstatic.

I felt myself reacting, against my will, to the emotional
excitement. My mind flashed back to the first Methodist
revival I had attended with skeptical adolescent assur-

ance in South Carolina—to go away blushing with angry shame because the orgiastic singing and shouting had made me tremble. It was the same sensation now—followed quickly by the same self-contempt. I hoped the Sheik el Melewi had not been watching me. This inward emotional stress was brief, and I soon focused my mind clearly enough to be quite sure of certain details which followed. All of the red-hot implements began almost immediately to fade and cool as they were waved in the air, but I saw one man with a poker, while it was still quite red, dart out his tongue and lick it repeatedly, but each time with lightning swiftness. There was actual contact, for fractional seconds at least, for I saw steam rise. Others had pierced the flesh of their breasts with long, sharply pointed spits and pins, and now leaped about with them thrust through and dangling, but none of these I saw was still red hot. They were stuck through transversely, not more than a quarter of an inch deep at any point, only through the skin and flesh, not deep enough to transfix the corded muscles, and out again at a point an inch or two beyond the spot where they were inserted. I saw none of those who waved knives stick them into their bodies. They slashed their shoulders and breasts with the edges of the knives so that the blood flowed, but did not cut themselves deeply. I looked back for the man who had been pinned to the pillar, but he was no longer there. He had released himself, or been released by the sheik, and I supposed was now leaping and howling with the others.

The frenzy lasted for about twenty minutes; then, without any signal which I could observe, it began gradually to subside. First one, then another, sank to the floor, until all were again seated, with their heads bowed almost to their knees, absolutely silent. The sheik went among them, throwing their cloaks over their shoulders. After a few moments of continued silence, he clapped his hands. They arose slowly, formed a procession, circled the hall, each bowing before him, and filed out.

The Rufai sheik followed them, and we saw no more of our hosts that night. When we returned to the recep-

THE MAR BEHNAN MONASTERY
Primitive Arabic Architecture in Its Purest Form

tion hall, we found that two clean pallets had been laid for us on the stone divans, without pillows, but with wadded cotton quilts for covering. Before going to bed, I went out and sat for a while on the hillside, under the stars and crescent moon. Jackals were howling. I wondered if, when beasts bayed the moon, they, too, were engaged unconsciously in a vague sort of worship. Was it all part of the same divine urge—the melancholy howling of the animals, the Methodist revival hymns, the frenzied chanting of the Rufai, the Melewi flutes and dances, the tomtoms in the African jungle, perhaps even the saxophones in the night clubs of New York? Invocation—of Pan—of God—of Allah—Priapus—but always the call to something cosmic, immense, beyond. A wolf on a cliff, or Debussy enraptured at his piano. Was it all the same? I felt I was about to discover something—to have a mystical illumination of my own. . . .

But when we awoke next morning, I was practically interested, most of all, in examing if possible, before we left the monastery, some of the Dervishes who had cut and burned themselves the night before. I wanted to see if there were any basis of fact in the stories brought back by travelers who had been persuaded that there was something physically supernormal in these ceremonies and their consequences. The Rufai sheik was courteously willing. He called in several who permitted me to examine their wounds as closely as I wished, and even to touch them. The wounds were all superficial and seemed already in process of healing, but not with any abnormal or "magical" rapidity. As for burns, they were negligible, for the simple reason, I believe, that all the implements, after being waved about in the air, were reduced in temperature, still hot enough, perhaps, to cauterize, but not to inflict burning sores. Nothing, indeed, could be more scientifically antiseptic than an iron heated red hot and then permitted partially to cool. I noticed on their chests and shoulders many old scars which had healed perfectly. The newly made wounds were real, but I did not observe one which would have prevented any normal, healthy individual from going about his business the next day. I asked the sheik how often they engaged in this rite, and he told me never more than once a month, and sometimes less frequently. I asked him if he considered that the ritual wounds healed with supernatural rapidity, and he said certainly not, that they were like any other wounds, but that at the moment they were inflicted the Rufai felt no pain because they were already in "the state." If they felt nothing, I asked him, what was the use of doing it?

"But we do feel something," he replied; "it is a kind of bliss in which the body and soul are both exalted."

My Arabic was not equal to these shades of meaning, but he repeated his words over and over, and when I was doubtful the Melewi translated carefully in French. "You must understand," he concluded, "that it is not an object—not a thing in itself—it is only a means—a way of unlocking a door." And with that I had to be content.

On the road back to Damascus, we stopped again at Hama for luncheon and sat in the main hotel dining-room, where the food and table service were European. The change of atmosphere was complete. French officers in uniform (some with their wives), tourists in sports costumes, commercial travelers, a few Syrians mostly in European clothes, occupied near-by tables.

It was an incongruous place for a lesson in the higher branches of Sufi mysticism, but it was there the Melewi taught me one which I shall never forget. We had been arguing about the Rufai. I had been stubbornly insisting there was a definite "wrongness" in any system which involved self-torture and mutilation. I had said that I found it repugnant in ascetic Christianity and even more repugnant in this strange Islamic sect which we had visited. I had quoted his own phrase that "the soul grows, like a flower, on the body's stem, and both are holy." I had expressed the utmost admiration for the paths of harmony and beauty which he and all the Melewi Dervishes followed—but I did not like the Rufai. And I did not understand how he—an esthetic aristocrat despite his true piety—could be so sympathetic toward their savage rites.

WATER WHEEL OF THE OLD TANNERIES AT HAMA

Now, as we sat at table, he resumed the conversation. "Speaking of Christianity," he said, "it contains many beautiful truths, but also a great error. There is not one single, straight and narrow path to God. There are many paths, of infinite number."

He took a napkin and twisted it round a sugar bowl so that it made a little cone-shaped mountain, which he invited me to consider.

"We will suppose," he said, "that the peak, the mountain-top, stands for Unity or God. And we will suppose, all round the wide base of the mountain, men who wish to attain the peak. From any spot at the base, the direc-

MENDICANT DERVISH OF AN ASCETIC ORDER VOWED TO POVERTY
AND SELF-TORTURE

tion to the top is not north, south, east, or west; it is upward. But the mountain is too steep for any mortal to climb straight upward; so here are some journeying eastward, and others westward, by winding paths, that mount gradually higher and higher. A party traveling east meets a party traveling west. 'Whither?' each asks the other party. 'To God!' both cry. And then, if they have not wisdom, each cries to the other: 'You are lost. Come, face about, and go with us.' And then, alas, my friend, they dispute and condemn, not knowing in their unwisdom that all paths lead to God if they mount only upward. I would bid you beware, my friend, of falling into such unwisdom, when you return to your own country and look back in memory on this older land."

Among the Yezidees

Chapter XIV

IN THE MOUNTAIN OF THE DEVIL-WORSHIPERS

"But, I repeat to you, *Effendim*, that I myself have seen it—"

The speaker was Najar Terek bey, a Turkish traveler and former cavalry captain, who had been my trusted friend in Stamboul, and whom I was overjoyed to find again at Aleppo.

We were drinking coffee in his little garden after a game of billiards, and he was telling me of things which, coming from almost any other man, I would have dismissed as fantasy.

We had been discussing the Yezidees, a mysterious sect scattered throughout the Orient, strongest in North Arabia, feared and hated both by Moslem and Christian, because they were worshipers of Satan.

He had told me how, three years before, he had visited the sacred stronghold of the Yezidees, in the mountains north of Baghdad, on the Kurdish border, near Mosul—of a strange temple, built on rock terraces hewn from the cliffs of the mountainside, which he had not been permitted to enter, but which was supposed to contain the great brazen image of a peacock and to lead into subterranean caverns where bloody rites were still performed in worship of the Devil—how he had seen one of their fabulous Seven Towers, or "Power Houses"—a high white cone-shaped structure with bright rays flashing from its pinnacle—and it was here that I interrupted him.

I interrupted him because I had heard of those Seven Towers more than once before, and I believed them to be as absolutely mythical as the Chinese "subterranean kingdom" or the caves of Sinbad. The tales I had previously heard, and which are widely current in the East, may be reduced to this:

Stretching across Asia, from Northern Manchuria, through Thibet, west through Persia, and ending in the Kurdistan, was a chain of seven towers, on isolated mountain-tops; and in each of these towers sat continually a priest of Satan, who by "broadcasting" occult vibrations controlled the destinies of the world for evil.

And now here was a man who, though he surely believed no such nonsense, calmly told me that, whatever might be their exact purpose, towers dedicated to the service of Satan actually existed, and that he had seen one of them with his own eyes.

He assured me further that in his opinion, though he had gone disguised as a Kurdish merchant, I might go openly and without unreasonable danger, and see much more than he had been permitted to see. The Yezidees, he had been told, were friendly to English-speaking people, because the English, installed in Irak, had put a stop to the murders and massacres of Yezidees which had been frequent under Moslem rule.

Their holy city, he told me, was called Sheik-Adi. No roads led thither, but it could be reached by mountain paths, on mule-back, from Mosul. We went into his library, and got out a map. Mrs. Seabrook and I had already counted on crossing into Irak, sooner or later, but had expected first to go back to Damascus and pick up there one of the guarded motor convoys of the British Nairn Transport Company, which carried passengers and the overland desert mail from the Beirut seaport to Baghdad. Terek bey told me, however, that while it was too dangerous to risk traveling direct from Aleppo to Mosul, we might save both time and money by crossing North Arabia in a hired car "on our own," following the valley of the Euphrates from Aleppo to Baghdad;

THE MEDIEVAL CITADEL AT ALEPPO

and that getting from Baghdad to Mosul afterward would be an easy matter.

He walked back with me that same night to the Baron Hotel, where Katie and I were stopping, and we routed out a young man known as George, who, though officially only head bell-boy, was the most competent person about the place. He found two garage owners, despite the late hour. Katie was keen for the proposed change in plans. We consulted, argued, bargained, and finally one of the garage men agreed to supply us with a car and driver for twenty gold pounds.

We should be able, they told us, to make it in three

days' hard going, down the Euphrates valley to Deir-er-Zhor, thence to Anah, then southeast across the desert to Baghdad.

This was a Wednesday night, and it was agreed that we should take a day for preparation and start at dawn on Friday.

Thursday at luncheon time, when we came back from shopping for smoked goggles, pith helmets, and tinned food, my friend Najar Terek bey was waiting to see me.

He had found an Arab who might give us further information about the Yezidees, and would take me to see him that afternoon. This man, D'wali Fadan by name, proved to be a cotton merchant who had lived in Mosul. We talked with him in his shop near the bazaar. He was voluble at first, but when we began to press him closely, he admitted that he had never actually been among the Yezidees. His information was from a "cousin" who had traded with them, and was vividly definite, but not easily credible.

He said the Yezidees were ruled by a prince called Mir Said Beg, who had murdered his own father for the succession. He told of a temple courtyard in which a black serpent was worshiped—of bloody sacrifices at the base of a white tower. And he told an even more fantastic tale of a custom among the Yezidees, how each night a young virgin was brought to the high priest, with a heavy "corset" of jeweled silver locked round her waist —and that no Yezidee took a maiden to bride until she had undergone certain abominable rites.

I didn't believe then that there was one grain of truth in that story—but I have now, in my actual possession a heavy silver Yezidee bridal girdle so wide that "corset" is a better name for it than belt—and the Yezidees themselves admitted to me, when I finally reached Sheik-Adi and gained somewhat of their confidence, that the "right of the first night" exists as a part of their law, though they declare it is not put into actual practice by the present Mir.

But I am getting too far ahead of the record, which must, even though it makes no pretense of being a travel story, include, at least in bare detail, the adventure which befell us in the valley of the Euphrates.

Our departure from Aleppo and the first few hours of our journey were uneventful. We traversed a barren plain, by a road that was only a trail, past villages with houses like beehives built of mud, cone-shaped, and came, after fifty miles or more, to the river, wide and yellow, flowing between banks of hard, baked clay.

We followed its southern bank along clay flats hard and level as the floor of a skating-rink. Daoud, our driver, a wiry little chap about thirty, seemed thoroughly dependable in his grease-smeared khaki and black sheepskin cap; but I was chagrined to discover that he was a Christian and therefore probably Armenian, though he denied it vigorously.

It was pleasant riding in the early morning, but by nine o'clock the heat and glare were damnable. Toward noon, cliffs of clay and sand, surmounted occasionally by gigantic ruins, began to appear at our right, following the river, and presently became high palisades, coming sometimes within a few hundred feet of the river's edge, then receding for more than a mile.

At intervals of every two or three hours, we saw old Turkish forts, some abandoned, and some garrisoned by handfuls of Arab troops put there by the French.

At one of these, where we stopped at noon to refill the boiling radiator and the water-bag slung to our windshield, a dozen or more of the desert gendarmes came out and buzzed around us.

They wanted to know how the rest of our convoy had been delayed, and recommended that we wait until it caught up with us. They were surprised to see a woman in the car. They were puzzled when they learned we were traveling alone.

They examined our passports, which were viséd to travel from French Syria into British Irak, without specifying the route, shook their heads as if it were none of their business, and let us go on.

As we rattled away, Daoud began muttering to himself. I asked him what was the matter, and he complained that we should never have started alone—that it might have been all right a month before, but that conditions changed and now it was *mal'un* [bad].

He began to push the car dangerously fast, and I called to him to go slower. He replied that there was another car somewhere ahead of us on the road with a French captain and chauffeur, and that if we could catch up with them it might be *zain* [good].

Presently, in early afternoon, the palisaded cliffs swept inward toward the river as if to block our route, and I supposed we would find a ferry or bridge there. But, instead, we turned to the right into a rocky pass, winding up among the cliffs. It was the first semblance of anything like a built road, and I imagine was cut thousands of years ago for chariot wheels.

Behind the cliffs we came into rising "bad lands," glaring white limestone crags which overhung our narrow road, sometimes cut out from the rock. The sun beat down from directly overhead, and when I took off my goggles and got the full glare, it was like riding through the clinkers and embers of some gigantic, white-hot furnace. I had to put on my coat, and Katie wrapped herself in a blanket, even covered up her hands, to protect them from being burned.

After an hour of this, as the road turned round a cliff, we saw a hundred yards ahead of us, at another turn, two Arabs, *kafiehs* wound round their faces and covering them to their eyes, with rifles ready in their hands—but sharpest of all in the glare were the brass buttons and insignia of their uniforms. We welcomed the sight of them. Not for one second did we mistake them for bandits. But they stopped us in great excitement, and it was there that we came up with the car in whose company Daoud had been so eager to travel.

It all but blocked the road. Its windshield had been smashed by bullets and its radiator deliberately ripped to pieces by other bullets. It was empty. Against its wheels, in the narrow shadow, lay the body of the chauffeur, covered with an *abba*, and already flies were swarming. The captain was missing. His body was found five days later, at the bottom of a nearby ravine. The Associated Press, at the time, gave a paragraph to the episode, and months later another paragraph, telling how the murderers were caught and duly hanged at Damascus.

It was a rotten situation, particularly to have brought

a woman into, and Katie was very pale and quiet, while Daoud was in a miserable funk. Not that I blamed him too much for it. I felt rather sick myself. But Deir-er-Zhor was only two hours distant, and plainly the sensible thing, if it were permitted, was to go on. The Arab gendarmes not only permitted, but advised us to do this. The posts were already being roused, and it wasn't likely there would be a second outrage on the same day in that immediate territory.

But Daoud, our driver, refused to agree. There was actually a green tinge to his brown, tanned face, dripping with perspiration beneath his black sheepskin cap. He wanted to turn back, spend the night at one of the desert forts, and go back to Aleppo next day, assuring me that it was "impossible," and that he would swear it had been impossible, and so my money would be returned to me. When he found me set against this, he declared that the only other safe thing was to remain where we were, under the protection of the two gendarmes, until others came, in whose company we could go to Deir-er-Zhor. But the gendarmes said that no troops might go on to Deir until the next day, as the news had already been sent in, and all would be occupied in the hunt for the bandits. So I finally succeeded in cursing and browbeating Daoud into cranking up the Ford and going on. And, of course, nothing further happened, except that we were disgusted with Daoud and in frequent risk of being overturned by his nervous driving.

The sun was still high in late mid-afternoon, when Deir-er-Zhor appeared, a big, flat-roofed desert town built on both sides of the river, the isolated metropolis of central North Arabia, its flatness relieved with domes and minarets and the tall wireless masts of the French army post, which were its only connection with the outside world.

At the gendarmerie, on the town's edge, the native sergeant, in khaki uniform, but bareheaded and barefooted, came running out to meet us. They had already learned the news, but he was keen to find out if we knew anything more. He was polite, friendly, chattered volubly in French, and exclaimed at *"le courage de Madame."*

There were no hotel accommodations for European travelers at Deir; so we put up at a native *khan*, where the Ford was parked in a courtyard, and we were given a room with iron-barred windows like a big prison cell, on a second floor—stone walls, floor, and ceiling. It was absolutely bare when Daoud dragged up our luggage. A boy of sixteen, naked except for his turban and a ragged belted shirt to his knees, came with a broom and a big earthen water-pot, with which he deluged and swept out the floor. Two iron cots were brought in, and on them later were spread pallets of straw, newly sewn into clean cotton cloth, with two quilts which were dubiously gray.

I was worried that we might not be permitted to go on next day; so while Katie lay down and rested, I went to call on the French commandant. He told me that we had taken a foolish risk, but that in his opinion it was probably safer to go on to Baghdad than to return to Aleppo. He regretted that he couldn't put us up for the night. He gave me a precious quart bottle of Périer water for Mrs. Seabrook, and took me to a near-by native cook-shop where we had excellent, cool German beer.

Feeling much better, I walked down through the town to see the river, made two or three photographs, just before sundown, and returned to Katie, who was sound asleep.

I was feeling remorseful about Daoud. As a matter of fact I had cursed him with every foul word I knew in Arabic and the few English ones I thought he would understand; so I had him sent for and let him superintend our dinner and share it with us—tinned stuff from our own basket, supplemented by a big bowl of mutton stew from the kitchen downstairs, and more beer which he sent a little rag-tailed girl running to get. He had brought in a low table, and we sat on our cots.

He was happy to be restored to favor, and promptly annoyed us by throwing bones, cucumber peelings, sardine tins, and other litter on the floor. But he knew the customs better than I, for when we had finished, the boy came again with water-jar and broom, cleaned up the débris, deluged the floor a second time, and swept it out thoroughly. We expected to be bothered by bugs—but as a matter of fact both of us were so tired that an army of them couldn't have kept us awake.

At Deir the river made a great loop northward, and instead of following it next morning, we struck out cross-country, so that the day's run was real desert, hard gravel and clay, sometimes level, sometimes broken by gullies and ridges so abominably rough that we had to low-speed.

The sun beat down until the leather cushions and the metal braces of the car-top were so hot it was painful to touch them. A wind like the breath of a furnace blew from the south. I had been in knickers and shirt-sleeves, but had to put on my coat, preferring to be dry-baked than grilled. Katie had long since been forced to put on her heavy woolen coat and gloves, as her skin actually blistered through her thin silk dress.

She had a long veil pinned over her helmet and wound round her head and shoulders. Its ends began to come loose and whip about in the wind. She couldn't find pins enough to hold it. It kept coming loose, slapping us both in the faces, pulling her helmet askew. I was

BOATS AND RAFTS ON THE EUPHRATES EAST OF DEIR ER ZHOR

sorry for her at first, then irritated, and presently I was God-damning all women, and we hated each other bitterly. It was worse than murders and bandits.

Things began to ping against my shoulder and the side of the car. I thought they were little stones, but they turned out to be grasshoppers. Soon we were running through clouds of them. They battered the windshield and came in at the side. Those which weren't stunned by the impact crawled all over us. We forgot our hatred as we fought them off. They spat "tobacco juice" like any Christian grasshoppers, but swarmed like

Pharaoh's plague. Presently they were gone as suddenly as they came. We had run through them, and left them behind. Katie and I grinned at each other sheepishly and made up our quarrel.

Early in the afternoon we came again to the Euphrates. Here and there were enormous ruins. Less frequently there were irrigated fields and signs of present habitation. At last, toward five o'clock, at a great bend of the river, far ahead, appeared what seemed a mighty fortress on the river bank, in the midst of walled parks or gardens. It was Anah with its groves of date palms.

We wound for three miles among the stone-walled groves, and finally arrived at the fort, built four-square around a huge colonnaded courtyard, garrisoned by some twenty native troopers. Here we were to spend the night.

In charge of the garrison was a sad young man in a long, dirty nightgown and red slippers, run down at the heel, who greeted us without enthusiasm. He turned out to be a Damascene who had lived in Algiers and Marseilles. He regarded his present post as an unutterably boring exile, and his melancholy was too deep to be cheered by a couple of chance visitors who would be gone again at dawn. He was eating his heart out with home-sickness.

But the spot which spelled loneliness and exile to him was like a little paradise to us that evening, for he installed us on a wide roof-top, with two long wooden couches and clean straw mattresses, with a manservant who made a fire in an angle of the wall, produced a tin kettle, heated water for us to wash with, and afterward brewed tea; he helped unpack our basket, brought fresh bread-flaps, and stood to serve us, as we dined picnic-fashion.

There was a gorgeous moon and a cool breeze. It was about ten o'clock when we lay down on the two couches on the roof, with the bright moon overhead, and we were slowly falling asleep when the man who had served us came tip-toeing to our baggage and bent over it. I won-

GOLDEN DOMES OF THE "FORBIDDEN" MOSQUE AT KADIMAIN

dered if he had come for petty thievery, but lay still and watched him. He thought we were asleep, but when he picked up two of our hand-bags and started away with them, I sat up and demanded what he was doing. He said: "There will come presently on the roof jackals and wild dogs. You need not fear them, but they would tear your luggage to pieces in search of food." With the aid of a ladder, he piled all our stuff on the top of a twelve-foot wall, out of reach. If the wild dogs came, we did not hear them.

Most of the next day was long, hot, flat, monotonous riding over the trailless desert, until we came in mid-afternoon to the embankments of the Berlin-Baghdad railway, abandoned in construction before the war, with a more recently built motor road paralleling it, which we followed.

I had hoped that our first sight of Baghdad would be its famous golden domes and minarets. Instead it was smoke from the ice factory, but as we got nearer, the domes and minarets appeared, mysterious and beautiful amid palm trees, lighted by the slanting rays of the sun and rich with the glamour of old Haroun el Reshid's court and the *Tales of a Thousand and One Nights*.

Our first closer impression of Baghdad enhanced the romantic spell, for we drove toward the southern bridge, through the purely native quarter of the city on the west bank of the Tigris—along a wide avenue, magnificently shaded by palm trees, lined on both sides by coffee shops with hundreds of divans before them, on which sat and reclined throngs of Arabs in long, sashed robes, some shaven-pated and bareheaded, others in turbans. Here might the ghosts of Sinbad and the hunchback tailor wander and feel themselves in the Baghdad of other days.

But when we crossed the wide, muddy river and turned into the new street which the British had cut through the center of the city, romantic dreaming gave way to real surprise. Crude frame buildings were everywhere, some with second-story false fronts, garish American motion-picture billboards, last year's Charlie Chaplin and Mae Murray—a tattooing establishment with signs in English and French, garage yards with high board fences and big English signs in box-car letters, motor cars honking everywhere, mostly flivvers. It was like a new western oil town at its worst. And this was Baghdad! Of course, it wasn't; but it was a part of our first impression.

We went to the Maude Hotel and were given a comfortable room with a balcony overlooking the river and another window directly over the hotel terrace, on which white-uniformed waiters were already laying the tables for dinner. While baths were being prepared, we got into pajamas and turned on the electric fan. It's all very well to talk of plain cool water as the best thirst-quencher, but we consumed two quarts of bubbling Apollinaris, liberally dosed with Holland gin and lime-juice, and it tasted better than the purest spring-water that ever flowed.

By the time we had had our baths, the terrace had been lighted in the dusk, and an orchestra was playing *Tosca*. We put on our dinner-clothes and went down to dine. The service and food were excellent, almost as elaborate as the Ritz.

The air was pleasant, like a moderately hot summer night in New York. It gave no hint of the deadly heat from which Baghdad suffers during the middle hours of the day. We dined and slept well and awoke refreshed.

My interest, at that time, was not in Baghdad. I was concerned only in seeing Mrs. Seabrook comfortably established, having her meet some of the Arabian families to whom we had letters—for she was more interested in that than in official British circles—and in getting on to Mosul and the Yezidees.

The first part of this program was settled most completely on the late afternoon of that day, when, after riding in an open carriage through a winding maze of covered bazaars and streets in one of the oldest quarters, we lifted the enormous iron knocker upon the gates of Howeja Mirzi Yacoub, Persian by birth, but lifetime inhabitant of Baghdad, and one of the ablest doctors in Irak.

Our letter was from his son, who was studying at the Turkish medical school in Constantinople, and with whom we had formed an intimate friendship.

How to describe Oriental hospitality—particularly when one comes recommended by a beloved son from whom there has been no recent news?

Dr. Yacoub, it seemed, was out, but the turbaned manservant, as soon as he gathered that our coming concerned, in some way, the son of the house, ran with the letter and our cards to *"El Sitt"*—the lady.

She could not have stopped even to open the letter, for the servant came rushing and beckoning down the stone steps into the courtyard where we stood waiting, and conducted us to a terraced roof-top—where stood the lady, who took us both literally to her bosom.

She was very large, motherly, swathed in folds of finest white muslin, hair hanging over her shoulders in two thick braids, gold anklets, bare feet in sandals of wood inset with silver—and two beautiful diamonds in her ears —but these were outshone by her fine, big face, which beamed with joy. We both loved her at first sight. She patted our hands.

"You are friends of my son—ah, happy welcome." She called down into the courtyard and sent a servant scurrying to meet her husband and bid him hasten. And, all the time, a thousand questions about her son. When had we seen him last? Was he happy? Was his color good? Had he been doing well with his studies? Had he been ill?

Katie assured her that the son was blooming with health, prospering in his studies, and that all was well with him.

This good news so overcame the dear old lady that she threw both arms around Katie's neck and cried so that tears ran in streams down her cheeks. And in no time at all Katie was crying with her. They hugged and sobbed as if their hearts were breaking. Here were two women who had never laid eyes on one another until five minutes before, now crying their eyes out in each other's arms—because the son of one of them was well and happy! Women are weird creatures—but I well understood that Katie would be safely looked after in Baghdad whether I went journeying on to the mountain of the Yezidees—or to the Mountain of the Moon.

We sat and talked more calmly. Dr. Yacoub arrived, a man of great charm and dignity. His welcome was less emotional on the surface, but he, too, was very glad to see us. Servants made coffee over a charcoal fire, on a lower roof in the courtyard.

Would we not come immediately and live with them? No? Well, then, we must come back many times. But even so, we could not leave the house on this first visit without taking with us a gift, for the sake of their son. We protested while they discussed what it should be. They led us into a big drawing-room, walls covered with huge Persian tapestries, gilded Louis Seize furniture on a hard earthen floor. The dear lady was for immediately tearing down and bundling up one of the finest hangings. Katie restrained her by physical force. Not to offend her, we accepted a small inlaid brass tray. But next day, the tapestry was sent to us at the hotel. And the Yacoubs were as a second mother and father to Katie when I left her a few days later for the country of the Yezidees.

PRINCIPAL ENTRANCE TO THE GREAT COURTYARD
OF THE MOSQUE AT KADIMAIN

I had counted on a certain Suleiman Pashati to help me in whatever arrangements were necessary about getting into the Yezidee mountains. I sent my letters to him, and next evening he called at the hotel. When he came in I thought there must be some mistake. He had been described to me as the elder son of one of the oldest and most old-fashioned princely families of the pure Baghdad strain. I had vaguely expected a turbaned prince with flowing robes and jeweled dagger, for there are many such in Arabia who hold to the old traditions of dress. Instead he looked like a rising young Wall Street broker, tailored by Fifth Avenue's best, and I found he had come in a swanky little Stutz roadster. He was affable and charming. His English, on the whole, was better than mine. He knew very little about the Yezidees, but he knew his Baghdad, and after reflecting a bit, his advice was shrewd and practical.

"You don't want to go to Gertrude Bell—you don't want to go to the British at all. They'd either stop you or send somebody in uniform along, which would be just as bad. It's in the Mosul region—Nineveh. The excavations. I know the man who ought to help you."

We went out and got into his roadster, drove north up Baghdad's main street, around a corner, and entered a little hand laundry which, with its counters and piled-up ticketed bundles, was not very much unlike laundries in that other Baghdad-on-the-subway. The proprietor was a spectacled, elderly man in his shirt-sleeves, who turned out to be an antiquarian. The laundry was his "sideline." He took us to a back room where there were a roll-top desk and a little iron safe. He dealt in Assyrian cylinders and other antiquities, in a small way, with most of the world's big museums. Before I left he showed me letters from the University of Pennsylvania and the British Archaeological Society. He had been many times to Mosul, in connection with the Nineveh excavations. He knew, if the man could be found, just the right person to help me, a certain Mechmed Hamdi— also once employed in connection with the work at Nineveh, who had been several times among the Yezidees, made a study of the cult, and written a pamphlet about it, he believed, in Arabic.

Luckily this Mechmed Hamdi was easily found next

day—a gray little badger of a man he proved to be, in a red fez and shabby frock-coat, with keen, likeable eyes— a real fund of scholarship—eager to be of service as soon as he discovered the matter concerned one of his pet subjects—in a word, an amiable, down-at-heel professor.

Ten minutes' conversation convinced me that he knew more about the Yezidees than any man I had yet met. Also he knew personally their ruler Said Beg, and exactly how to get from Mosul to Sheik-Adi. We liked each other, and in less than ten more minutes he had agreed— for a very modest consideration—to make the trip with me.

For a professor, he handled the arrangements very well. Some mornings later—after a wholly uneventful journey by third-class railroad carriage to the railroad head a half-day north of Baghdad, and then by easy stages in an old Pugeot, cheaply hired, to Mosul—we found ourselves on mule-back, with a pack mule and guide in front of us, ambling northeast among green foothills and valleys gay with flowers, toward higher and more rugged hills, in the shadow of the Kurdish mountains.

During the previous days, Mechmed Hamdi had supplied me from the rich store of his sound knowledge such facts as he thought I should know in advance concerning the strange sect we were going to visit. And he continued his discourse as we ambled along on our mules. It was practical rather than academic. I would find the Yezidees trustworthy, he said, and hospitable, but there were certain things always to be remembered when among them which, if forgotten, could lead to serious trouble.

One must take care never to pronounce the name of Shaitan [Satan] and must avoid the use of any words or syllables, whether in English, French or Arabic, which could, by any chance, be mistaken for that word—such Arabic words, for instance, as *khaitan* [thread] and *shait* [arrow].

One must neither wear nor exhibit any article of clothing that was blue—no necktie of blue, for instance, no ring with a blue stone in it—for blue is taboo and anathema among the Yezidees, because it is supposed to have magical properties inimical to Satan. Blue amulets and charms, particularly blue beads, are worn universally among Moslems as a protection against devils and to ward off the evil eye. All babies and almost every domestic animal in certain parts of Arabia have a necklace or collar of blue beads, and I have even seen a woman, in the bazaar at Baghdad, with a string of blue beads on her Singer sewing-machine, to prevent demons from breaking or tangling the thread. Blue, therefore, was a color accursed among the Yezidees, who worshiped the Arch-Demon.

A third prohibition was that one must take care never to spit in a fire or to put out a dropped match by stepping on it with the foot, for to them all fire is sacred.

Since they were confessedly worshipers of Satan, I asked Mechmed Hamdi why was it forbidden to pronounce his name.

It was prohibited in their scripture, their Khitab al Aswad [Black Book], he said, of which he himself had studied the copy of a partial translation made from Kurdish into Arabic more than a hundred years before by one of their own priests in the Sinjar. In the Black Book, Shaitan says:

> Speak not my name nor mention my attributes, lest ye be guilty, for ye have no true knowledge thereof; but honor my symbol and image.

The basis of the Yezidee belief, as Mechmed Hamdi outlined it to me, was briefly this:

God created seven spirits "as a man lighteth one lamp after another," and the first of these spirits was Satan, whom God made supreme ruler of the earth for a period of ten thousand years. And because Satan was supreme master of the earth, those who dwelt on it could prosper only by doing him homage and worshiping him.

Since the true name was forbidden, Mechmed Hamdi told me, they referred to Shaitan as Melek Taos [Angel Peacock] and worshiped him in the form of a brass bird.

I asked Mechmed whether he had ever seen this bird, and he said absolutely no, and that he knew of no man not a Yezidee who had ever seen it, but that it was supposed to be rudely carved, more like a rooster than a peacock, mounted on a brass pole, of such size as one man might easily carry.

While the name of Shaitan was forbidden, he said— so much so that if a Yezidee hears it spoken, their law commands him either to kill the man who uttered it or kill himself—yet we could talk as freely with them about Melek Taos "as we could to a Christian about Jesus."

Pushing steadily forward and upward, by winding stony paths, we were gradually leaving the valleys below us, rising to more rugged, jagged, rocky hills; but still there were mulberry and olive trees, so that the route, while wild, was not desolate. In early afternoon we halted by a spring, had lunch, and allowed the mules to rest. We planned to reach Baadri, the stronghold of Said Beg, easily an hour or so before sunset.

In the late afternoon, we passed one or two stone villages along the slopes, which Mechmed said were Yezidee. I saw, at a distance, women cultivating the fields. They were unveiled, some in black, others in tucked-up robes of bright red or yellow. A man leading three pack donkeys tried to avoid saluting us, but mumbled *Marhaba* [a rough "hello"] as he passed. He also was Yezidee, in baggy white trousers, black tunic which reached to his knees, a wide, red sash, and a red cotton turban wound round his rusty felt cap.

Now and again, but rarely, we passed others afoot, usually carrying a sack or some rude farm implement. These first worshipers of Satan were evidently a habitually peaceful people engaged in tilling their soil, but if they showed no open hostility toward us, neither were they friendly.

Toward five o'clock, on a mountainside several miles ahead of us, we had our first view of the castle of Said Beg, ruler and "Black Pope" of the Yezidees. It was a boxlike, flat-roofed structure, apparently unornamented, like a blockhouse or fortress, and so indeed it seemed as we gradually drew closer. It stood isolated on a slope, and the little village of Baadri with clustering low stone houses lay several hundred yards below it.

The castle gate stood open, unattended. We dismounted and entered a big, bare rectangular courtyard, where servants came, greeted us civilly, and went out to look after our mules, while one went to announce our arrival.

A few moments later, Said Beg himself appeared. He was a man of perhaps fifty, in black tunic and big red turban, with a large nose and a long, sparse dark beard. Immediately he recognized Mechmed Hamdi, shook hands with him, and bade us both a hospitable welcome.

It was hard to convince myself that I was actually in the presence of the ruler of the Devil-Worshipers—the man whose name was surrounded, among superstitious Moslems, by tales as terrifying as those told in Saladin's day of the Old Man of the Mountain, King of the Assassins—the monster who devoured young silver-girdled virgins nightly, and who, as J had been told in Aleppo, had murdered his own father to become Mir—for he seemed no different from any other grave and courteous Oriental host, and in the most matter-of-fact way set about making us feel at home and comfortable.

He evidently made no distinction between English and American, and told me that I was welcome because my countrymen had stopped the murder and persecution of his people and that now a Yezidee could journey safely even to Baghdad and could walk openly in Baghdad's streets without fear of being set upon by Christians or Moslems and slain.

We would please excuse him that night, because, not forewarned of our coming, he had other necessary occupations, but his home was ours, and on the morrow he would accompany us to Sheik-Adi, to visit the temple and shrines of his people.

Our luggage was taken into a big rectangular hall. We washed ourselves in water poured from earthen jugs by a servant in the courtyard. Pallets and cushions were brought into the hall and arranged for us, and a little later a brass tray laden with dishes was brought in and deposited on the floor—grilled mutton, a sort of pilaff, quantities of ripe olives, a big bowl of clabbered milk—and presently we lay down to sleep as safely and soundly in Satan's castle as I had ever slept in the houses of the godly.

Chapter XV

IN THE COURTYARD OF THE SERPENT

I WAS awakened at dawn, after a sound sleep in the castle stronghold of Mir Said Beg, by a servant who announced that the mules were already saddled for our journey further up the mountain to the temple of Satan and the sacred shrine at Sheik-Adi.

It was for this "unholy" pilgrimage that I had ventured, with some misgivings, to the slope of Mount Lalesh.

Fortune had favored me, and now the Mir himself, supreme ruler of the Devil-Worshipers in all Asia, black-bearded, in scarlet turban, with a great black cloak swathed round him against the morning mists, was condescending to be my guide. At his side rode his adolescent son, who, if he followed historical precedents, might in later years slay the Mir and rule as Black Pope in his stead. Behind them I rode with my friend the learned Mechmed Hamdi of Baghdad, and in our rear, on a donkey, one of Mir Said Beg's servants followed.

We were approaching a sanctuary which few Arab Moslems or Christians have ever seen, but which they all discourse about with voluble superstition as a nest of diabolical mysteries from which one might not return alive. Now that I was actually among the Yezidees, as guest of their own prince, I knew that there was nothing to fear, and wondered as we rode how many of the other

wild tales would turn out to be untrue—the Courtyard
of the Black Serpent—the Tower of Satan from which
occult vibrations of evil were broadcast to sway the destinies of the world—the temple hewn from the solid rock,
leading down to vast subterranean caverns stained with
the blood of human sacrifice.

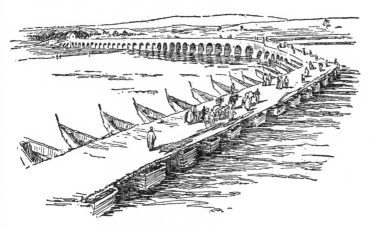

LONG BRIDGE OF ARCHES AND PONTOONS
Spanning the Tigris at Mosul

Phantasm and embroidery, doubtless; but experience
had already taught me that often, in Arabia, the seemingly wildest fictions prove on closer examination to be
based on distorted fact. So now, as we mounted toward
the shrine of Satan, I had high hopes of seeing "some
strange thing"—perhaps many.

The ride from Baadri to Sheik-Adi, the Mir had told
us, would take only an hour. A stony bridle path, winding upward among ravines and rocks, had left the castle
out of sight behind, and still mounted, twisting, through
wild, barren scenery—but when we crossed a ridge and

finally had our first glimpse of sacred Sheik-Adi, clinging to the terraced slope of a mountain, it was not wild and desolate—for among the walls and rocks were foliage and grass, many mulberry trees and olive trees in full leaf.

The entire hillside was dotted with hundreds of uninhabited stone huts—shelters, the Mir told us, for Yezidee pilgrims who visited the shrine. The temple itself, in their midst, appeared as a collection of rambling walls, surrounding terraced courtyards and flat-roofed buildings, above which there was a glimpse of two small whitewashed, cone-shaped domes.

Behind it and above, surmounting a higher ridge, was a white fluted tower shaped like a sharpened pencil-point —and from its top brilliant, dazzling rays of light, as if from a heliograph, actually flashed toward us! The sight of it thrilled me, for this, whatever its exact purpose, I knew was undoubtedly one of the "Towers of Shaitan," the fabulous "power houses" which figure in the tales and myths of Arabia, Persia, and Turkestan. I hoped we would be permitted to see what was inside it.

Meanwhile the path, which we now followed on foot, leading our mules, took us between old crumbling walls and under arches to a larger archway which gave into a wide courtyard, around which was built a flat-roofed monastery in which the priest in charge of the temple and his associates lived. He came out, an old graybeard, in white robes and red sash and turban, kissed the Mir Said Beg's hand, and then saluted us.

Like any sacristan of a Christian cathedral, the old priest of Satan offered his services to conduct us through the temple. Mir Said Beg and his son left us. Mechmed

Hamdi and I followed our new guide down a flight of stone steps, through a gateway which he unlocked for us, into a little rectangular walled yard whose northern wall was the face of the actual temple, built against and into the living rock of the mountainside. This was the "Courtyard of the Serpent." And the serpent's actual dominating presence was there—though it was not alive. It was a stone serpent standing on its tail, carved in high relief, and glistening black in the sunlight on the gray wall, at the right of the temple door. Many other symbols were carved in the façade of the temple—a two-edged beheading axe, a harrow, a pair of scissors, and square Kurdish symbols. The façade of the temple faced south. In the southeast corner of the courtyard, sunk into the pavement, was a small rectangular pool. But most of all I was interested in the black serpent on the wall. The priest observed this and signed for me to inspect it as closely as I liked. He did not seem to regard it with exaggerated reverence. He told me that it was *alamt el akl* [symbol of wisdom], and I was sure it must be the lineal descendant, mythologically, of that same serpent which tempted Eve. The priest had touched it casually as he spoke, and he was not annoyed when I ventured respectfully to stroke its tail. I wanted to see what its glistening black substance was—whether it had been carved, as I had at first supposed, in relief from the rock, or was perhaps of some inset metal. It was the same stone as the rest, cut in relief, and some of the black came off on my finger. Whereupon this amiable priest of Satan explained to me—with the astounding matter-of-factness which I think has no parallel in western psychology—that in the old days the serpent had been kept polished with black lead, but that now they did it with harness-blacking made by the *Engleysi* and bought in Mosul. The black lead was more durable, but the harness-blacking gave the snake a finer appearance. I duly admired it. And then he conducted us into the temple.

It was a gloomy rectangular stone chamber, perhaps fifty feet long, shaped like a shoe-box, its length lying east and west. The first thing I noticed was dozens of little flickering points of light at irregular spots in the wall. These came from small iron dishes, set in niches, in which lighted wicks floated in olive oil. These, he told us, were kept continually burning. The arrangement of the temple was curious and difficult to describe. Down its middle, from end to end, ran a row of stone pillars, and between these pillars from base to base of each ran a low wall, which one could almost step over.

It divided the chamber longitudinally into two separate parts with floors on a different level—that nearer the door being a few feet lower. In a corner, on the lower level, another rectangular pool was sunk.

There was no altar of any sort, but midway in the northern wall was an iron grating and behind it a dark inner chamber, hewn, I think, from the rock. There was no entrance directly into it, but farther along the north wall was a door, giving inward against the mountain, to which the priest led us. Through this door we entered a small square chamber, over which was the smaller of two cone-shaped domes we had seen from outside, and under the dome was a sarcophagus-like tomb. At the right was a small closed door which led apparently into the bowels of the mountain, while at the left was an open door leading to the dark chamber which I had peered into through the iron grating. We entered this chamber and found, beneath the larger of the two domes, another tomb, covered with a black pall, which, the priest told us, contained the remains of Sheik Adi, the founder of their sect. Beyond it another door led to a third inner chamber, where were stored many earthen jars of oil for the lamps.

Mechmed Hamdi began telling me in French, which the priest could not understand, of the supposed cavern or crypt, hidden in the bowels of the mountain, beneath our feet, which he had wanted to see on former occasions. He said he had been refused on the ground that strangers could be permitted to enter it only by special order of the Mir Said Beg himself. The closed door from the adjacent chamber was supposed to lead to it.

Now that Said Beg was here and seemed friendly disposed, we decided that it could do no harm at least to make the request. This Mechmed Hamdi did, in politest Arabic, suggesting that if the priest were not too greatly inconvenienced, and if Said Beg graciously permitted it, we would like to see the lower chambers.

The priest seemed uncertain, but was willing that we should consult the Mir himself. And so we did when we went back and found him awaiting us in the upper courtyard.

He told us we might descend the steps and look in, but that there was nothing to see—"it was just a cave." The priest procured a torch, and we reëntered the temple, went through the little door, down a very old flight of damp stone steps, through a dungeon-like passage. At the foot of the steps where we stopped and stood, we found ourselves in a vaulted cavern, partly natural, it seemed, and partly hewn from the rock, and around a corner the sound of rushing water—a sound which we had heard as a murmur in the upper temple, but had supposed to come from some near-by stream flowing down the mountainside. We could not see the whole of the cavern, or guess how far it extended. Its floor at the foot of the steps was covered with water, which I guessed from the slope to be not more than ankle-deep. But the priest made it an excuse to deter us from going farther, declaring that there was no use getting our feet wet, since there was nothing more to see. I peered about by the light of the torch to see whether I could observe any inscriptions on the wall, any signs of an altar, niches, or other indications that the place was used for ritual purposes—and though the light was flickering and bad, I was pretty surely convinced that there was nothing of the kind within our range of vision. It was a place admirably suited to the weird and dreadful rites which Arab Moslems assured me were conducted there in the worship of Satan—including, they insisted, human sacrifice—but I must admit that there was nothing to offer the slightest intimation that it was currently used for such purpose. Except for stimulating the imagination and making one wonder what secret scenes, in recent or earlier times, that mysterious cavern of Satan had witnessed, our partial penetration of it was interesting chiefly as establishing the fact that the whole temple edifice was constructed over subterranean caverns and streams and springs, some of the water of which was led into the pools we had seen in the temple and courtyard above. I learned later that the Yezidees believed these waters flowed by a subterranean river across all Arabia, underneath the desert, from the miraculous spring of Zem-Zem in Mecca. The fountain of Zem-Zem, like the Kaaba, with its black stone, was holy to the ancient idolatrous Arabs many centuries before Mecca became the sacred city of Islam. I found that the Yezidees regarded both fire and water as sacred elements.

I would have given a month of my life to explore those caverns completely, and shall always wonder what I might have found around the angles of the rocks—what other chambers, what altars, what relics of ancient or modern sacrifice. I have since had nightmare dreams of wading ankle-deep through the water at the foot of the stairs, of turning a corner and, beneath a great vault like a cathedral, coming upon a dreadful red, fiery altar —but actually there and wide awake, the only thing which made me believe there might possibly be an altar of some sort in the cavern was the fact that there was no sign of one, or even an emplacement for an altar, in the temple above.

Hamdi was of the firm opinion that rites of some sort were still practiced there—but it was only an opinion. We saw nothing actually to confirm it.

Another mystery was the fluted cone-shaped tower, with its light-flashing pinnacle, on the mountain above, which we went to see after we had climbed up from the crypt and emerged from the temple.

It rose from the flat roof of a big vault of whitewashed masonry, so that the roof made a wide platform around the tower's base. The tower itself was likewise of white-washed stone, and the glistening peak which cast fiery rays of light in all directions was a highly polished ball of burnished gold or brass. When the sun was overhead, a man looking across the valleys from any direction, east, west, north, or south, would be bound to see its darting heliographic rays. Here was a most practical explanation of the belief in the "power house" from which occult emanations or vibrations were sent out to cast a Satanic spell upon the world.

We entered the vault beneath the tower and there found the *turbah* of another of the old devil-worshiping saints, placed immediately beneath the tower's hollow, domelike shaft. But otherwise it was empty. I looked about for the sinister figure who was supposed to sit in the tower day and night, weaving his potent incantations. I asked outright the innocently worded question whether any priest ever came there to pray, and I was thrilled when our guide answered that the regular priests did not, but that the *kolchaks*, who I learned later were the *fakirs* or miracle workers of the Yezidees, often came to this *turbah* and remained in it making magic for many days! So that part of the fabulous tale was literally true— though it scarcely followed that, whatever the *kolchaks'* belief in their own diabolical powers, their incantations had been directly responsible for the World War, the Russian Revolution, or the Wall Street explosion, which were among the events a certain captain of the British secret service—since dismissed and shut up in a sanitarium, I am told, because he had become cracked on occult mysticism and magic—had assured me were directly attributable to the "controlling emanations sent out by the priests of this infernal cult." He had assured me as well that, to his personal knowledge, a man had been murdered—at long distance—in the Savoy Hotel in London, by similar Yezidee priestcraft. I am so constituted as not to be able to believe these things—but there are thousands of highly educated people, not in sanitariums, either, who do believe them; and I suppose that if they had seen what I saw in the Mountain of the Yezidees, their worst suspicions would have been confirmed.

THE YAMI EL KABIR MINARET
AT MOSUL

More interestingly definite than the reputed magical influence of the tower was a ceremony which the priest described to us as having taken place less than a month previous, and which he said was repeated every spring. I wish indeed that I could say I had witnessed it. It concerned a bull, of which I had heard in Aleppo; but it seemed that it was a white bull, instead of black as I had been told. This bull, the priest now told me, was decorated with garlands of red flowers, a vein in its throat was opened, and it was led or dragged in procession round and round the tower, on the wide stone platform, until the tower's white base was bathed in the crimson circle of its spurting blood. It was *zain k'tir*, he said—"very beautiful"—nor did he seem a bloodthirsty wretch in saying it, but rather was like some benevolent Italian village padre describing to sympathetic travelers the beauties of a procession of the Madonna which they had missed by arriving after Easter. I began to have a fondness for the old man such as I had not felt toward the more exalted Mir Said Beg, whom, though he had been a most courteous host, I did not find sympathetic or lovable as an individual. The story, by the way, that he had murdered his father for the succession, I was reliably informed in Baghdad later, was not true, though it is generally believed by the natives of Irak. The former Mir, Ali Beg, died peacefully some ten years ago in his bed. But Ali Beg's father and grandfather before him had both been murdered when their sons or nephews became old enough to rule—in one case through the connivance of son and mother—and it seems that there was some ancient law by which the son of a Mir was exculpated by his people if he thus slew his father, and automatically became Mir in his father's stead.

During the three days we remained on Mount Lalesh among the Yezidees, I was not fortunate enough to gain the intimate friendship of Mir Said Beg, though we returned to his castle that afternoon and remained his guests. But something like a friendship sprang up between me and the old priest, whose name was Nadir Lugh. He invited us to come again when we took leave that afternoon, and the following day, with the Mir's permission, accompanied this time only by a servant

Mechmed Hamdi and I rode up to see him. We made no further exploration of the temple or its environs—I think we had already been shown everything it is permitted any unbeliever to see—but sat and "visited" with him, on a stone bench in the upper courtyard, in the shade of a mulberry tree, with our backs comfortably against the wall.

Mechmed Hamdi had told me that while it was forbidden, at least theoretically, on pain of death to pronounce the name of Shaitan, we might freely mention their Satanic god by his other name, Melek Taos [Angel Peacock]; and Nadir-Lugh, when he found me eager to hear whatever he might be free to tell concerning the cult he served, was amiable and loquacious. I discovered that not only was a part, at least, of their doctrine not secret, but that they taught it willingly and had made native converts from other religions.

I had begun by asking Nadir-Lugh to tell us of their great "saint" and founder, Sheik Adi, who lay buried in the temple—but there was a preliminary point that he was first determined to make clear to us.

"Do you believe in God?" he asked me with startling directness—and it seemed to me the strangest of questions, coming from a priest of Satan. I did not know whether he wanted me to answer yes or no, so I replied truthfully, that I supposed I did, but that I was not quite sure what I meant by God.

"Well, we, of course, also believe in God," he told me; 'but our difference from all other religions is this—that we know God is so far away that we can have no contact with Him—and He, on his part, has no knowledge or interest of any sort concerning human affairs. It is useless to pray to Him or worship Him. He cares nothing about us.

"He has given the entire control of this world for ten thousand years to the bright spirit, Melek Taos, and Him, therefore, we worship. Moslems and Christians are wrongly taught that he whom we call Melek Taos is the spirit of evil. We know that this is not true. He is the spirit of power and the ruler of this world. At the end of the ten thousand years of his reign—of which we are now in the third thousand—he will reënter paradise as the chief of the Seven Bright Spirits, and all his true worshipers will enter paradise with him."

I liked his casual and simple explanation. Whatever its merits or demerits as a doctrine, it was logically and admirably stated.

Having established this point of Satanic theology to his satisfaction and ours, he went on to tell us about Sheik Adi. He reckoned, as nearly all Arabs do, whatever their sect, by the Islamic calendar, and told us that Sheik Adi, founder of the Yezidees, had been born near Baalbek—ancient City of the Sun whose colossal ruins lie on the western skirt of the desert near Damascus—in the fifth century, which would make it the twelfth by Christian reckoning.

Sheik Adi had traveled in Persia, where a revelation had come to him through fire (possibly contact with the Zoroastrian fire worshipers) and had founded the Yezidee cult here where we sat, on Mount Lalesh.

For many years Sheik Adi had ruled, and the cult had grown—and then he had decided to make another pilgrimage. In his absence, Melek Taos himself had taken a human form exactly resembling that of the absent Sheik Adi and had appeared among the Yezidees, who believed that he was indeed their Sheik who had returned among them. For three years Melek Taos was the ruler—and when the real Sheik Adi returned from his pilgrimage, the Yezidees, believing him to be an impostor, fell upon him with their swords and slew him; whereat Melek Taos resumed his own true form, told them that Sheik Adi, whose sacrifice at their hands completed the founding of the religion, would be with them on the Day of Judgment, and that he should always be revered as their greatest saint.

The old priest then told us how Sheik Adi would appear and save them on that last day.

"The souls of all true Yezidees will be carried into paradise in a wicker basket on the head of Sheik Adi, and will submit to no reckoning or trial in the last judgment."

I ventured to ask if it were proper for him to explain why their Bright Spirit was worshiped in the form of a peacock, and this is the extraordinary tale he told me:

Jesus was a spirit who came to earth and took the form of a man, to wage war on Melek and wrest the earth from his dominion. When Jesus hung on the cross, being crucified, the magic was such that if he had been able to carry out his purpose and die in the form of a man, it would have given him power and dominion. Melek thwarted this with his greater magic by taking Jesus from the cross alive, expelling him from earth, and hung on the cross in his stead a figure without substance which seemed to the watchers to be Jesus.

When this figure without substance seemed to die and

was laid in a tomb, it dissolved and disappeared. The two Marys came to the tomb, found it empty, and were astonished.

Melek then appeared to them as an angel and told them to have no fear for their friend Jesus, who had been taken from the cross and sent safely away to other worlds.

They refused to believe Melek, and in order to convince them of his power, he slew a peacock which was in the garden, took out its entrails, cut it into pieces, and then brought them all together again to make a living bird more glorious and beautiful than the one which he had slain.

Then he himself entered the body of this bright bird and flew away. Therefore he is called Angel Peacock, and the bird is his symbol.

"Was it ever permitted," I asked, "for profane eyes to look upon this symbol?"

This he did not answer directly, but said that the image was kept in a secret place in the mountains of the Sinjar, many days' journey to the west, and only brought to the temple on Mount Lalesh at certain times. I did not question him any further on this score. He was so very amiable in answering other questions that for courtesy's sake I did not want to press him on any that he chose to avoid. In fact I begged that if, in my ignorance, I asked questions about things which were secret or forbidden he would forgive me.

When I questioned him about the origin of the Yezidees as a people—who seemed to me mixed Arab and Kurdish—he declared that they were the children of Adam, but not of Eve!

"How could that be?" I eagerly inquired—and sup-

posed that I was going to hear some new tale of that
amazing Lilith, whom medieval monkish legend describes
as a beautiful fiend in the form of woman, who was
Adam's first wife before Eve was created, and who left
him to become the paramour of the Serpent. But the old
priest's tale ran otherwise.

It seems that Adam and Eve had a quarrel about their
children—the same sort of quarrel that many husbands
and wives still engage in, a sort of clash between paternal
and maternal jealousy. Adam said: "These children are
entirely mine. I am their real parent. From me comes
their life. You are nothing but the vessel in which they
were carried until they were big and strong enough to
come out of it."

Eve retorted: "You are all wrong. The children are
entirely mine. They grew as a part of my body, and you
had nothing whatever to do with it."

So Adam and Eve, unable to agree, decided to put
their difference to a practical test.

Adam made an *oya* [a sort of rude pottery jug] and
put into it earth and water, mixed to make a thick mud,
to which he added some of the "vital juices" from his
body, and sealed it up.

Eve also made an *oya*, filled it with mud, put some of
her "vital blood" into it, and likewise sealed it up. And
the two jars were buried "like ostrich eggs" in the warm
sand and left there for the period of thrice three months.

At the end of that time Adam dug up his jug, and was
about to break it open, when something began kicking and
crying inside, the jug cracked and broke open "like an
egg," and a baby boy appeared—the son of Adam alone.

But when Eve dug up her jug, there was no sound or

movement, and when she took a stone and broke it, there was nothing inside but dry, dead dust.

Eve was then humbled and Adam took her again to wife, and together they had many children, who became idolaters, Jews, Moslems, and Christians—the progeny of Adam and Eve.

But from the son who had been born to Adam alone, without Eve's coöperation, came the race of the Yezidees.

Nadir-Lugh's old wrinkled face beamed when I told him how one of the greatest *Engleysi* scientists, Professor Haldane of Oxford, had predicted that, in another hundred years, babies might actually be grown in laboratory jars—an experiment strikingly similar to that which he had recounted as having taken place in the Garden of Eden—except that Professor Haldane was of the opinion that it would require the vital fluids of both male and female, merged, to make the experiment successful.

The old man gave due consideration and replied that now this might be true, as human beings were at the present day constructed—but that since Adam was originally created complete, containing within himself both the male and female principle, as the nipples on man's breasts still show, it was quite likely that the original experiment took place just as it had been related.

He added that in paradise all differences of sex would again be wiped out, and that each soul would inhabit an angelic body which would be neither male nor female, but the perfect union of both in one.

While we were so frankly on the subject of sex, I asked him to tell me, if he would, of the marriage customs and ceremonials of his people.

He told me that each Yezidee who could afford it was

permitted to have four wives, but that many of them had only one—that on the occasion of a marriage there was a great dance which lasted all day long, in which both men and women "leaped," but that during this wild rejoicing the bride was shut up all alone, in a dark room which no single ray of light was permitted to penetrate, and that the first light she saw was the torch carried by the bridegroom when he entered to release her.

In the religious part of the ceremony, he said, earth and water were mixed into a loaf of bread and broken over the bride.

I was wondering meanwhile about the stories that among the Yezidees the Mir had the same right as medieval feudal lords in Christendom to lie with the bride on the first night, before the husband. I supposed that if there was such a custom, the Yezidees themselves must regard it as proper, and that, therefore, there could be no harm in asking.

The priest replied that there was indeed such a law, but that it was an ancient law and that, so far as he knew, in his own lifetime it had never been put into actual practice.

As for the silver bridal girdle or "corset" in which I expressed an interest, I might see one of them for the asking, he said, at Baadri, or in any of the villages.

As we rode returning to the castle of Said Beg that afternoon, I told Mechmed Hamdi that I would very much like to go down into Baadri, or to some other village, and see not only the girdles, but something of the common everyday life of the Yezidees. He advised me against it and doubted that the Mir would permit it, even though he himself was friendly to English-speaking people. He said that the Yezidees had been persecuted and murdered, and reviled and hated so long by all other Arabs, that while they would certainly offer us no hurt or insult—knowing that we were among them with the permission of the Mir and stopping under the Mir's roof —yet we would not be really welcome, and that it would be uncomfortable.

I felt that he was right. Already I had seen much more than I had dared to hope, and assented willingly to his suggestion that we return the following day to Mosul.

When the Mir Said Beg learned that we were preparing to depart on the next morning, he came at once to the reception hall which had been converted into our guest-room and asked if we had been shown everything I wished to see.

He was under a great debt of gratitude, he said, to the English, with whom he insisted on identifying me, because they had stopped the persecution which his people had endured for centuries, and he was happy that I had come to visit Mount Lalesh. Was I certain that I had seen everything I wished?

I told him there was one thing more which I had heard about in Aleppo and wanted very much indeed to see, if it was proper and possible, and not inconvenient. I knew perfectly well that he would think I meant the image of Melek Taos, the brazen Angel Peacock, and after a slight, embarrassing pause, I quickly explained that I had heard of the unique beauty and design of the girdle worn by Yezidee brides, and that since I was a great admirer of Oriental craftsmanship, I should like very much to examine one.

He was surprised but well enough pleased, I think, that just after he had been expressing such friendship for the English, he would not be forced to refuse a last request. It was quite easy, he said. He called a servant, and then went out himself. And I think he sent down into the village. At any rate he came back in about half an hour with a really beautiful piece of crude, barbaric jewelry in his hand, which jangled as he walked—quite the widest belt I have ever seen or expect to see—two broad, curved silver bands, fastened together at the back with a broad piece of black leather, and joined at the front with a long silver pin which went through like a loose rivet, with a little ball at the top, fastened by a chain. The silver part of the belt was not like a double buckle, lying flat in front, but was curved so as to encircle the waist like a corset when locked in place by the pin. It was heavily bossed and crudely set with a number of big red and yellow stones. Closer examination showed that it was of no great intrinsic value. The silver was backed with lead alloy, and the stones, of course, were of the kind described as semi-precious—but it was savagely, barbarically magnificent.

When I handed it back to Said Beg and thanked him, he put his hands behind him and said: "No, no! You will take it with you as a souvenir of Mount Lalesh." And so, after much protestation and thanks, I did. And I still keep it as one of the strangest of my Arabian mementoes.

I wish that I might write of having actually witnessed some secret, mysterious Yezidee ceremonial or ritual—but I did not, nor do I believe any stranger among them

ever has; so I confine myself to this record of what I did
see and hear, with deep gratitude to Mechmed Hamdi of
Baghdad, who by his previous acquaintance with Mir
Said Beg made even this much possible.

YEZIDEE BRIDE'S GIRDLE

Barbaric Silver, Set with Uncut Jewels

Index

Index

Abba, 29, 34, 40, 92, 172, 186
Abdullah, Amir, 5, 25, 26, 138
  author's meeting with, 141
  description, 141
  visit to Mitkhal, 140
Abilene, Kan., 7
Ablutions, 38, 39
Adam and Eve, children of, 328
Adham, Dervish Sheik, 257, 258, 267
Adi, Sheik, 319, 325, 326, 327
Agal, 34, 92, 141, 142
Ahmed, Arab interpreter, 235
Airplanes, 21, 23
Akil, 172, 195
  initiation ceremony, 212
  jahil and, 201
Aleppo, 218, 273, 289
  citadel (ill.), 291
Ali, brother of Gutne, 145
Ali, King, 225
Ali and the Prophet, 243
Allah, 52, 254, 268, 278
  "in the face of Allah," 21
  "in the name of Allah," 48
Allah Akbar, 199, 279
Allenby, General, 187
Amir, Sheik, 189
  killing his brother, 190
Amman, 22, 25, 31
Amulets, 48, 49, 58, 309
Anah, 292, 300
Angel Peacock, 310, 325
Anklets, 58
Annezy, 85, 86
  killing of Ali by, 145
  Sheik with infected eye, 101
Antar, 197
Antiquarian at Baghdad, 307
Anz, 185, 188
Arabia, reason for author's journey to, 7, 11
Arabic, 23
  learning, 11

Arabs, first sight of, 8
Arak, 11
Arch of Ctesiphon in Tigris valley (ill.), 200
  on the lower Tigris (ill.), 91
Architecture, primitive Arabic (ill.), 281
Archway in street to the north of Damascus (ill.), 271
Aristocrats, Arabian, 30
  men as, 70-71
Arslan, Amir Amin, 11, 13, 23
  on the beauty of Gutne, 144
  on the golden calf, 208
  letters from, 24
  on reincarnation, 215
  story of two assassins, 116
  theory of the Salib, 52
  visit to Roualla camp, 96
Asafœtida, 100
Ascetics, 242, 243, 283
Asia (periodical), 5, 207
Asia (ship), 12
Aspirin, 100, 104
Assarah, Sahr, 110
Asses, 62
Atlanta, Ga., 9
Atrash, Ali, 178
  on a reincarnation detail, 215
Atrash, Hussein Pasha, 5, 185, 186, 194
  children, 186
Atrash, Mansour, 216
Atrash, Mustapha, 178, 181
Atrash, Sultan Pasha, 5, 169, 176, 232
  attack on French tank, 181-184
  author's meeting with, 177
  brothers, 178
  castle, 175, 178
Atrash, Thoukan, 180
  family, 231
  Shekib Wahhab and, 225
Azem Palace courtyard (ill.), 266

Baadri, 311, 331
Baalbek, 326
 capitals and architrave of temple
  (ill.), 46
 Temple of Bacchus at (ill.), 170
Babies, 329, 330
Baby camels, 57
Babylon, sacred bull (ill.), 193
Bacchus, Temple of (ill.), 170
"Bad lands," 295
Baghdad, 26, 291, 292
 first sight, 302
 Maude Hotel, 303
 mosque of Merdjan (ill.), 63
Baghdad railway, 302
Bakhir bey, 219
Bakhlin, 210, 219
Ballad of Gutne, 85
Bandits, 273, 295, 296
Banner of Islam, 196
Barokat, 73
Basrah, corner of (ill.), 151
Bathing, 74
Battles, 85, 86
Bazaar at Damascus (ill.), 121
Beauty, 243, 244
 Gutne's, 143, 144
Bedawi, 40
Bedbugs, 39
Bedouin Arabic, 53
Bedouin clothes, 40
Bedouins, 10
 allegiance, 139
 character, 123
 girl, unveiled (ill.), 32
 Jews and, 123, 124
 religious rites, 43
 women, 66, 70, 78
 women beauties standing on
  camels (ill.), 144
Beds, 26, 37, 173, 185
 tucking in the guest, 39
Beduw, 21. See also Bedouins
Beg, Mir Ali, 324
Beg, Mir Said, 5, 292, 308, 316, 319,
  332, 334
 as host and as man, 324
 stronghold, 311, 313
 welcome from, 312
Beirut, 10, 11, 12
 Druse girl in, 228
Beit-Lachem (Bethlehem), 25
Bektashi, 243, 260
Bell, Gertrude, 307

Beni Hassan, 143, 153
 encampment and blackening, 88
 noted beauty, 81, 83
Beni Maruf, song of, 176, 183, 231
Beni Sakhr, 24
 girl of the tribe (ill.), 32
 religious customs, 43
 riding in ghrazzu, 127, 130
 Roualla and, 95, 96
 wife of a warrior (ill.), 78
 wild adventure among, 127
Bethlehem, 25
Bible, 195, 205
Birds, eating, 187
Bissot, 126
Black Book, 309
Black pepper, 100
Black Pope of the Yezidees, 311
Blackening, 88-91
Blackness, significance, 92
Bliss, 248, 283
Blood feud, 77, 124, 125, 126
Blue, 309
Boccaccio, 113
Body, care of, 75
Bodyguard, 30, 32, 37
Book of Wisdom, Druse, 202, 204,
  210
Borzoi, 56
Bosphorus, 12
Bowls, 73
Brass bird, 310
Bread-flaps, 38, 40, 56, 72, 173
Breakfast, 40
Bridal raiment, 152
Bridge at Mosul (ill.), 315
British headquarters, 27, 29
Brother, killing, 92-93, 190, 191
Bteddin palace, 226
Buffalo Bill, 130
Bull, sacred (ill.), 193
Burial, among the Druses, 192, 195
Bustard, 109

Cadillac car, 170, 185
Calf. See Golden calf
Camel boy, 86
Camel corps, French, 123
Camel dung, 72
Camel milk, 38, 57
Camel rider, dramatic arrival, 127
Camel-stick, 59, 60, 128
Camel throne, 86

Camels, 21
  angry, 62
  baby, 57
  bad name, 55
  gift of a hundred, 113
  going without water, 62
  groaning and moaning, 61-62
  last camel slain to feed a guest, 112
  picture of three men on, 7
  riding a camel, 58, 60
  rising, 59
  sleeping, 57
  wasted whole carcass, 97
  white, 54-56, 150
Camp and coffee fire (ill.), 115
Camphor, 100
Capture, 125
Cattle-stealing, 120
Caverns in the Mountains of the Yezidees, 320, 321
Charity, 112, 113
Charms, 101, 103
Chastity, 79, 80, 82, 202
Chelebi, Mohamet Bakhir, 244, 250, 257, 267, 268, 269
Cherbourg, 8
Chibeh, 276
Child-bearing, 68
Children, 68
  naked, 98
Chin, tattooing, 78
Chinese-Druse babies, 215
Chivalry, 134
Chrallah, 58-62, 65
  moans, 61
  riding, 59
Christian girl in the scullery, 226
Christian mysticism, 254
Christian nomad tribe, 52
Christianity, one error in, 284
Christians, 47
  Bedouins and, 52
  Druses, Moslems and, 196
  idolatry, 210
Cigarettes, 31, 37
Circassian girls, 226, 245, 246
Citadel at Aleppo (ill.), 291
Cleanliness, 75
Clothing, 75, 76
Club, 79
Coats, U. S. Army, 76
Coffee, 31, 71
  ceremony among the Druses, 172

Coffee,
  drinking, 34, 37
  making, 72
  serving, 34
  spilling, 173
Coffee-pot, upsetting, 108
Coffin, 196
Colonnades, Azem Palace, Damascus (ill.), 266
  Sultan Selim courtyard (ill.), 229
Colt, 29, 93
Companionship among women, 69
Constantinople, 12
Contagious diseases, treatment, 101
Convoy, 120, 291
Cooking, 72
Corset of silver, 292, 331, 332, 333, 334 (ill.)
Cotton Flower, 143
Courier, warning of a raid, 127
Courtesy, Haditha's, 108
Courtship of Gutne, 147, 148
Courtyard of the (Black) Serpent, 315, 317. *See also* Colonnades.
Cowardice among the Druses, 173
Cows, 208
Crete, 12
Crime, 117
  Druses and, 189
Crops guardian (ill.), 94
Crusades, 52
Ctesiphon, arch of, in Tigris valley (ill.), 200
  on lower Tigris (ill.), 91
Cupping, 101

Dakhile. See *Dakhilak*
Dagger, gift of, 49, 58
Daidan Helmy's leap, story of, 255
Dairymaid, 245, 246
Dakhilak, dakhile, 10, 23, 44, 96
Damascus, 120
  archway on street to the north (ill.), 271
  Azem Palace courtyard (ill.), 266
  great bazaar (ill.), 121
  oasis gardens (ill.), 24
  Sultan Selim courtyard (ill.), 229
  tales about the Druses, 192, 193
  Yelbogha Mosque, niche (ill.), 260

Damascus banker, 96
Dance, Melewi, 245, 246, 250
Dance-floor of the Dervishes, 237, 249, 250
Daoud. *See* Izzedin
Daoud, a driver, 293, 294, 296, 298
Dates, 40
David, 25
Dawwa, 100
Deir-er-Zhor, 292, 296
  boats and rafts on the Euphrates east of (ill.), 299
  khan at, 297
Demoniac possession, 194
Dervish, term, 242
Dervishes, 235
  Bedouin's she-goat and the Dervish, 50-52
  faith, 253, 254
  hospitality, 238
  Howling, 243, 273
  palace at Syrian Tripoli (ill.), 249
  palace courtyard and fountain (ill.), 256
  sects, 243, 274
  Whirling, 236, 250-253
Desert, 31
  character, 37
  strange things, 95
Desert vampire, 67, 81
Devil-worshipers, 289. *See also* Yezidees
Dhai, 59
Dhaif, 23
Dinner, 38
Dirdar, 107
Dirt, 74
Divan, 66, 68, 70
Divorce, 80
Djebel, 169, 170
Djinns (*jinns*), 31, 201
Dogs, wild, 301
Donkeys, 54
Doughty, C. M., 10
Dray, Dr. Arthur, 5, 235, 236, 237, 241, 245, 246, 249
Dress, Bedouin, 40
  Bedouin women, 79
  Mitkhal's, 34
  skins, 53
Drinking-water, 74-75
Druses, 9, 10, 153
  administration of justice, 188
  among the, 169

Druses,
  aristocracy, 217
  Christians, Moslems, and, 217
  elders, 172, 195, 197, 201, 202
  France and, 171
  girl tragedies, 228, 229
  honor, 189
  justice, 191
  love and romance, 230
  number of souls fixed, 217
  peasants, 194
  race purity, 217, 227, 228
  religion, 202
  tales about, 192, 193
  temple and religion, 203
  unchanging character and number, 217
  village wedding, 230-231
  war lord of, 169
  war-song, 176, 182-183
  warriors, 175 (ill.), 176
  women and marriage, 217, 226, 227
Duwish, Faisal, 225

Eating, 38, 173
  birds and fingers, 187
  camel carcass, 97
  at a Druse funeral, 199, 201
Eden, Garden of, experiment, 329, 330
El Khour. *See* Khour
Elders. *See* Akil; Druses
Encampment, 32
  blackening ceremony, 88
Etiquette, 35, 73
Euphrates River, 291
  adventures in the valley, 293
  boats and rafts on (ill.), 299
Eve and Adam, children of, 328
Evil eye, 309
Evil spirits, 194
Excrements, medical value, 100
Eye, infected, 101
Eyelashes on animals, 56

Fadan, D'Wali, 292
Fahim, 275
Falcon, 109
  Boccaccio's tale, 113
  joke about, 133
Falsehood, 115
Fantasia, 115
Farengi, 21, 23, 31, 35, 40
Faris, Sheik. *See* Turkan

Farm labor, 71
Fasting, 212
Fate, 205
Fatima, tomb of (ill.), 24
Feast, untouched, 212
Feet, care of, 75
Fellaheen, 71, 93
Feruki, Sami Pasha, 181
Festival, Bedouin (ill.), 144
Firdoos, 257, 267
Fire, among the Yezidees, 309
  sacredness, 321
  worshipers, 326
Fire-Eaters, 243
First aid, 99
Fleas, 39
Flesh, temptation of, 213
Flirtation, 79, 81
Food, 38, 40, 71-72
  camel carcass, 97
  Christian, 26
Ford car, 27, 139, 142, 296
Foreign entanglements, 27
Formality, 73
Fouad. *See* Obeyid; Taimani
Fountain in Dervish palace (ill.), 256
Frankness, 77
French captain and chauffeur killed, 294, 295
French in Syria, 171
French language, 27, 34
Friendliness, 35
Fuel, 72, 174
Fugitives, 53
Fundamentalism, 52
Funeral at Ibadyah, 195
Furja, 81
  ballad sung by, 85, 86-87
  story told by, 83
Furtak Ben Klaib, blackening of, 88-91

Gabriel, Angel, 206
Garlic, 100
Gateway in Syrian Tripoli (ill.), 239
Gendarmes, 294, 295, 296
Generosity, 106
  farengi tale, 113
George, 291
German archeologist, 120
German doctor, 101
Ghouls, 201

Ghrazzu, 43, 53, 71, 93, 110
  adventure in, 127
  laws of, 125
  Sirdieh and, 129
Ghrazzwat, 26
Gifts, 23, 305
  dagger, 49, 58
  declining, 73
  hundred camels, 113
  Koran, 48
Goat stew, 273, 277
Goats, breaking the legs of, 110
  story of lame she-goat, 50-52
God, 45
  Dervish idea, 247, 253
  Druse doctrine, 206
  first symbol of, 211
  many paths to, 284-285
  no god but God, 45-48
  Yezidee belief, 325
Golden calf, worship of, 153, 192, 203, 207
  author's theory, 211
  calumny, 208
  Israelites and, 211
Goren, 117
Gouraud, General, 182
Grasshoppers, 299
Gravy, 38
Greenwich Village, 9
Greyhound, 109
Groaning of camels, 61-62
Guests, 44
  in the Djebel, 182
Guide, 21
Gumbaz, 34, 40, 42, 97
Gutne, 85, 86, 143
  beauty, 143, 144
  Meteb's love for and price of gift in marriage, 149, 150, 151
  Shalan and, 154, 162
  song of, 145
  taunts to the women, 158
  Trad Ben Zaban and, 155, 162
  whipped by Shalan, 159
  wooing, 147, 148

Haditha Pasha, history of, 106
  story about his mare, 117
Hair, 75
Hakim, 204, 206, 211
  deification, 208
  symbol of his incarnation, 210
Hal, 252, 262
Haldane, Professor, 330

Haltita, 100
Halvah, 201
Hama, 273, 283
  water wheel at (ill.), 284
Hamdi, Homeja Mechmed, 5, 307, 312, 314, 316-317, 319, 325, 334
Hamza, 204
Hand-kissing, 87, 221
Hands, washing with sand, 38, 39
  washing with water, 173
Hanjar, Adhan, 182
Hareem, 36, 39, 67, 77
  Dervish palace, 238
  Druse, 174
Harmony, 247; divine, 248
Hassan, 163, 164
Hatim, Sheik, 113
Hauran, 21
  plains, 169
Headcloth, 34
Heeaki winietche, 83-85
Hejin, 55, 56, 129
  ancestry, 57-58
  speed, 60-61
Hejra, 52
Helmy, Daidan, story of his leap, 255
Hijab, 102, 103
Himyarite inscription (ill.), 109
Historian, Druse, 207
Hodja el Vatan, 47
Honor, code of, 117, 119, 120
  among thieves, 134
Hormat Hamra, 155, 156
Horseback, 54
Horses, 54
  method of riding, 40, 41
  speed of camels compared with, 60
  urine, 100
Hospitality, 27, 35, 36, 44, 110
  Dervishes, 238
  Oriental, 304
  tales of, 110, 111
Howling Dervishes, 243, 273
Humor of the Bedouins, 52
Hundred camels, tale of, 113
Hunger, unsatisfied, 212
Hyena, 274

Ibadyah, funeral, 195
Iblis, 211
Ibn el Ghanj, 143, 145
Ibn Saud, 139
Idolatry, 209, 210

Ikh, 59
Incense, 278
Indian war-whoops, 130
Inscription, Himyarite (ill.), 109
Intimate relations, 77
Irak, 110, 290
Iron collar, 192, 194
Islam, 43, 47
Ispahan, 259
Israelites, 211
Izzedin, Daoud, 5, 9, 12-13, 169
  at Mukhtara, 218
  uncle, 195
Izzedin, Suleiman bey, 5, 10, 207

Jackals, 301
Jahil, 172
  akil and, 201
Jelal-ed-Din, 244, 250, 251, 254
Jemel Pasha, 237
Jeremiah, 25
Jerid and Thirya, 66
Jerusalem, 45
Jesus, as God, 45-46
  Melek and, 327
Jewelry, 78
Jews, Bedouin opinion of, 123
  God of, 45-46
Jinns (djinns), 31, 201
Job, 172
Jumblatt, Fouad, 223
Jumblatt family, 218
  palace, 218, 223 (ill.), 225
  son (Fouad) of the family, 221
Justice, administration, 66
  divine, 215
  Druse, 188, 191

Kaaba, 321
Kadimain, domes of "forbidden" mosque (ill.), 301
  entrance to courtyard of mosque (ill.), 306
Kafieh (kafiyeh), 29, 34, 77, 98, 99, 172, 186, 231
Kansas, 7
Karma, 215
Katie, 9, 11, 13, 169, 172, 221, 290, 291, 295, 296, 297, 298, 299, 300, 305
Khair Inshallah, 108
Khaki coats, 76
Khitab al Aswad, 309
Khour, El, 106
Kismet, 205

Kissing the hand, 87, 221
Kitab el-Hikmet, 202, 210
Killing, among the Bedouins, 125, 126
Kolchak, 322
Konia, 244, 245, 257, 268, 269
Koran, 49, 205
  present of minute copy, 48
  sorcery with, 101, 195
Kurdish mountains, 308
Kurieh, 169, 175, 178, 183

Labne, 245, 246
Lalesh, Mount, 314, 324, 328
Lamb, worship of, 209
Lanterns, 38
Laundry in Baghdad, 307
Laws of the desert, unwritten, 116-117
Leap, a lover's, 255
Lebanon, 195, 217
Lejah, 193, 194
Letters, writing, 74
Lice, 39
Liheh, 188
Lilith, 329
Little Whirlwind, 56
Losing face, 54
Love, 81
  Firdoos and Daidan Helmy, 257
  Gutne's story, 143
  Mara, 230
  resisting the arts of, 213
Luncheon in Dervish palace, 241
Lying, 115

Madness, 259, 263, 264, 268
Magi, 7
Magic, 101, 192, 194
  Yezidee, 322
Magician, 226
Mansour, the slave, 5, 30, 31, 33
  approval of writer's Bedouin dress, 40
  impudence, 50
  Moslemism and, 48-50
  property, 94
  shooting his brother, 92-93
  status, 92
Mar Behnan Monastery (ill.), 281
Mara, love story of, 230
Mares, 54
  gift of white virgin mare, 147
  Haditha's, 117
  white Arabian, 30, 31

Marhaba, 311
Maronite shepherd, 192
Marriage, 80
  Druses, 227, 230   [151
  high price asked for Gutne, 150,
  Yezidees, 330
Marseilles, 8
Maruf, song of, 176, 183, 231
Marys, the two, at the tomb, 328
Mazir, 56
Mecca, 44, 47, 139, 249, 321
  bowl from, 73
Medicines, 99, 100, 104
Medina, 49
Mehari, 123
Melboos, 274, 275, 276
Melek Taos, 310, 325
  Jesus on the cross and, 327
  worship of, 326
Melewi, Sheik Shefieh el, 5, 235, 243
  description, 236
  journey to Rufai, 270, 273
  monasteries and monks, 245
  palace, 236
Memory, survival from former incarnation, 216, 217
Menzil, 72, 77, 88
Merdjan, mosque of (ill.), 63
Mesned, 262
Meteb, 145, 148
  exile, 153
  flight with his sister, 152
  love for Gutne, his sister, 149
Methodist revival, 279
Mevlevi, 235
Minaret of Yami el Kabir (ill.), 323
Mitkhal Pasha el Fayiz, 5, 23, 24, 26
  administering justice, 66
  description, 34
  dress, 34
  encampment, 32
  hospitality, 34
  mode of welcome, 33
  palace, 41
  picture in group (ill.), 115
  search for, 29
  tent (ill.), 42
  tent described, 36
  visit from Amir Abdullah, 140
  warned by courier of raid, 127, 129
  wives, 77

Mnashid, 113
Moat, 21
Modesty, male, 76
Mohamet, 47, 243
Molasses for a wound, 99
Monastery of Mar Behnan (ill.), 281
Moses, 124
Moslems, 46, 47
Mosques, Kadimain, domes (ill.), 301
  Kadimain, entrance to courtyard (ill.), 306
  ruins of an eighth-century mosque (ill.), 180
  Yelbogha mosque, niche (ill.), 260
Mosul, 289, 290, 292, 308
  bridge of arches and pontoons at (ill.), 315
  minaret of Yami el Kabir (ill.), 323
  ruins of Qara Serail (ill.), 70
Muezzin calling to prayer (ill.), 50
Mukaad (*mukhaad*), 36, 52, 79, 96
  among the Druses, 172
Mukhtara, 218
  Jumblatt palace, 218, 223 (ill.), 225
Mukhtara, Veiled Lady of, 218
Murder, 21, 91
Musician, Dervish, story of, 255
Mysteries, 214
  Druse, 202, 204
Mysticism, 274
  Christian, 254
  of the Dervishes, 242, 243, 253, 254

Nadir-Lugh, 5, 324
  on marriage customs of the Yezidees, 330
  on Yezidee doctrine, 326, 327
  tale of Adam and Eve, 329
  "visiting" with, 325
Nairn convoy, 120, 291
Najar, Said, 195
Najib Abu Faray, 216
Naked woman (with ill.), 213
Nakedness, 76
Naples, 9
Nargheela, 71
Nasr'b hbal, 148
Natives, white men and, 35
Nazara, 52

Needle's eye, 41
Nefud, 37
Negro body servant, 29
Negroes, 92
New York, 9
Night, 39, 255
Nightingale, 246
Nineveh, 307
Nose-ring, 78
Nur-Adesh, 275
Nusralla ibn Gilda, 210

Obeyid, Adham, 172
Obeyid, Ali bey, 5, 171, 203
  sons, 172
  wife and daughter, 174
Obeyid, Fouad, 172, 181, 185
Omens, 108
Oneness of God, 45-48
Orah, 231
Oya, 329

Palmyra, 120, 123
Pantheism, 253
Paradise, 246
Pariah, 90
Partridges, dish of, 187
Pashati, Prince Suleiman, 5, 306
Passports, 294
Peacock, Angel, 310, 325
Peacock, story of, 327, 328
Pepper, 100
Personal affairs, 44
Personal survival of death, and memory of former life, 216, 217
"Petting," 79
Philadelphia (Amman), 25
Physicians, 101, 105
Pir, 244
Pommels of camel saddles, 58
Power, 248
Power Houses, 289, 316, 322
Prayer rugs, 43
Praying, 43, 44
  call of a muezzin (ill.), 50
  Druses, 205
  story of Bedouin's she-goat, 50-52
Prime minister, 27
  Syrian, 28
Prisoners, 125
Prisons, 188
Privacy, 76
Promises, 119

Prophet, legend of the, 243
Prophets, 206
Punishment, 124
    Druse, 188, 189

Qara Serail, ruins (ill.), 70

Rabeyba, 85, 109
Rahla, 26, 43
Raiding, 53, 120
Rakaby Pasha, 27, 142
    personality, 27
    "politeness," 27-28
Ramtah, 21
Rape, 91, 124
Reading and writing, 74
Reincarnation, 214
    detail of the theory, 215
    interesting cases, 216
Religion, 43, 45-48
    forms and rites, 207
Renaud, Captain, 176
Renault car, 270
Rice, 38
Riding, 40, 41, 54
Right of the first night, 293, 331
Robber-saint, 106
Robbery, 21, 120
    attempt at, 22
Roualla, 95, 96, 136, 137
    Gutne and, 155
    Meteb's coming to, 153
    Spartan discipline, 98
    Trad Ben Zaban and, 160-162
    visit to camp of, 96
Rufai, 243, 273
    red-hot irons and their effect, 279, 283
    ritual ceremony, 277
    self-torture cells, 275, 276
    sheik, 274
Rugs, 37
Ruins, eighth-century mosque (ill.), 180
    Qara Serail at Mosul (ill.), 70

Sacy, Silvestre de, 192
Saddle pommels, 58
Saddlebag, 58
Sadee, 243
Said bey, 219, 225
Saint, robber, 106
Salaam aleikum, 37, 73, 172
Saladin, 218
Salib, 52
Salutation, 73

Samarkand, 8, 259
Sand, bathing in, 75
    writing in, 74
Sand waste, 37
Satan, 309
    his priests on seven towers, 290.
        See also Yezidees
Scimitar, 73, 131, 154, 162
    Dirdar's, 107
Scouts, 132
Scribe, 74
Seabrook, Mrs. *See* Katie
Seal, letter, 74
Seduction, 79, 91
Sema Zan, 250, 251, 252, 253
Serpent of stone, 317
Seven Bright Spirits, 326
Seven Towers, 289
Sex relations, 77
    Bedouin pre-marriage, 79
    Druses, 202
Shaitan, 309, 310, 325
Shalan Pasha, 153
    Gutne and, 154, 162
    Gutne's reckless words and his honor, 158
    whipping of Gutne, 159
Sheep dung, 100
Sheik-Adi, city, 290, 293, 312, 314
    ceremony of the bull, 323
    first glimpse, 316
    priest of the temple, 5, 316, 324
    temple, 317, 318
    temple crypt, 319
    tower with burnished ball, 321
Sheiks, 11
Shereefian ruler, 138
Shibli, Sheik, 230
Shihab, Amir Beshir, 226
Sirdieh, 85, 86-87
Shuweifat Druse girl episode, 228
Sinjar, 328
Sirdieh, 129
    attack, 77
    vengeance "for the eyes of Gutne," 143, 147
Sirhan, Sheik, 107
Sitt Nazira el Jumblatt, 5, 218.
    See also Veiled Lady.
Sitt Zainab Umm Yahyah el Atrash, 231
Skins, wearing, 53
Slaves, 92, 187
    status, 95
Sleeping, 39

Smyrna, 9
Songs, Druse funeral, 197
  hundred camels for a song, 113
  Maruf, 176, 183, 231
Sorcerer, 194
Souieda, 170, 171, 176
  family of Suli bey, 201
Soul and divine justice, 215
Spinning as she rode, 83
Stallions, 54
Stamboul. *See* Constantinople
Standard, tribal, 86
Stealing, 117, 119
Sterilizing wounds, 99
Stone-mason, anecdote of, 189
Street scene (ill.), 103
Stutz roadster, 307
Subterranean waters, 320
Sudanese slave story, 95
Sufi philosophy, 242, 283
Suleiman bey. *See* Izzedin
Suli bey, family, 201
Suwaree, 58
Syria, French and, 171
Syrian Tripoli, 235. *See also*
  Tripoli

Taimani, Fouad, 21
  scouting for news, 26
Talaha, 149
Tanks, French, 181-184
Tattooing the chin, 78
Teeth, care of, 75
Tekkeh, 237, 245, 252
Temptation, resisting, 212
Tents, 32
  luxury of the chief's, 36
  method of pitching and using, 36
  Mitkhal's (ill.), 42
Terek bey, Najar, 289, 291, 292
Tesseri, 251
Thirst, quencher of, 303
  unquenched, 212
Throne on camel back, 86
Thum, 100
Tigris River, 302
  bridge of arches and pontoons at
    Mosul (ill.), 315. *See also*
    Ctesiphon.
Tomatoes, 107
Tombs, Druse, 199
  Fatima's (ill.), 24
  guarding, 201
  Zobeide's (ill.), 85
Torture, 124, 275, 276, 279, 283

Tower of Satan, 315, 316
Trad Ben Zaban, 148
  Roualla and, 160-162
  Roualla *ghrazzu* and, 155
Trader with English foods, 107
Trance, Dervish, 252
Transjordania, 25, 138
  village street (ill.), 103
Tripoli, Syria, 235, 245
  gateway (ill.), 239
  palace-monastery (ill.), 249
True believers, 46-48
Truth-speaking, 116
Tuaregs, 124
Turbah, 322
Turkan, Sheik Faris, 203
Turkish forts, 294
Turks, 181, 187
Turuk, 274

Um-el-Akmid (-Akmit), 26, 40,
  88, 138
Ummrumman, 216
Unitarians, 206
Unity, 45-48, 248
Unwritten laws, 116-117

Vampire of the desert, 67, 81
Veiled Lady of Mukhtara, 5, 218
  French and, 225
  reception, 220
  unveiling, 222
Verdun, 9
Vermin, 39

Wahabi, 52, 94, 107, 139, 225
Wahhab, Shekib, 224
Wands planted as signals, 88, 90
War-song, Druse, 176, 182-183
Washing hands, with sand, 38, 39
  with water, 173
Water, sacredness, 321
Water wheel at Hama (ill.), 284
Waverly Place, 9
Wedding, Druse, 230-231
Weygand, General, 221
Wheat fields, 93-94
Whirling dance of Dervishes, 250-
  253
Whirling Dervishes, 236. *See also*
  Dervishes
White camels, 54-56, 150
White men, natives and, 35
White virgin mare, 147
Widow of a sheik, story of, 111

Wit, women's, 79, 81
Wives, 66
  plea for second wife, 68
  relations with, 77
Women, 33
  Bedouin, 70
  Bedouin beauties standing on
    camels (ill.), 144
  burden of child-bearing, 68
  dress, 79
  Druse, 174
  Druse, marrying, 217, 226, 227
  infidelity, 80
  intercourse, 77, 78
  naked woman (with ill.), 213
  peculiarities, 299, 305
  trinkets, 78
  wit and humor, 79, 81
Work, 71
World's Fair, 8
Worship, unconscious, 281
Wounds, treatment, 99, 101
Writing a letter, 74
Writing in the sand, 74

Xenophon, 109

Ya hoo, 278, 279
Yacoub, Dr. and Sitt Mirza, 5, 304
Yahh, 59
Yami el Kabir minaret (ill.), 323
Yamile, 264, 265
Yelbogha Mosque, niche (ill.), 260
Yezidees, 289
  belief, 311, 325
  bride's girdle, 331, 332, 333, 334
    (ill.)
  castle of the ruler, 311
  friendliness, 290
  information about, 308
  marriage customs, 330
  origin as a people, 328, 330
  paradise, 327
  priestcraft, 322
  tales about, 292
  things to be avoided by a visitor,
    309

Zain k'tir, 324
Zem-Zem, 321
Zikr, 251
Zionists, 123
Zjeyd, generosity, 113
Zobeide's tomb (ill.), 85